2 All-Star
Teacher's Edition

Linda Lee

★ **Kristin Sherman** ★ **Grace Tanaka** ★ **Shirley Velasco**

Second Edition

ALL-STAR 2 TEACHER'S EDITION
Published by McGraw-Hill, a business unit of The McGraw-Hill Companies, Inc., 1221 Avenue of the Americas, New York, NY, 10020. Copyright © 2011, 2005 by The McGraw-Hill Companies, Inc. All rights reserved. No part of this publication may be reproduced or distributed in any form or by any means, or stored in a database or retrieval system, without the prior written consent of The McGraw-Hill Companies, Inc., including, but not limited to, in any network or other electronic storage or transmission, or broadcast for distance learning.

Some ancillaries, including electronic and print components, may not be available to customers outside the United States.
This book is printed on acid-free paper.

1 2 3 4 5 6 7 8 9 0 WDQ/WDQ 1 0 9 8 7 6 5 4 3 2 1 0

ISBN   978-0-07-719719-3
MHID   0-07-719719-4

Vice president/Editor in chief: *Elizabeth Haefele*
Vice president/Director of marketing: *John E. Biernat*
Director of sales and marketing, ESL: *Pierre Montagano*
Director of development: *Valerie Kelemen*
Marketing manager: *Kelly Curran*
Lead digital product manager: *Damian Moshak*
Digital developmental editor: *Kevin White*
Director, Editing/Design/Production: *Jess Ann Kosic*
Lead project manager: *Susan Trentacosti*
Senior production supervisor: *Debra R. Sylvester*
Designer: *Srdjan Savanovic*
Digital production coordinator: *Cathy Tepper*
Typeface: *11/13 Frutiger LT Std*
Compositor: *Laserwords Private Limited*
Printer: *Worldcolor*
Cover credit: *Andrew Lange*

The Internet addresses listed in the text were accurate at the time of publication. The inclusion of a Web site does not indicate an endorsement by the authors or McGraw-Hill, and McGraw-Hill does not guarantee the accuracy of the information presented at these sites.
www.mhhe.com

www.mhhe.com

TABLE OF CONTENTS

Contents

Welcome to the Teacher's Edition and To the Teacher iv

Teaching Strategies xi

Pre-Unit Getting Started 2

Unit 1 Describing People 5

Unit 2 Going Places 28

Unit 3 Dollars and Cents 50

Unit 4 Plans and Goals 72

Unit 5 Smart Shopping 94

Unit 6 Food 116

Unit 7 Relationships 138

Unit 8 Health 161

Unit 9 Home and Safety 183

Unit 10 Work 203

Worksheets 224

Target Grammar Pages 244

Workbook Answer Key 262

Unit Tests 280

Unit Tests Audio Script 300

Unit Tests Answer Key 303

Welcome to the *All-Star Second Edition* Teacher's Edition

This Teacher's Edition provides support to teachers using the Second Edition of the *All-Star* Student Book. Each unit of the Teacher's Edition begins with a list of the unit lessons and a list of the Big Picture Expansion Activities to be used with the Big Picture in each unit. Hundreds of additional expansion activities, including activities addressing multi-level classes, literacy, and students needing a challenge, are clearly marked throughout the book.

The *All-Star* Second Edition Teacher's Edition offers step-by step procedures for each lesson. Seasoned teachers can use the instructions as a quick refresher, while newer teachers, or substitute teachers, can use the step-by-step instructions as a helpful guide for carrying out the Student Book activities in the classroom.

The Teacher's Edition provides:
- Step-by-step notes for each Student Book activity
- More than 200 clearly marked expansion activities, including activities addressing multi-level classes, literacy, and students needing a challenge
- Culture/Civics, Grammar, Literacy, and Pronunciation Notes
- Reproducible Big Picture Expansion Activity Worksheets for additional Reading and Grammar practice
- Notes and Answer Keys for the Target Grammar section
- Answer Keys for the Workbook
- Unit Tests, Unit Test Audio Scripts, and Unit Test Answer Keys

New to the Second Edition
- **Updated content** provides full coverage of all major *revised* standards including CASAS, Florida, LAUSD, EFF, and Texas.
- **NEW comprehensive, carefully sequenced grammar program** connects target grammar to the content to enrich learning and provide full coverage of grammar standards.
- **NEW robust listening program** addresses the latest CASAS standards and prepares students for the types of listening items on CASAS tests.
- **NEW Work-Out CD-ROM with complete student audio** provides a fun, rich environment with over 25 hours of interactive learning and the entire *All-Star Second Edition* student audio program in downloadable MP3 files.
- **NEW Teacher Resource Center** offers downloadable and printable Study Guides and Learner Persistence Worksheets, EZ-Tests, Big Picture PowerPoint Slides, full Teacher Audio for Tests in downloadable MP3 files, and other materials to support teaching.
- **NEW Interactive Correlations Chart** allows teachers to easily cross-reference standards with Student Book, Workbook, and Study Guide pages.

Hallmark *All-Star* Features
- Dynamic Big Picture scenes present life-skills vocabulary and provide lively contexts for activities and discussions that promote all-skills language development.
- Predictable sequence of seven two-page lessons in each unit reduces prep time for teachers and helps students get comfortable with the format of each lesson.
- Flexible structure, with application lessons addressing family, work, and community topics in both the Student Book and Workbook, allows teachers to customize each unit to meet a variety of student needs and curricular objectives.
- Comprehensive coverage of key standards, such as CASAS, Florida, LAUSD, EFF, and Texas, prepares students to master a broad range of critical competencies.
- Multiple assessment measures like CASAS-style tests and performance-based assessment offer a variety of options for monitoring and assessing learner progress.

TO THE TEACHER

Series Overview

All-Star is a four-level, standards-based series for English learners, featuring a picture-dictionary approach to vocabulary building. Big Picture scenes in each unit provide springboards to a wealth of activities developing all of the language skills.

An accessible and predictable sequence of lessons in each unit systematically builds language and critical thinking skills around life-skill topics. *All-Star* presents family, work, and community topics in each unit, and provides Alternate Application lessons in its workbooks, giving teachers the flexibility to customize the material for a variety of student needs and curricular objectives. *All-Star* is tightly correlated to all of the major national and state standards for adult instruction.

The Complete *All-Star* Program

- The **Student Book** features ten 14-page units that integrate listening, speaking, reading, writing, grammar, math, and pronunciation skills with life-skills topics, critical thinking activities, and civics concepts.

- The **Student Work-Out CD-ROM with full student audio** extends the learning goals of each Student Book unit with interactive activities that build vocabulary, listening, reading, writing, and test-taking skills. The CD-ROM also includes the full Student Book audio program.

- The **Teacher's Edition with Tests** includes:
  - Step-by-step procedural notes for each Student Book activity
  - Notes on teaching the Target Grammar Pages
  - Expansion activities addressing multi-level classes, literacy, and students that need to be challenged
  - Culture, Grammar, and Pronunciation Notes
  - Two-page written test for each unit (Note: Listening passages for the tests are available on the Teacher Audio with Testing CD and on the Online Teacher Resource Center.)
  - Audio scripts for all audio program materials
  - Answer keys for Student Book, Workbook, and Tests

- The **Workbook** includes supplementary practice activities correlated to the Student Book. As a bonus feature, the Workbook also includes two alternate application lessons per unit that address the learner's role as a worker, family member, and/or community member. These lessons may be used in addition to, or as substitutes for, the application lessons found in Lesson 6 of each Student Book unit.

- The **Teacher Audio with Testing CD** contains recordings for all listening activities in the Student Book as well as the listening passages for each unit test.

- The **Online Teacher Resource Center** provides teachers with the tools to set goals for students, customize classroom teaching, and better measure student success. It includes:
  - EZ-Tests that allow teachers to create customized tests online
  - An Interactive Correlations Chart that allows teachers to easily cross-reference standards with Student Book, Workbook, and Study Guide pages
  - Big Picture PowerPoint slides that present the Student Book Big Picture scenes
  - A Learner Persistence Kit that sets and tracks student achievement goals
  - A Post-Testing Study Guide that moves students toward mastery and tracks their progress using the reproducible Study Guide Worksheets
  - Downloadable MP3 files for the Testing audio program

TO THE TEACHER

Overview of the *All-Star Second Edition* Program

UNIT STRUCTURE

Consult the **Welcome to *All-Star* Second Edition** guide in the Student Book. This guide offers teachers and administrators a visual tour of one Student Book unit and highlights the new features of the second edition.

All-Star Second Edition is designed to maximize accessibility and flexibility. Each unit contains the following sequence of seven two-page lessons that develop vocabulary and build language, grammar, and math skills around life-skill topics.

★ Lesson 1: Vocabulary
★ Lesson 2: Vocabulary in Action
★ Lesson 3: Talk about It
★ Lesson 4: Reading and Writing
★ Lesson 5: Conversations
★ Lesson 6: Application
★ Lesson 7: Review and Assessment

Each unit introduces several grammar points. A Target Grammar  icon in the lessons refers teachers and students to the Target Grammar Pages at the back of the book where they can find explanations of the grammar points and contextualized practice.

SPECIAL FEATURES OF EACH UNIT

★ **Target Grammar Pages:** Throughout each unit, students are directed to the Target Grammar Pages in the back of the book, where the grammar point they have been exposed to in the lesson is presented and practiced in manageable chunks. Students learn the target grammar structure with clear charts, meaningful examples, and abundant practice activities.

This approach gives teachers the flexibility to introduce grammar in any of several ways:

1) At the beginning of a lesson
2) At the point in the lesson where the grammar appears in context
3) As a follow-up to the lesson

★ **CASAS Listening:** Each unit has at least two activities that simulate the CASAS listening experience.

★ **Pronunciation.** The introductory activity in Lesson 5 (Conversation) of each unit is Pronunciation. This special feature has two major goals: (1) helping students hear and produce specific sounds, words, and minimal pairs of words so they become better listeners and speakers; and (2) addressing issues of stress, rhythm, and intonation so that the students' spoken English becomes more comprehensible.

★ **Window on Math.** Learning basic math skills is critically important for success in school, on the job, and at home. As such, national and state standards for adult education mandate instruction in basic math skills. In each unit, a box called Window on Math is dedicated to helping students develop the functional numeracy skills they need for basic math work.

TWO-PAGE LESSON FORMAT

The lessons in *All-Star* are designed as two-page spreads. Lessons 1–4 follow an innovative format with a list of activities on the left hand page of the spread and picture dictionary visuals supporting these activities on the right hand page. The list of activities, entitled Things to Do, allows students and teachers to take full advantage of the visuals in each lesson, enabling students to achieve a variety of learning goals.

TO THE TEACHER

BIG PICTURE SCENES

Each unit includes one Big Picture scene in either Lesson 2 or Lesson 3. This scene is the visual centerpiece of each unit, and serves as a springboard to a variety of activities in the Student Book, Teacher's Edition, and Work-Out CD-ROM. In the Student Book, the Big Picture scene introduces key vocabulary and serves as a prompt for classroom discussion. The scenes feature characters with distinct personalities for students to enjoy, respond to, and talk about. There are also surprising and fun elements for students to discover in each scene.

The Teacher's Edition includes a variety of all-skills "Big Picture Expansion" activities that are tied to the Student Book scenes. For each unit, these expansion activities address listening, speaking, reading, writing, and grammar skills development, and allow teachers to customize their instruction to meet the language learning needs of each group of students.

Finally, the Work-Out CD-ROM program draws on the Big Picture to enhance student learning. Students listen to new conversations taking place within the Big Picture scenes, and then work through a series of interactive activities based on these conversations. They also receive immediate feedback on their work.

CIVICS CONCEPTS

Many institutions focus direct attention on the importance of civics instruction for English language learners. Civics instruction encourages students to become active and informed community members. Throughout each *All-Star* unit, students and teachers will encounter activities that introduce civics concepts and encourage community involvement. In addition, Application lessons provide activities that help students develop in their roles as workers, parents, and citizens. Those lessons targeting the students' role as citizen encourage learners to become more active and informed members of their communities.

CASAS, SCANS, EFF, Florida, LAUSD and Other Standards

Teachers and administrators benchmark student progress against national and/or state standards for adult instruction. With this in mind, *All-Star* Second Edition carefully integrates instruction elements from a wide range of updated standards, including CASAS, SCANS, EFF, LAUSD, Texas, and the Florida Adult ESOL Standards. Unit-by-unit correlations of these standards appear in the Student Book Scope and Sequence and in the Online Teacher Resource Center. Here is a brief overview of our approach to meeting the key national and state, and district standards:

★ **CASAS.** Many U.S. states, including California, tie funding for adult education programs to student performance on the Comprehensive Adult Student Assessment System (CASAS). The CASAS (www.casas.org) competencies identify more than 300 essential skills that adults need in order to succeed in the classroom, workplace, and community. Examples of these skills include identifying or using appropriate nonverbal behavior in a variety of settings, responding appropriately to common personal information questions, and comparing price or quality to determine the best buys. *All-Star* comprehensively integrates all of the CASAS Life Skill Competencies throughout the four levels of the series.

★ **SCANS.** Developed by the United States Department of Labor, SCANS is an acronym for the Secretary's Commission on Achieving Necessary Skills (www.doleta.gove/SCANS/). SCANS competencies are workplace skills that help people compete more effectively in today's global economy. The following are examples of SCANS competencies: works well with others, acquires and evaluates information, and teaches others new skills. A variety of SCANS competencies are threaded throughout the activities in each unit of *All-Star*. The incorporation of these competencies recognizes both the intrinsic importance of teaching workplace skills and the fact that many adult students are already working members of their communities.

★ **EFF.** Equipped for the Future (EFF) is a set of standards for adult literacy and lifelong learning, developed by The National Institute for Literacy (www.nifl.gov). The organizing principle of EFF is that adults assume responsibilities in three major areas of life—as workers, as parents, and as citizens. These three areas of focus are called "role maps" in the EFF documentation. In the parent role map, for example, EFF highlights these and other responsibilities: participating in children's formal education, and forming and maintaining supportive family relationships. *All-Star* addresses all three of the EFF role maps in its *Application* lessons.

TO THE TEACHER

NUMBER OF HOURS OF INSTRUCTION

The *All-Star* program has been designed to accommodate the needs of adult classes with 70–180 hours of classroom instruction. Here are three recommended ways in which various components in the *All-Star* program can be combined to meet student and teacher needs.

★ **70–100 hours.** Teachers are encouraged to work through all of the Student Book materials. Teachers should also look to the Teacher's Edition for teaching suggestions and testing materials as necessary. Students are encouraged to "Plug in and practice" at home with the Work-Out CD-ROM for each unit.

  Time per unit: 7–10 hours

★ **100–140 hours.** In addition to working through all of the Student Book materials, teachers are encouraged to incorporate the Workbook and Work-Out CD-ROM activities for supplementary practice. Students are encouraged to "Plug in and practice" at home with the Work-Out CD-ROM for each unit.

  Time per unit: 10–14 hours

★ **140–180 hours.** Teachers and students working in an intensive instructional setting can take advantage of the wealth of expansion activities threaded through the Teacher's Edition to supplement the Student Book, Workbook, and Work- Out CD-ROM materials. Students are encouraged to "Plug in and practice" at home with the Work-Out CD-ROM for each unit.

  Time per unit: 14–18 hours.

ASSESSMENT

PURPOSES OF ASSESSMENT

J. Michael O'Malley and Lorraine Valdez-Pierce describe six purposes of assessment in *Authentic Assessment for English Language Learners* (Addison-Wesley, 1966), similar to those listed below.

★ **Screening** determines if the student is at the right level for the English language instruction provided. Some students' language level may be too advanced for an adult ESL program, and their needs better met in an academic program or in adult high school.

★ **Placement** tests determine at what level a student should be placed. Adult ESL programs often give an entrance test of some kind to place the student. Screening and placement can be done with the same instrument. Many programs use CASAS or BEST Plus tests for this purpose.

★ **Monitoring achievement** allows the learner and the instructor to see how well particular information has been learned. An end-of-unit test can demonstrate if the student has been successful in learning specific instructional content.

★ **Measuring performance** involves assessing how well learners accomplish specific tasks using prior knowledge and recent learning. Such tasks are usually productive (speaking/writing) and may involve presentations, reports, or projects.

★ **Program evaluation** can involve a variety of assessments in order to determine the effectiveness of a program as a whole. Programs may look at overall improvement in test scores, examples of student projects, and surveys of students and instructors in evaluating program effectiveness.

★ **Accountability** is required for programs receiving state and federal funds. Federal reporting standards, as described by the National Reporting System (NRS), require that programs demonstrate student progress. This progress is often measured by standardized testing (e.g., CASAS), but may also be substantiated by alternative methods of assessment.

ALL-STAR UNIT TESTS

The Teacher's Edition contains a reproducible unit test for each of the ten units in *All-Star*. Each two-page test assesses students' knowledge of the vocabulary and language structures taught within the unit. Each test is worth 20 points.

Each unit test consists of four sections: Listening, Grammar, Reading/Vocabulary, and Writing. The Listening section includes two short conversations, each followed by multiple-choice questions about the conversation. The Grammar section focuses on structures learned in the unit. Students are asked to choose the correct answer to complete sentences. The Reading/Vocabulary section includes different types of reading passages and multiple-choice questions

TO THE TEACHER

about those passages. Finally, the Writing section might ask students to write two sentences about a topic introduced in the unit, or to fill out a form or an application similar to one in the unit. The audio portion of each test is provided on the *All-Star* Teacher Audio CDs and in the Online Teacher Resource Center.

The Unit Test Audio Script and Unit Test Answer Key are included at the end of the Teacher's Edition.

MULTIPLE FORMS OF ASSESSMENT

The *All-Star* program offers teachers, students, and administrators the following wealth of resources for monitoring and assessing student progress and achievement:

★ **Standardized testing formats.** *All-Star* is correlated to the CASAS competencies and many other national and state standards for adult learning. Students have the opportunity to practice answering CASAS-style listening and reading questions in Lesson 7 of each unit (*What do you know?*), in Lesson 7 of the Workbook (*Practice Test*), and in the Work-Out CD-ROM program. Students practice with the same item types and bubble-in answer sheets they encounter on CASAS and other standardized tests.

★ **Achievement tests.** The *All-Star* Teacher's Edition includes end-of-unit tests. These paper-and-pencil tests help students demonstrate how well they have learned the instructional content of the unit. Adult learners often show incremental increases in learning that are not always measured on the standardized tests. The achievement tests may demonstrate learning even in a short amount of instructional time. Twenty percent of each test includes questions that encourage students to apply more academic skills such as determining meaning from context, making inferences, and understanding main ideas. Practice with these question types will help prepare students who may want to enroll in academic classes.

★ **Performance-based assessment.** The *All-Star* Student Book and Workbook provides several ways to measure students' performance on productive tasks, including the *Writing Spotlights* in the Workbook. The Teacher's Edition suggests writing and speaking prompts that teachers can use for performance-based assessment. These prompts derive from the Big Picture scene in each unit, which provides rich visual input as the basis for the speaking and writing tasks asked of the students.

★ **Portfolio assessment.** A portfolio is a collection of student work that can be used to show progress. Examples of work that the instructor or the student may submit in the portfolio include writing samples, speaking rubrics, audiotapes, videotapes, or projects. The Study Guide Worksheets in the Online Teacher Resource Center can be included in a student's portfolio.

★ **Self-assessment.** Self-assessment is an important part of the overall assessment picture, as it promotes student involvement and commitment to the learning process. When encouraged to assess themselves, students take more control of their learning and are better able to connect the instructional content with their own goals. The Student Book includes *Learning Logs* at the end of each unit, which allow students to check off the vocabulary they have learned and skills they have acquired. The Workbook provides self-check boxes for each lesson, encouraging students to monitor their own progress on individual activities and across units.

★ **Other linguistic and non-linguistic outcomes.** Traditional testing often does not account for the progress made by adult learners with limited educational experience or low literacy levels. Such learners tend to take longer to make smaller language gains, so the gains they make in other areas are often more significant. These gains may be in areas such as self-esteem, goal clarification, learning skills, and access to employment, community involvement and further academic studies. The SCANS and EFF standards identify areas of student growth that are not necessarily language based. *All-Star* is correlated with both SCANS and EFF standards. Like the Student Book, the Workbook includes activities that provide documentation that can be added to a student portfolio.

TO THE TEACHER

About the Authors and Series Consultants

Linda Lee is lead author on the *All-Star* series. Linda has taught ESL/ELT in the United States, Iran, and China, and has authored or co-authored a variety of successful textbook series for English learners. As a classroom instructor, Linda's most satisfying teaching experiences have been with adult ESL students at Roxbury Community College in Boston, Massachusetts.

Kristin Sherman is a consultant and co-author on the *All-Star* Student Book series. Kristin has 15 years teaching experience in both credit and non-credit ESL programs. She has taught general ESL, as well as classes focusing on workplace skills and family literacy. She has authored a number of student books, workbooks, and teacher's editions for English learners. Her favorite project was the creation of a reading and writing workbook with her ESL students at the Mecklenburg County Jail in North Carolina.

Grace Tanaka is professor and coordinator of ESL at the Santa Ana College School of Continuing Education, in Santa Ana, California, which serves more than 20,000 students per year. She is also a textbook co-author and series consultant. Grace has 25 years of teaching experience in both credit and non-credit ESL programs.

Shirley Velasco is principal at Miami Beach Adult and Community Education Center in Miami Beach, Florida. She has been a classroom instructor and administrator for the past 28 years. Shirley has created a large adult ESL program based on a curriculum she helped develop to implement state/national ESL standards.

Teaching Strategies

Repetition: On almost every page of *All-Star*, students have the opportunity to listen to and repeat new vocabulary and structures. They need this structured practice in a low-anxiety environment before they are asked to manipulate this language in reading, writing, listening, or speaking activities. Repetition allows them to learn the pronunciation of individual words, internalize word order, and better approximate the stress and intonation pattern of native speakers. Although the audio program provides for repetition, students may need more frequent repetition drills to reinforce pronunciation or word order. One strategy is to say the new word or phrase and have the class repeat chorally, then call on individual students. You can use the Big Picture Power Point Slides, found in the Online Teacher Resource Center, to introduce or review new language in this way.

When students are practicing conversational structures, you can lead them through a progression of activities. First, you read one role and the students respond chorally. Then, divide the class into two: one half reads one role chorally, and the other half responds chorally. Then model the conversation with a student, or have two students model the conversation for the class. Finally, students can practice with partners. In this way, they acquire confidence as they gradually become more independent in using the new language.

Modeling: Before students are asked to produce language in a new context, they need the opportunity to see it demonstrated and then to practice it in a structured setting. Whenever there is an activity that calls on students to personalize the language, the instructor should model how this is done. For example, if students are asked to talk to a partner and complete the sentence "I'm wearing _____ shoes." You should point to your shoes and say, "I'm wearing . . ." You can then pause and prompt students to say the color of your shoes. Repeat the sentence, including the color of your shoes. After you have modeled the new language, more advanced students can provide additional examples of appropriate responses (e.g., "I'm wearing brown shoes."). Less proficient students can follow their examples.

Elicitation: Elicitation is an effective tool in making the classroom more learner-centered. When students contribute their ideas, they feel more secure about their abilities in the new language, and valued for what they already know. Asking questions and eliciting responses from the class will keep students more actively engaged in learning. More advanced students are often eager to respond, whereas the less proficient may be more reluctant. One way to level the playing field is to provide a sentence stem for the answer (e.g., "My name is _____."), and then have more advanced students model appropriate responses. Less proficient students can follow the pattern set by the students before them. Another strategy is to accept partial or one-word answers and provide the rest of the sentence (e.g., "Tien." "Your name is Tien."). Allowing students to discuss the topic in small groups or pairs before you elicit responses from the whole class is also an effective strategy (see *Modeling*).

Error correction: When and how often to correct students is the subject of much debate. Research suggests that it is repeated exposure to accurate input rather than correction that helps a student internalize new language. Too much correction can cause a learner to feel insecure about his or her language ability and reluctant to take the risks necessary to becoming more fluent in a new language. When accuracy is the goal, as in the repetition of listening activities or completing a multiple-choice assessment, correction should be immediate and constructive. When fluency is the goal, as in conversation practice with a partner, correction should be minimized, as it interrupts the conversational flow and can make students more self-conscious. In many cases, students can self-correct if you provide a model of accurate language. For example, if a student says, "Hello. I Carlos," you can respond, "Hi, Carlos. I'm Isabel." By emphasizing the correct form in your response, you can help students monitor their own speech. This technique is often referred to as "counsel correction." Another strategy is to pause before the error, gesturing for students to fill in the correct form.

Pair/group work: Students at a beginning level are often reluctant to work in pairs or small groups, as they are insecure about their own language abilities and may be accustomed to a teacher-centered approach. However, pair and group work activities allow each student more opportunities to engage in conversation in English. To encourage student participation in these activities, walk around and listen to all of the pairs or small groups as they are working. Asking questions or helping with pronunciation makes students feel that the activity is purposeful and personally beneficial. Such monitoring also prepares students to speak in front of the whole group and in authentic situations outside the classroom. To maximize interaction among the students, you can vary the seating arrangements or use strategies such as counting off that match students with different partners each time. Alternatively, you can engineer the groupings so that students complement each other, perhaps placing a more communicative student with one who has stronger literacy skills.

TEACHING STRATEGIES

Using the audio program: Every unit in *All-Star* includes substantive listening practice for students on realistic topics. This practice is important not only for assessment purposes, but also to help students become accustomed to listening to and comprehending voices other than that of the instructor. Such activities prepare students to navigate more successfully in the real world with other native speakers. Units are structured so that students first listen to vocabulary or conversational models as they associate the sound with the context, then repeat the new language. When they have mastered the scripted conversation, they are then asked to personalize the new language in describing their own experiences.

Using the interactive Work-Out CD-ROM: The Work-Out CD-ROM provides additional language practice and reinforces the learning goals of each unit of the Student Book by integrating language, literacy, and numeracy skill-building with computer practice. The Work-Out CD-ROM allows students to interact with the language in a variety of ways. The activities support visual learning through pictures and text as well as auditory learning through recorded conversations, monologues, and jazz chants. The drag and drop, and scrambled sentences activities require students' kinesthetic interaction to move words and pictures to appropriate locations on the screen. Students can use the CD-ROM at their own pace and receive instant feedback to their answers. Students can track their completion of the Work-Out CD ROM activities with a reproducible checklist, which can be found in the Online Teacher Resource Center.

Using realia: Adult students attend to and retain information when it is made relevant to their own needs and experience. Using real material such as authentic documents, maps, pictures, and objects not only helps students relate language learning to their own lives, it also appeals to a variety of learning styles. *All-Star* includes forms that help students develop competence with authentic documents. Wherever possible, other realistic diagrams and visuals have been included in the units to help students place the language in real world contexts. Bringing in other authentic materials related to the unit topic can make concepts more tangible and reinforce learning.

How to work with reluctant learners: Sometimes adult students enter literacy and low beginning classes having had little experience in an educational setting. Others may have had negative experiences in school, or may feel that learning English at this stage in their lives is a burden rather than an opportunity. Such students may be reluctant at first to participate in class activities. Recognize that these students have a wealth of experience and knowledge on which to draw, and include activities that are relevant to their everyday lives. For example, when students begin a unit on families, ask them to bring in photos of the people in their families. When they begin to learn about jobs, ask them to talk about the kind of work they do. Help them use the language provided in the unit to talk about their own jobs. With every topic, be sensitive to the needs of your students. For example, students who may have lost family members or whose families have been left behind can either tell about their relatives or about the people they live with now.

PRE-UNIT: NICE TO MEET YOU

OBJECTIVE
Introduction: Nice to meet you.

1 Practice the Conversation

- Welcome students to the class and introduce yourself. Follow the model in the first line of the conversation: *Hi. My name is _____*, and gesture to yourself.
- Have students look at the picture. Read the conversation, turning from side to side, or pointing at the pictures in the book to indicate when A is talking or when B is talking.
- Say the lines a second time. Pause after each line and have students repeat.
- Read A's lines and have students respond chorally with B's lines. For variation, divide the class in half, with one side reading A's lines and the other reading B's lines. Have students use their own names.
- Model the activity with a student. Read A's lines and substitute your own name. Cue the student to respond with his or her name.
- Have the students practice the conversation in pairs. Have them switch partners four more times to practice the conversation.
- Walk around the room to monitor the activity and provide help as needed.

Culture Note:
- Newcomers may be unfamiliar with introductions in American culture. Point out that we usually use our first and last names when we meet someone for the first time, and that we give our first name first rather than our last name. It is customary for both men and women to shake hands when they are introducing themselves.

EXPANSION ACTIVITY: Introduction Lines
- Have students form two lines facing each other. Have the two students facing each other practice the conversation.
- Have the first person in one line move to the other end of the line. Everyone should be facing a new partner to practice the conversation again.
- Continue a few more times.

2 Complete the Conversations

- Have students look at the useful expressions. Read each expression and have students repeat.
- Have students look at the first conversation. Go over the directions. Read the first two lines of the conversation and elicit the third line (*How do you spell that?*). Point out that this expression is written on the line.
- Have students complete the conversations.
- Put students in pairs to check their answers.
- Read the conversations aloud or play the audio. Have students check their answers.
- Read the conversations or play the audio a second time if necessary.
- Go over the answers with the class.

LISTENING SCRIPT

Pre-Unit, Activity 2: Complete the Conversations

Use a question or sentence from the box to complete the conversations. Listen again and check your answers.

1.
A: What's your name?
B: Keiko.
A: How do you spell that?
B: K-e-i-k-o.

PRE-UNIT: NICE TO MEET YOU

2.
A: Where are you from?
B: I'm from Mexico. What about you?
A: I'm from China.

3.
A: What languages do you speak?
B: Russian, French, and English.
A: Really? That's interesting!

4.
A: Do you like to watch flicks?
B: I'm not sure. What is a flick?
A: It is a movie.
B: Then yes, I do.

5.
A: Please turn to page 12.
B: Could you repeat that?
A: Please turn to page 12.

6.
A: Would you be interested in studying tomorrow?
B: I'm sorry. I don't understand your question.
A: Do you want to study with me tomorrow?
B: Yes, thank you.

ANSWER KEY:
1. How do you spell that?
2. What about you?
3. That's interesting!
4. What is
5. Could you repeat that?
6. I'm sorry. I don't understand your question.

Language Notes:
- Point out that three of the useful expressions (*Could you repeat that?*, *What is _____?*, and *I'm sorry. I don't understand your question*) are used when communication is not successful, in other words, when the listener doesn't understand what is said.
- Often students will ask for repetition of an entire sentence (*Could you repeat that?*) when they really just need clarification of one word or phrase. Point out that asking about the word or phrase is often more effective in clarifying what the speaker is saying.

EXPANSION ACTIVITY: What is that?
- Write ten nouns or gerunds on the board that may be unfamiliar to your students (possible words: *hot rods, pop, rap, hip-hop, hanging out, potlucks, banana splits, telemarketers, flea markets, gumbo, knitting, talk radio*).
- Call on students and ask: *Do you like _____?* Complete the sentence with an unfamiliar word. Have students practice responding *I'm not sure. What's _____?*
- Be prepared to provide simple definitions for the words you have chosen.

PRE-UNIT: NICE TO MEET YOU

❸ Follow Instructions 003

- Have students look at the pictures. Elicit the action words they know.
- Have students listen and look at the pictures while you say the words or play the audio.
- Say the words or play the audio a second time. Pause after each word or phrase and ask the students to repeat and point to the correct picture.
- Put students in pairs and have one say a word or phrase as the partner points to the correct picture. Reverse roles and repeat the activity.
- Give instructions in random order and have students comply.
- Go over the instructions and the example at the bottom of the page.
- Put students in pairs. Have them take turns giving and following instructions. Walk around the room to monitor the activity and provide help as needed.

EXPANSION ACTIVITY: Get it right!

- Write instructions on the board.

    Read all the instructions.
    Take out a piece of paper.
    Write your name.
    Underline your first name.
    Circle your last name.

- Have students follow your written instructions and then check their work with a classmate.

LISTENING SCRIPT

Pre-Unit, Activity 3: Follow Instructions

Look at the pictures. Listen to the classroom instructions. Listen again and repeat.

1. Listen to the words.
2. Say, "Hello."
3. Write your name.
4. Sign your name.
5. Check True or False.
6. Take out a piece of paper.
7. Practice the conversation.
8. Raise your hand.
9. Underline the word.
10. Circle the word.
11. Hand in your homework.
12. Listen and repeat.

UNIT 1: DESCRIBING PEOPLE

UNIT OVERVIEW

LESSON	STUDENT BOOK PAGE	TEACHER'S EDITION PAGE
1. Giving Personal Information	4	6
2. Talking About People	6	9
3. At a Park	8	12
4. Likes and Dislikes: Bio Poems	10	15
5. Meeting People	12	18
6. Taking Phone Messages	14	22
7. What Do You Know?	16	25

Big Picture Expansion Activities

FOCUS	TITLE	SUGGESTED USE
Speaking	Memory Game	Lesson 3
Reading	Greg Works Hard	Lesson 4
Grammar	Simple Present Tense	Lesson 4
Writing	Describing People	Lesson 6
Speaking	Assessment: Talking about the Big Picture	Lesson 7

Big Picture Expansion Activity Worksheets

FOCUS	TITLE	TEACHER'S EDITION PAGE
1. Reading	Greg Works Hard	224
2. Grammar	Simple Present	225

DESCRIBING PEOPLE • 5

LESSON 1: Giving Personal Information

OBJECTIVE
Giving personal information

VOCABULARY

address	employee I.D.	last name
birth certificate	badge	middle name
birthplace	eye color	occupation
date of birth	first name	sex
diploma	hair color	signature
driver's license	height	weight

 TARGET GRAMMAR

Simple present of *be*, statements *page 144*

THINGS TO DO

1 Learn New Words 004

- Have students look at the pictures, and elicit the words they know.
- Have students listen and look at the pictures while you say the words or play the audio.
- Instruct students to circle the words that are new to them.
- Say the words or play the audio a second time. Pause after each word or phrase and ask the students to repeat and point to the correct picture.
- Put students in pairs and have one say a word or phrase as the partner points to the correct picture. Reverse roles and repeat the activity.
- Call on students and ask them personal information questions: *What's your first name? What is your date of birth?*

LISTENING SCRIPT

Lesson 1, Activity 1: Learn New Words

Look at the pictures. Listen to the words. Listen again and repeat.

1.	birth certificate	It's a birth certificate.
2.	birthplace	His birthplace is Kingsville, Texas.
3.	date of birth	His date of birth is March 2, 1975.
4.	first name	His first name is Robert.
5.	middle name	His middle name is Manuel.
6.	last name	His last name is Garza.
7.	sex	His sex is male.
8.	driver's license	It's a driver's license.
9.	address	His address is 1521 Market Street, San Francisco, California, 94821.
10.	hair color	His hair color is brown.
11.	eye color	His eye color is brown.
12.	height	His height is 5'10".
13.	weight	His weight is 160 pounds.
14.	diploma	It's a high school diploma.
15.	signature	There's a signature on the diploma.
16.	employee I.D. badge	It's an employee I.D. badge.
17.	occupation	His occupation is nursing assistant.

6 • UNIT 1   STUDENT BOOK PAGES 4–5

Unit 1: Lesson 1

> **EXPANSION ACTIVITY:**
> **Write It Out [Low-Level]**
> - Have students write the words from Activity 1 down the left side of a piece of paper except for *birth certificate, driver's license, diploma,* and *employee I. D. badge.* Point out that those words refer to documents, not personal information.
> - Have students write their own personal information next to the appropriate word.
> - Point out that this exercise will prepare them for Activity 3.

❷ Use the Words

- Go over the directions.
- Model the conversation with a student. Have the student read A's lines. Cue the student to ask about the numbered information below. Demonstrate how to substitute different names in B's first line, and different addresses in the last line.
- Have students work in pairs and practice the conversation asking about the numbered information.
- Walk around the room to monitor the activity and provide help as needed.
- CHALLENGE: Have more advanced students add to each conversation by asking additional questions or providing additional information. For example, students may add to the example conversation in this way: *His address is 1521 Market Street. His house is across from the city park.*

> **ANSWER KEY:**
> 1. What's his first name? His first name is Robert. What's his middle name? His middle name is Manuel.
> 2. What's his date of birth? His date of birth is March 2, 1975. What's his birthplace? His birthplace is Kingsville, Texas.
> 3. What's his height? His height is 5'10". What's his weight? His weight is 160 pounds.
> 4. What's his eye color? His eye color is brown. What's his hair color? His hair color is brown.

🎯 TARGET GRAMMAR

Simple present of *be*, statements

The Target Grammar point is used in Activities 2–5. Presentation and practice of this grammar point appears on Student Book page 144. Answer Keys appear on Teacher's Edition page 246.

> **EXPANSION ACTIVITY:**
> **Invent a Character [Challenge]**
> - Have students search through magazines to find a picture of an intriguing person. Have students create an identity for this person, including the information from Activity 2. Encourage students to include additional information based on the vocabulary words, such as the person's occupation and educational background.
> - Have partners interview each other about their character, with partners pretending to be the characters they've created. Invite partners to share their pictures and interviews with the class.

❸ Interview

- Explain the directions. Be sure to say that students will be writing their partner's answers.
- Read the questions aloud and have students repeat.
- Go over the example. Model the activity with a student. Ask the questions. Write the student's answers on the board.

Unit 1: Lesson 1

4 Tell the Class

- Tell the class about the student: His/Her first name is; His/Her last name is; His/Her eyes are; His/Her birthplace is.
- Have students work in pairs to practice asking and answering the personal information questions.
- Call on students to tell about their partners.

> **EXPANSION ACTIVITY: Beanbag Toss**
>
> - Tell students that when you ask a question they should respond with information about themselves.
> - Model the activity. Call on a student and toss him or her a beanbag or ball. Ask a question (*What is your eye color?*). Elicit the answer (brown). Have the student toss the beanbag back to you. Toss the beanbag to another student and continue the activity.
> - Once students understand the activity, have them toss the beanbag to each other and ask and answer questions.

5 Circle *True* or *False* 005

- Go over the directions.
- Play the audio and have students circle *True* or *False* for each question.
- Replay each statement one at a time and have the class give the correct answer.
- Replay the statement if necessary to help students understand the information.

> **LISTENING SCRIPT**
>
> **Lesson 1, Activity 5: Circle *True* or *False***
>
> *Listen. Then circle True or False.*
>
> 1. Robert's middle name is Manuel.
> 2. His birthplace is New York.
> 3. He is a high school student.
> 4. His eyes are brown.
> 5. He is five feet nine inches tall.
> 6. Robert is a nursing assistant.

> **ANSWER KEY:**
>
> 1. True; 2. False; 3. False; 4. True; 5. False; 6. True

> **EXPANSION ACTIVITY: Find Someone Who**
>
> - Write sentences with *be* on the board. Use these sentences or create your own: He/She is an only child. He/She is a parent. They are homeowners. He/She is a singer or musician. He/She is happy at his/her job. They are sports fans. You and he/she are _____.
> - Have the students copy the sentences.
> - Tell students that they will write down the name of a student for whom the statement is true next to each statement. For statements using *they*, students will need to write the names of two or more people. Explain that for the final statement, the student must find someone who has something in common with him- or herself and rewrite the sentence beginning with *We are*.
> - Model how to do the activity. Walk around the class and ask a student a question. Write his or her answer on the board.
> - Have the students walk around the class and talk to other students. Call on students to tell what they found out about each other. Monitor for correct use of *be*, having peers correct each other.

LESSON 2: Talking About People

OBJECTIVE
Talking about people

VOCABULARY

bald	heavy	short hair
beard	light brown	slim
blond	long hair	straight hair
curly hair	medium height	tall
dark brown	mustache	
gray	short	

TARGET GRAMMAR

Simple present of *have*, statements   *page 145*

THINGS TO DO

1 Learn New Words 006

- Have students look at the pictures and elicit the words they know.
- Have students listen and look at the pictures while you say the words or play the audio.
- Instruct students to circle the words that are new to them.
- Say the words or play the audio a second time. Pause after each word or phrase and ask the students to repeat and point to the correct part of the picture.
- Put students in pairs and have one say a word or phrase as the partner points to the correct picture. Reverse roles and repeat the activity.
- Walk around the class and stand next to a student. Make a statement about the student using one of the new words: *He has curly hair.* Elicit *yes* or *no* from the other students. Continue with other statements about students.

LISTENING SCRIPT

Lesson 2, Activity 1: Learn New Words

Look at the picture. Listen to the words. Listen again and repeat.

1. long hair — She has long hair.
2. short hair — He has short hair.
3. straight hair — He has straight hair.
4. curly hair — She has curly hair.
5. bald — He is bald.
6. beard — He has a beard.
7. mustache — He has a mustache.
8. tall — He is tall.
9. medium height — He is medium height.
10. short — He is short.
11. slim — She is slim.
12. heavy — He is heavy.
13. blond — His hair is blond.
14. light brown — Her hair is light brown.
15. dark brown — His hair is dark brown.
16. gray — Her hair is gray.

EXPANSION ACTIVITY:
Describe Yourself [Low-Level]

- Model the activity by describing yourself: *I have curly hair. I am short. My hair is gray.*
- Have students write three sentences about themselves using the new words.
- Have students take turns describing themselves in pairs.
- Call on students to describe their partners.

Unit 1: Lesson 2

❷ Listen and Write

- Have students look at the picture and describe each person.
- Play the audio and have students write the answers on the lines.
- Play the audio a second time. Have students check their own answers.
- Have students check their answers in pairs.
- Go over the answers with the class, playing the audio for each description again if desired.

LISTENING SCRIPT

Lesson 2, Activity 2: Listen and Write

Listen. Write the correct name under each picture.

1. Robert is slim. He has short curly hair and a mustache.
2. Lisa has long blond hair and she's medium height.
3. Estela is short and slim.
4. Rick is short and heavy.
5. Dan is heavy, and he has short straight hair.
6. Paul has dark brown hair, and he is slim.
7. Sam has long straight hair, and he is tall.

ANSWER KEY:

From left to write in the picture: Lisa, Dan, Sam, Estela, Rick, Robert, Paul

ⓞ TARGET GRAMMAR

Simple present of *have*, statements
The Target Grammar point is used in Activities 2, 3, and 4. Presentation and practice of this grammar point appears on Student Book page 145. Answer Keys appear on Teacher's Edition page 246.

EXPANSION ACTIVITY: Add One

- Write the sentences from Activity 2 on the board.
- Put students in groups of four. Tell students that they will take turns starting the activity. The first student reads a sentence from Activity 2. The next student repeats that sentence and adds a sentence to describe another quality that can be seen in the picture. The third student repeats the first two sentences and adds another. Continue until no one can add anything new. Then a student will read the next sentence from Activity 2.
- Model the activity. Have a student read the first sentence. Repeat it and add information: *Robert is slim. He has short curly hair and a mustache. He has brown hair.* Elicit another sentence about Robert from a student: *He has a purple shirt.*
- Have students continue the activity in their small groups.
- Walk around the classroom to monitor the activity and provide help as needed.
- Call on students to add information about each picture.
- LOW LEVEL: Have students who need practice listening or writing listen to their classmates tell about the picture. Have them write down what they hear. After students have finished describing a person, have the students read their notes about what they heard. Have the class confirm whether the notes were accurate.

❸ Practice the Conversation

- Have students listen and look at the conversation while you read it or play the audio.
- Say the words or play the audio a second time. Pause after each line and ask the students to repeat.

Unit 1: Lesson 2

- Model the conversation with a student. Have the student read B's lines. Demonstrate how to substitute a different person (*Robert*) in the first line, and a different description (*He has a mustache*) in the third line. Cue the student to repeat the same changes in B's lines.
- Point out that the expression *You can't miss him* means that you will definitely see and recognize him.
- Have students work in pairs and practice the conversation making substitutions with the names and descriptions in the boxes below.
- Walk around to make sure they understand the activity and provide help if needed.

> **LISTENING SCRIPT**
>
> **Lesson 2, Activity 3: Practice the Conversation**
>
> *Listen to the conversation. Listen again and repeat.*
>
> A: Would you give this book to Robert?
> B: I'm sorry. I don't know Robert.
> A: He has a mustache. You can't miss him.
> B: A mustache?
> A: Right.

> **Grammar Note:**
> - Students may get confused over the use of the verbs *be* and *have* in physical descriptions. Point out that we use *have* when we are talking about the particular type of hair, eyes, or other body part that belongs to someone: *He has long hair; She has blue eyes.* We use *be* before adjectives that describe someone's height and weight: *He is tall, We are slim* or someone's hair or eyes directly: *His hair is long; Her eyes are blue.*

> **EXPANSION ACTIVITY:**
> **Classmates [Multi-Level]**
> - Have students practice the conversation using information about their classmates.
> - Model the activity with a student using a real book. Substitute the name and description of a student in your class. Have the student find that classmate and give him or her the book.
> - Continue with other students, or have them take turns practicing the conversation in pairs. Have more advanced students play the role of A and lower-level students play the role of B.

4 Write

- Go over the directions and the example with the class.
- Have students write one sentence each about a classmate.
- Have each student read his or her sentence to the class and have students guess who the person is.

> **EXPANSION ACTIVITY:**
> **Who Is It? Mingle**
> - Make Activity 4 more challenging by having students circulate and ask and answer questions about their classmates.
> - CHALLENGE: Have advanced students write sentences that tell what the mystery person is NOT. For example: *This person is not short, and she doesn't have blond or black hair. Her eyes aren't green or blue.*

LESSON 3 — At a Park

OBJECTIVE
At a park

VOCABULARY

afraid	happy	slide
angry	laptop	swing
basketball	nervous	tired
bored	radio	toy
camera	relaxed	
cell phone	sad	

TARGET GRAMMAR

Simple present, questions *page 146*

THINGS TO DO

1 Learn New Words 009

- Have students look at the pictures and elicit the words they know.
- Have students listen and look at the pictures while you say the words or play the audio.
- Instruct students to circle the words that are new to them.
- Say the words or play the audio a second time. Pause after each word and ask the students to repeat and point to the correct part of the picture.
- Put students in pairs and have one say a word or phrase as the partner points to the correct picture. Reverse roles and repeat the activity.
- Call on students and ask them questions using the words: *Who is afraid? Who is tired? Who is playing basketball?*

LISTENING SCRIPT

Lesson 3, Activity 1: Learn New Words

Look at the picture. Listen to the words. Listen again and repeat.

1. happy — He looks happy.
2. relaxed — He looks relaxed.
3. sad — She looks sad.
4. nervous — He looks nervous.
5. afraid — She is afraid.
6. bored — He looks bored.
7. angry — She looks angry.
8. tired — He looks tired.
9. radio — She has a radio.
10. slide — It's a slide.
11. swing — It's a swing.
12. basketball — He has a basketball.
13. camera — He has a camera.
14. toy — It's a toy.
15. laptop — He has a laptop.
16. cell phone — She has a cell phone.

EXPANSION ACTIVITY: To Tell the Truth

- Say a sentence about the picture that isn't true: *There are 15 people in the picture.* Have students correct the sentence: *There are 27 people in the picture.*
- Have students write five sentences about the picture that are not true.
- Have students in pairs or teams read one sentence at a time and have the other partner or team correct the sentences.
- Walk around to monitor the activity and provide help as needed.

Unit 1: Lesson 3

❷ Talk About the Picture

- Go over the directions and the examples with a student. Have students confirm the information using the picture.
- Have students write their ideas, then share them with a partner.
- Have each student present one idea to the class.

> **EXPANSION ACTIVITY: But Why? [Challenge]**
>
> This activity builds on Activity 2.
> - Have partners discuss the people in the picture, telling not just how each person feels, but why. Tell them to use their imaginations to decide why each person feels the way he or she does.
> - Have each pair tell the class about why one person in the picture is feeling a certain way.

❸ Practice the Conversation 010

- Have students listen and look at the picture while you read it or play the audio.
- Say the words or play the audio a second time. Pause after each line and ask the students to repeat.
- Model the conversation with a student. Have the student read B's lines. Demonstrate how to substitute a different person (Amy) and feeling (happy) in the first line, and a different reaction (That's great) in the second line. Cue the student to substitute a different reason (She likes the slide).
- Have students work in pairs and practice the conversation using the names and situations in the boxes.
- Walk around to make sure they understand the activity and provide help if needed.

LISTENING SCRIPT

Lesson 3, Activity 3: Practice the Conversation

Listen to the conversation. Listen again and repeat.

A: Is Lynn nervous?

B: Yes, she is. She is afraid of the dog.

A: That's too bad.

> **EXPANSION ACTIVITY:**
> **Charades [Low-Level]**
>
> - Tell the students that you are going to act out one of the words on the list (happy).
> - Mime this feeling (by smiling, skipping, etc.) and elicit the word.
> - Have volunteers come to the front of the class. Whisper a word and have them act it out until the other students name the word correctly.

> **BIG PICTURE EXPANSION ACTIVITY:**
> **SPEAKING—Memory Game**
>
> - Have students look at the Big Picture in their books (Student Book pages 8–9). Divide the class into teams. Have each team create yes/no or Wh- questions about the picture: *Is there a girl on the slide? Who is angry?* Make sure that each team creates enough questions so that each member can ask at least one question. Encourage students to ask about specific details in the picture.
> - Have students close their books. Within each team, they should answer the created questions based on their memory of the picture.
> - Next, have each team ask another team its questions about the picture. Every student should ask one question and the game should continue until each student has had a chance to ask and answer questions about the picture. Each correct answer earns a point.
> - Small prizes for the winning team may increase enthusiasm for the game and the energy level of the class.

Unit 1: Lesson 3

> **TARGET GRAMMAR**
>
> **Simple present, questions**
> The Target Grammar point is used in Activity 3. Presentation and practice of this grammar point appears on Student Book pages 146–147. Answer Keys appear on Teacher's Edition page 246.

④ How About You?

- Have students look at the chart.
- Model the activity by talking about yourself: *I am often happy.*
- Have students check the boxes to describe themselves.
- Have students take turns sharing their answers in pairs.
- Call on a few students to share their answers with the class.
- CHALLENGE: Have students write sentences or a paragraph about something that makes them feel bored or nervous. Have them draw an illustration for their writing and share their ideas and picture with a partner.

> **EXPANSION ACTIVITY: Where or When**
>
> - Have students draw lines to divide a blank piece of drawing paper into four quadrants. Have them label each quadrant with an emotion, such as *happy, nervous,* and so on.
> - Have students draw or write in each quadrant about a place or time that makes them feel the emotion listed there.
> - Have students share their ideas in pairs.

LESSON 4

Likes and Dislikes: Bio Poems

OBJECTIVE
Likes and Dislikes: bio poems

VOCABULARY

baseball	motorcycles	soccer
housework	music	swimming
loud noises	pets	

TARGET GRAMMAR
Simple present, statements *page 148*

THINGS TO DO

1 Learn New Words 011

- Have students look at the pictures and elicit the words they know.
- Have students listen and look at the pictures while you say the words or play the audio.
- Say the words or play the audio a second time. Pause after each word or phrase and ask the students to repeat and point to the correct picture.
- Put students in pairs and have one say a word or phrase as the partner points to the correct picture. Reverse roles and repeat the activity.
- Call on students and ask them questions about their likes and dislikes: *Do you like soccer?*

LISTENING SCRIPT

Lesson 4, Activity 1: Learn New Words

Look at the pictures. Listen to the words. Listen again and repeat.

1. music	She likes music.
2. swimming	She likes swimming.
3. loud noises	She doesn't like loud noises.
4. soccer	He likes soccer.
5. baseball	He doesn't like baseball.
6. housework	He doesn't like housework.
7. motorcycles	He likes motorcycles.
8. pets	He doesn't like pets.

TARGET GRAMMAR

Simple present, statements

The Target Grammar point is used in Activities 1, 2, and 3. Presentation and practice of this grammar point appears on Student Book pages 148–149. Answer Keys appear on Teacher's Edition page 246.

Unit 1: Lesson 4

> **EXPANSION ACTIVITY:**
> **Draw the Picture [Low-Level]**
>
> - Have the students work in small teams. Explain that a member from each team will draw a picture of a new word from Activity 1 on the board and the other students will guess what it is.
> - Have the students determine in which order they will draw by labeling each member in their group A, B, C, etc.
> - Have Student A from each team go to the board. Tell them that they will draw a picture, but they may not speak or write letters or words.
> - Point to or whisper one vocabulary word from the list of new words to the Student As. When you say "go" they should all begin to draw a picture of the word on the board.
> - The first student to raise his or her hand and correctly guess the word gets a point for his or her team.

❷ Read and Take Notes 012

- Have students look at the chart. Elicit the type of information they will find in the poems (name, description, likes, dislikes, languages, occupation, last name).
- Have students look at the poems. Point out the shape of the poem (a diamond). Ask: *What is on the first line of each poem?* (a first name).
- Have students listen and look at the pictures while you read the poems or play the audio.
- Read the poems or play the audio a second time. Have the students read along silently.
- Ask questions about Yuko: *What color hair does she have? What does she like? What does she dislike?* Point out that the information about Yuko is written on the chart.
- Have students complete the chart with the information about Paul and Abel.
- Have students check their answers in pairs.
- Call on students and ask questions about Paul and Abel.

- **LITERACY:** Explain that in poems, writers often ignore conventions of grammar and punctuation. Authors may use sentence fragments or run-on sentences to express their ideas. Have students find and circle the proper names in the poems. Point out that each one retains its capital letter, despite the informality of the poem.

> **LISTENING SCRIPT**
>
> **Lesson 4, Activity 2: Read and Take Notes**
>
> *Listen to the poems. Then read the poems and take notes in the chart.*
>
> 1.
> Yuko
> my classmate
> brown hair, brown eyes, intelligent
> likes music, swimming, and Japanese food
> doesn't like pets, loud noises, and the color yellow
> speaks Japanese and English
> a student
> Tanaka
>
> 2.
> Paul
> my friend
> tall, slim, good-looking
> likes cars, loud music, and soccer
> doesn't like baseball, housework, and homework
> speaks Chinese, French, and English
> a student
> Ho
>
> 3.
> Abel
> my husband
> tall, dark, handsome
> likes cameras, motorcycles, and good food
> doesn't like American coffee, alarm clocks, and pets
> speaks Spanish and English
> a businessperson
> Diaz

Unit 1: Lesson 4

EXPANSION ACTIVITY: Guess Who?

- Tell the students that they are going to write sentences about Yuko, Paul, and Abel using the information in the poems.
- Model the activity. Write a sentence about one person: *This person is a businessman who likes good food.* Have the students look at the poems to find out who it is. Elicit that you are writing about Abel.
- Have the students write five sentences about the people in the poems. Have them take turns reading their sentences to a partner, who must guess who it is.
- For variation, divide the class into teams after they have written sentences. Have team members take turns reading sentences to members of the other team. Set a time limit (five seconds, for example). The team earns a point for every correct answer given within the time limit.

3 Write

- Go over the directions with the class.
- Have students look at the descriptions of what should be written on each line. Ask questions to familiarize students with the format: *What do you write on line 1? What do you write on line 2?* Point out that they can write about themselves, in which case they should write *myself* on line 2.
- Have students write a poem about themselves or someone they know well.
- Call on students to read their poems aloud to the class.

**EXPANSION ACTIVITY:
Who Am I? [Multi-Level]**

- Have the students write poems about themselves, but tell them to omit the names on the first and last lines. Have more advanced students work with lower-level students to help them brainstorm ideas and write the correct form of the poem.
- Collect the poems and redistribute them.
- Have students read the poems to the class. Have the students guess who wrote the poem.

**BIG PICTURE EXPANSION ACTIVITY:
READING—Greg Works Hard**

- Make copies of Worksheet 1 (Teacher's Edition page 224) and distribute them to students.
- Have students look at the Big Picture in their books (Student Book pages 8–9). Have students read the story, or read the story aloud line by line and have students repeat.
- Instruct students to complete the activities and then check their answers with a partner.
- Go over the answers with the class.

ANSWER KEY:

A. 1. False; 2. True; 3. False; 4. True; 5. True; 6. False
B. 1. no; 2. no; 3. young; 4. at a table; 5. his computer; 6. yes

**BIG PICTURE EXPANSION ACTIVITY:
GRAMMAR—Simple Present Tense**

- Make copies of Worksheet 2 (Teacher's Edition page 225) and distribute them to students.
- Have students look at the Big Picture in their books (Student Book pages 8–9). Instruct students to complete the activities and then check their answers with a partner.
- Go over the answers with the class. For each "no" answer, have students tell the correct information about the person.

ANSWER KEY:

A. There <u>are</u> many things to do in Sun County City Park. Some people <u>play</u> basketball. Some people <u>sit</u> and <u>talk</u>. Today, two children <u>are</u> on the slide. Someone <u>has</u> a camera. One woman <u>is</u> angry. A man <u>is</u> tired. Many people <u>are</u> happy. The park <u>is</u> a nice place to visit.
B. 1. yes; 2. yes; 3. no (he is nervous); 4. yes; 5. yes; 6. no (she has a radio); 7. yes; 8. no (he has blond hair); 9. no (he doesn't have a mustache); 10. no (he is young)

LESSON 5 — Meeting People

OBJECTIVE
Meeting people

PRONUNCIATION
Vowel Sounds in *Slip* and *Sleep*

❶ Practice Pronunciation: Vowel Sounds in *Slip* and *Sleep* 🎧 013

A. Listen to the words. Listen again and repeat.

- Go over the introductory comment.
- Write *slip* and *sleep* on the board. Say each word several times. Exaggerate the length of the sound in *sleep*. Point out that people learning English often have trouble hearing the difference between the two sounds.
- Have students look at the list of words.
- Read the words or play the audio.
- Read or play the audio a second time. Have the students repeat the words. Have the students circle the words that have the long E sound as in *sleep*.
- Have students check their answers in pairs. Go over the answers with the class.

ANSWER KEY:
Circle: 2. these, 3. meet, 6. leave, 7. me, 9. feet, 12. sleep, 14. easy, 15. he

---

LISTENING SCRIPT
Lesson 5, Activity 1A: Practice Pronunciation: Vowel Sounds in *Slip* and *Sleep*

A. Listen to the words. Listen again and repeat.

1.	this	9.	feet
2.	these	10.	slim
3.	meet	11.	slip
4.	live	12.	sleep
5.	fifth	13.	is
6.	leave	14.	easy
7.	me	15.	he
8.	fit	16.	his

Circle the words with the long vowel [E] sound.

B. Listen to the pairs of sentences. Listen again and repeat. 🎧 014

- Have students listen as you read the sentences or play the audio.
- Read the sentences or play the audio a second time and have students repeat.
- Ask students which sentences have words with the long E sound (the ones on the right).

LISTENING SCRIPT
Lesson 5, Activity 1B: Practice Pronunciation: Vowel Sounds in *Slip* and *Sleep*

B. Listen to the pairs of sentences. Listen again and repeat.

1.	This is for you.	These are for you.
2.	Did you slip yesterday?	Did you sleep yesterday?
3.	I want to live.	I want to leave.
4.	Is he shopping?	Easy shopping?

Unit 1: Lesson 5

C. Listen as your partner says a sentence from each pair in Activity B. Circle the sentence you hear.

- Have students look at the pairs of sentences in Activity C. Point out that they are the same sentences as in Activity B.
- Read the two sentences in C 1: *This is for you/These are for you*. Ask how they are different (the first one is about a single object; the second is plural).
- Now read just one of those sentences. Ask the students to circle the one you read.
- Ask the students to raise their hands if they circled A. Then ask them to raise their hands if they circled B. Tell them the correct answer.
- Put the students in pairs. Tell them that they will take turns reading a sentence from each pair in Activity C. Tell them that listeners should circle the sentence that they hear. Speakers will check to see that they have circled the correct sentence.
- Walk around the classroom to monitor the activity and provide help as needed.

> **EXPANSION ACTIVITY: Categories**
> - Put a chart like the one below on the board.
>
> | Category | Words with Vowel Sound in "Slip" | Words with Vowel Sound in "Sleep" |
> |---|---|---|
> | Country | Finland | Ethiopia |
> | First Name | Jill | Eileen |
> | Food | pickle | bean |
> | Things in a Home | dishes | tea kettle |
>
> - Put students in pairs or small groups and have them copy and complete the chart. Encourage them to list as many examples as they can.
> - Walk around to monitor the activity and provide help as needed.
> - Have volunteers come to the board and fill in the chart.

- For variation, have each group read one example for each category. Have them take turns until they have exhausted their lists. The group that can give an example after the other groups are finished wins.
- CHALLENGE: Have advanced students create one or more new categories and brainstorm words for each vowel sound.

❷ Practice the Conversation: Greeting a Friend 🎧 015

- To set the context for the conversation, ask questions about the picture: *Who are these people? Where are they?*
- Read the conversation or play the audio.
- Check comprehension by asking questions: Do they know each other? What is B's name? How is his class?
- Read or play the conversation again. Pause after each sentence and ask students to repeat.
- Divide the class in half. Have half the class read A's part and half the class read B's part. Then have them cover the conversation in their books and try it again. Switch parts and repeat.
- Model substituting items with a more proficient student. Read A's part substituting *How is it going?* for *How are you?* Have the student read B's lines. Cue the student to substitute *Pretty good!* by pointing to the phrase below.
- Put students in pairs and have them practice the conversation. They should take turns playing both parts, substituting the different phrases from the boxes and using their own ideas. Then have them close their books and practice again.

Unit 1: Lesson 5

LISTENING SCRIPT

Lesson 5 Activity 2, Practice the Conversation: Greeting a Friend

Listen to the conversation. Listen again and repeat.

A: Hi, David. How are you?
B: Fine, thanks. And you?
A: Not bad. How's your class?
B: Good. I like it.

EXPANSION ACTIVITY: Greetings and Pleasantries

- Have students write down several greetings and pleasantries in their native language, such as ways to say *hello, how are you,* and so on.
- Have students use a bilingual dictionary of their native language or the Internet to look up the literal translation of each phrase. For example, in Arabic, *As-salamu 'alaykum* means *hello*, but the literal translation is *peace be upon you.*
- Have students share their culture's linguistic traditions with the class. Point out any similarities that occur between the various languages of your students.

Culture Notes:

- Point out that this conversation is between friends. *How's it going? How are you doing?* and *How are things?* are other less formal ways to ask *How are you?*
- When we answer a question like *How are you?* we may respond more formally *(Very well, thanks)* in business situations or with people we don't know, or more informally *(Pretty good/Not too bad)* in casual situations or with friends.

❸ Practice the Conversation: Making Introductions 🎧 016

- Repeat the basic procedure from Activity 2.
- To set the context, ask questions: *Who is in the picture? What is their relationship?*
- After students have listened to and repeated the conversation, check comprehension by asking more questions: *Who is the man? Who is Sally Smith?*
- Have students continue practicing the conversation, making substitutions from the numbered items and using their own ideas.

LISTENING SCRIPT

Lesson 5, Activity 3: Practice the Conversation: Making Introductions

Listen to the conversation. Listen again and repeat.

A: Hello, Mr. Carter. How are you?
B: Fine, thanks. And you?
A: I'm very well, thank you. Mr. Carter, this is my friend Sally Smith.
B: How do you do, Ms. Smith?
C: How do you do, Mr. Carter? It's nice to meet you.

Culture Notes:

- Make sure students notice the difference between the formality of the expressions in Activity 3 and the more casual nature of the responses in Activity 2. Point out that in Activity 3, the speakers address each other with a title (Mr., Ms.) and last name. It may be helpful to brainstorm situations that require greater formality (introducing/greeting a teacher, supervisor, someone you don't know well, parents of friends).
- Point out that in Activity 3, the speakers use the phrase *How do you do?* Explain that typical responses may include the usual answers such as *fine, thank you* or *very well,* but a person may also respond with the same phrase: *How do you do?* Explain that the phrase is more a social courtesy than a question that requires an answer.

Unit 1: Lesson 5

> **EXPANSION ACTIVITY: Role-Play [Challenge]**
> - Put students in groups of three.
> - Assign each group a situation to role-play (introducing a date to your parents, a neighbor to your husband or wife, a coworker to your child, your sister to your boss).
> - Have the small groups practice an introduction.
> - Walk around the classroom to monitor the activity and provide help as needed.
> - Have volunteers perform their role-play for the class.

4 Practice the Conversation: Introducing Yourself 017

- Repeat the basic procedure from Activity 2.
- To set the context, ask questions: *Who is in the picture? Where are they?*
- After students have listened to and repeated the conversation, check comprehension by asking more questions: *Where does Paul live? Where does Cora live?*
- Have students continue practicing the conversation, making substitutions from the numbered items and using their own ideas.

> **EXPANSION ACTIVITY: Meet and Greet**
> - Have students look at the conversation in Activity 4 for a minute or two to remember as much as they can.
> - Divide the class into two equal groups. Have one group stand and form a circle, facing out. Have the members of the second group from a circle facing the first group.
> - Have the students practice introducing themselves to the classmates facing them. Have them follow the model in Activity 4, substituting their own ideas when possible.
> - After the first conversation finishes, have the inside circle turn counter-clockwise so that each student is now facing a new classmate. Have them introduce themselves again, rotating and continuing for several rounds.

> **LISTENING SCRIPT**
>
> **Lesson 5 Activity 4: Practice the Conversation: Introducing Yourself**
>
> *Listen to the conversation. Then listen and repeat.*
>
> A: Hi, my name is Paul. I live on the fifth floor.
>
> B: Hi. Nice to meet you. I'm Cora. I live on the second floor.
>
> A: Nice to meet you, Cora. Do you know Mary? She lives on the second floor, too.
>
> B: Yes, I do. She's a good friend of mine.

LESSON 6: Taking Phone Messages

OBJECTIVE
Taking phone messages

WINDOW ON MATH
Calculating Time

1 Read the message

- Go over the directions.
- Have students look at the form and read the words *While You Were Out.* Ask questions: *What kind of information can we get from a form like this?* Elicit that message forms usually tell who called, when, and why. Go over each feature of the form as needed.
- Have students answer the questions and then check their answers in pairs.
- Go over the answers with the class.

ANSWER KEY:

1. No; 2. Yes; 3. No; 4. I don't know; 5. Yes; 6. No

EXPANSION ACTIVITY:
Role-Play the Conversation [Multi-Level]

- Have groups reread the message form from Activity 1. Have them write the phone conversation that happened between Sergei and the woman who took the message. Ask them to include information about why Sergei will be late, as well as why Anna cannot answer the phone herself at the time of the call. Have lower-level students retell the information that happened. Have intermediate and advanced students write the conversation.
- Have each group perform their role-play for the class.

2 Write

- Go over the directions and read the questions aloud.
- Have students answer the questions and then check their answers in pairs.
- Go over the answers with the class.

ANSWER KEY:

1. 2/13/2012; 2. 10:30 A.M.; 3. He is going to be late.; 4. 415-555-6437; 5. CTI Bank

EXPANSION ACTIVITY: Memory Game

- Give students one minute to study the details of the message form in Activity 1.
- Have students close their books and write one question about the phone call and its answer on a slip of paper.
- Have students give their papers to you. Divide the class into small groups of three or four students.
- Draw one paper at a time and ask the question to the class. Have groups write down their answer and then reveal it at the same time. Award a point to each group with the correct answer. When an answer is in question, appoint a student to look it up in the book.
- LOW-LEVEL: Allow students to use their books to write answers for each question.

3 Listen and Write 018

- Play the audio and have students fill out the message form.
- Play the audio a second time. Have students check their own answers.
- Have students answer the questions and then check their answers in pairs.
- Go over the answers with the class, playing the audio again if desired.

Unit 1: Lesson 6

LISTENING SCRIPT

Lesson 6, Activity 3: Listen and Write

Listen to the phone conversation. Complete the message form. Use the information in the box.

Woman:	Hello? Adult Learning Center.
Man:	Hi. Could I speak to Ms. Morgan?
Woman:	Sorry. Lena is not here right now. Can I take a message?
Man:	Yes. This is Henry Temple. I'm calling from the Reseda Adult School. I want to talk to her about her class.
Woman:	Okay, Mr. Temple. I will have her call you back. What's your number?
Man:	My number is 947-555-7855. Thank you!
Woman:	You're welcome. Good-bye.

ANSWER KEY:

FOR Ms. Morgan; Mr. Henry Temple; OF Reseda Adult School; PHONE 947-555-7855, √ Telephoned, √ Please Call

EXPANSION ACTIVITY: Take a Message

- Write and record two or three short telephone conversations in which a person calls and leaves a message. You may have a student help you with the recording, or have pairs of students write and record their own messages.
- Play each message for the class. Have students fill out blank message forms like the one in Activity 1.
- Have partners check to see if they filled in the same information on the form.
- Replay each conversation to help students check their work. Then go over the answers as a class.

WINDOW ON MATH

Calculating Time

A Complete the sentences.
- Point out the topic, *Calculating Time,* and go over the time equivalents.
- Have students complete each sentence.
- Have partners read the sentences to each other to check their work.
- Go over the answers as a class.

B Answer the questions.
- Have students read each question and write an answer.
- Have partners check their answers together.
- Go over the answers as a class.

ANSWER KEY:

A. 1. 120 minutes; 2. 300 seconds; 3. 2 minutes; 4. 4 hours and 35 minutes
B. 1. 3:10; 2. 9:50; 3. 11:20; 4. 2:45; 5. 11:10; 6. 11:45

EXPANSION ACTIVITY: Daily Routine

- Have students brainstorm various activities that they do during the day and list them on the board, including a specific time for each action.
- Have partners ask and answer questions with each other based on the times on the board, using Activity 3B in the Window on Math as a model.

Unit 1: Lesson 6

BIG PICTURE EXPANSION ACTIVITY:
WRITING—Describing People

- Have students look at the Big Picture in their books (Student Book pages 8–9).
- Have students write a paragraph about someone in the picture. Encourage them to be creative and imagine where the people are from, what their occupations might be, and how they are feeling. Direct them to use the vocabulary and grammar they've learned in this unit.
- Walk around the room to monitor the activity, check punctuation, and provide help as needed.
- Instruct students to read their paragraph to a partner. Have the partner identify who the student wrote about.

LESSON 7: What Do You Know?

1 Listening Review 019

- Go over the directions with the class.
- Read the items or play the audio and have the students mark their answers on the Answer Sheet.
- Walk around to monitor the activity and help students stay on task.
- Have students check their answers with a partner.
- Go over the answers with the class.

LISTENING SCRIPT

Lesson 7, Activity 1: Listening Review

Listen to the question and choose the correct answer: A, B, or C. Use the answer sheet.

1. What color is your hair?
   A. My hair is long.
   B. My hair is curly.
   C. My hair is brown.
2. What's your last name?
   A. Robert Manuel Garza
   B. Garza
   C. California
3. How are you today, John?
   A. Oh, that's nice.
   B. How did you do it, Ms. Johnson?
   C. Fine, thanks. How are you?
4. Would you give this book to Maya?
   A. She has curly brown hair.
   B. That's a good book.
   C. I'm sorry. I don't know Maya.
5. Is Sara bored?
   A. Yes, she is.
   B. No, thank you.
   C. That's too bad.

ANSWER KEY:
1. C; 2. B; 3. C. 4. C; 5. A

TESTING FOCUS: Dictation Strategies

- Tell students that because they will hear the following sentences three times, they can focus on something different each time they listen. Explain that the first time, they should just listen for the meaning and not write anything down. The second time they should write down what they hear. The third time they should add to or correct the sentence as they listen.

2 Listening Dictation 020

- Copy the numbers and lines from the Listening Dictation section on the board.
- Read the first exchange: *What color are your eyes? They're brown*. Have a more advanced student write the answer on the board. Have students copy the sentence in their books.
- Play the audio and have students write the sentences they hear. Repeat as many times as necessary.
- Put students in pairs to compare answers.
- Have volunteers write the sentences on the board.

LISTENING SCRIPT

Lesson 7, Activity 2: Listening Dictation

Listen and write the sentences you hear.

1. A: What color are your eyes?
   B: They're brown.
2. A: You look happy!
   B: I am. I just got good news!
3. A: Hi, I'm José. I'm from Chile.
   B: Nice to meet you, José. My name is Barbara.
4. A: What does Tara look like?
   B: She is tall and heavy. She has short brown hair.
5. A: What's your middle name?
   B: It's Maria.

Unit 1: Lesson 7

③ Grammar Review

- Go over the directions.
- Read the first sentence. Elicit the appropriate completion. Have students circle B for item 1.
- Have students answer the rest of the questions.
- Put students in pairs to compare answers.
- Go over the answers with the class.

ANSWER KEY:

1. B; 2. B; 3. A; 4. C; 5. B; 6. A

LEARNING LOG

- Point out the four sections of the Learning Log: *I know these words, I can ask, I can say,* and *I can write.*
- Have students check what they know and what they can do.
- Walk around to note what students don't know or can't do. Use this information to review areas of difficulty.

BIG PICTURE EXPANSION ACTIVITY:
SPEAKING—Assessment: Talking about the Big Picture

- You can use the Big Picture as an individual assessment to place new students in open entry classes, to diagnose difficulties, or to measure progress.
- Work with one student. Show the Big Picture (Student Book pages 8–9) to the student. Ask: *What do you see in the picture?* or say: *Tell me about the picture.* Tell the student you want him or her to speak for as long as possible. Wait a moment for the student to prepare to answer. If the student has difficulty, use prompts: *What do you see in the park? What are the people doing?*
- You can use a rubric like the one below to rate beginning speakers.

4	Exhibits confidence, begins speaking without prompting Uses some complex sentences, although may make mistakes with irregular forms Can use more than one tense
3	Uses sentences, although form may be incorrect Can speak for a sustained length of time Responds to prompts, but doesn't need them to begin speaking
2	Can use nouns and verbs Uses phrases Answers informational questions
1	Can name objects Uses single words Can answer *yes/no* questions
0	Cannot say anything independently May be able to point to objects when prompted

Unit 1: Lesson 7

TEACHER'S NOTES:

Things that students are doing well:

_____
_____
_____
_____
_____
_____

Things students need additional help with:

_____
_____
_____
_____
_____
_____

Ideas for further practice or for the next class:

_____
_____
_____
_____
_____
_____

UNIT 2: GOING PLACES

UNIT OVERVIEW

LESSON	STUDENT BOOK PAGE	TEACHER'S EDITION PAGE
1. Identifying Places and Community Activities	18	29
2. Giving Directions	20	32
3. At a Train Station	22	36
4. Train Maps and Schedules	24	39
5. Getting Travel Information	26	42
6. Locating Community Agencies	28	45
7. What Do You Know?	30	47

Big Picture Expansion Activities

FOCUS	TITLE	SUGGESTED USE
Speaking	Creating Conversations	Lesson 3
Grammar	*Wh-* Questions	Lesson 3
Reading	A Letter Home	Lesson 4
Speaking	Assessment: Talking about the Big Picture	Lesson 7
Writing	Describing Activities and Locations	Lesson 7

Big Picture Expansion Activity Worksheet

FOCUS	TITLE	TEACHER'S EDITION PAGE
3. Grammar	*Wh-* Questions	226
4. Reading	A Letter Home	227

LESSON 1: Identifying Places and Community Activities

OBJECTIVE
Identifying places and community activities

VOCABULARY

bank	get cash	medical center
buy groceries	get something	post office
buy medicine	to drink	restaurant
buy stamps	get something	see a doctor
cash a check	to eat	socialize
check out books	library	study
community	mail letters	supermarket
center	mail packages	take classes
drugstore		

TARGET GRAMMAR

Present continuous *page 150*

THINGS TO DO

1 Learn New Words 021

- Have students look at the pictures, and elicit the words they know.
- Have students listen and look at the pictures while you say the words or play audio.
- Instruct students to circle the words that are new to them.
- Say the words or play the audio a second time. Pause after each word or phrase and ask the students to repeat and point to the correct picture.
- Put students in pairs and have one say a word or phrase as the partner points to the correct picture. Reverse roles and repeat the activity.

LISTENING SCRIPT

Lesson 1, Activity 1: Learn New Words

Look at the pictures. Listen to the words. Listen again and repeat. Which words are new to you? Circle them.

1.	library	There are many books at the library.
2.	study	Tom studies at the library every day.
3.	check out books	Janet often checks out books from the library.
4.	post office	They sell stamps at the post office.
5.	buy stamps	Carlos buys stamps at the post office.
6.	mail letters	Maria mails letters at the post office.
7.	mail packages	Barb mails packages at the post office.
8.	bank	I have money in the bank.
9.	get cash	Lee gets cash at the bank.
10.	cash a check	Sue cashes her check at the bank.
11.	drugstore	They sell medicine at the drugstore.
12.	buy medicine	Ana buys medicine at the drugstore.
13.	supermarket	They sell food at the supermarket.
14.	buy groceries	Laura and Sofia buy groceries at the supermarket.
15.	medical center	Doctors work at the medical center.
16.	see a doctor	Jack sees a doctor at the medical center.
17.	community center	There are many activities at the community center.
18.	socialize	Greg and Emily socialize at the community center.
19.	take classes	Luz takes classes at the community center.
20.	restaurant	I like to eat dinner at a restaurant.
21.	get something to drink	Pamela often gets something to drink at a restaurant.

Unit 2: Lesson 1

| 22. | get something to eat | Pat often gets something to eat at a restaurant. |

EXPANSION ACTIVITY: Chain Story

- Tell the students that they will make a chain story. Each person will say a sentence about where they do the actions in Activity 1. The next person repeats that sentence and adds a new one.
- Model the activity. Say a sentence: *I study at the library*. Call on a student. Have the student repeat your sentence and add a new one (*I study at the library. I mail letters at the post office.*).
- The next student repeats the previous student's sentence only and adds a new one.
- CHALLENGE: Have students repeat all of the sentences given previously and then add a new sentence.
- Continue the activity until everyone has participated. Students may repeat activities or places. This exercise will prepare students for Activity 2.

Culture Note: Socializing

- Lead a discussion about the ways people socialize in the United States. Point out that it is very common for men and women to socialize together freely, and that many people have friends of the opposite sex. Ask students to discuss typical forms of socialization and friends in their own cultures, and whether it is considered acceptable for men and women to interact freely in all situations.

❷ Listen and Write

- Have students look at the pictures. Ask questions about each picture: *Where is the person? What is he or she doing?* Elicit the names of each place and the actions that are happening.
- Play the audio and have students write the answers in the blanks.
- Play the audio a second time. Have students check their own answers.
- Have students check their answers in pairs.
- Go over the answers with the class, playing the audio for each question again if desired.

LISTENING SCRIPT

Lesson 1, Activity 2: Listen and Write

Look at the pictures. Listen and write the names.

1. He is at the restaurant. He is getting something to eat.
2. She is at the community center. She is taking classes.
3. They are at the supermarket. They are buying groceries.
4. She is at the post office. She is mailing packages.
5. She is at the library. She is checking out books.
6. They are at the community center. They are socializing.
7. He's at the library. He's studying.
8. He's at the medical center. He's seeing a doctor.
9. She's at the drugstore. She's buying medicine.

ANSWER KEY:

1. Pat; 2. Luz; 3. Laura and Sofia; 4. Barb; 5. Janet; 6. Greg and Emily; 7. Tom; 8. Jack; 9. Ana

🎯 TARGET GRAMMAR

Present continuous

The Target Grammar point is used in Activities 2 and 3. Presentation and practice of this grammar point appears on Student Book pages 150–151. Answer Keys appear on Teacher's Edition page 248.

Unit 2: Lesson 1

EXPANSION ACTIVITY: Beanbag Toss
- Tell the students that when you say a place, they should respond with an activity that happens there.
- Model the activity. Call on a student and toss a ball or beanbag as you say a place: *restaurant*. The student must respond with a complete sentence including an activity you can do there (*You (get something to) eat at a restaurant*).
- Have that student toss the beanbag to another student and say a place. Continue until everyone has participated.

Grammar Note:
- Point out to students that with the present continuous, pronouns are often contracted with *be*, especially in spoken English. For example, in item 1, *He is getting something to eat* can also be expressed as *He's getting something to eat*. In item 7, *He's studying* can also be expressed as *He is studying*. If students ask, go over the spelling rules for adding the *-ing* ending, although they will not need to apply the rules in this lesson.

3 Practice the Conversation 023

- Go over the directions.
- Model the conversation with a student. Have the student read A's lines. Cue the student to ask about one of the people in a box below. Demonstrate how to substitute a different location in B's first line and different activities in the second line.
- Have students work in pairs and practice the conversations asking about the people in the boxes.
- Walk around the room to monitor the activity and provide help as needed.

EXPANSION ACTIVITY: Guess the Activity [Multi-Level]
- Have students each draw a picture of someone doing one activity. On the back of the picture have them write a sentence describing the activity. Have advanced students help lower-level students write their sentences.
- Collect the pictures. Hold them up one at a time and have the class guess what the people are doing.

4 Interview
- Read the directions.
- Review expressions of frequency: *every day, every week, every month, a few times a year*
- Go over the example with a student as your partner. Then model substituting another action from one of the pictures and have the student respond.
- Have students work in pairs to take turns asking and answering the questions.
- Call on students to tell about their partners.

EXPANSION ACTIVITY: Vote with Your Feet [Low-Level]
- Write the expressions of frequency (*every day, every week, every month, a few times a year*) on pieces of paper and tape them around the classroom.
- Tell students that you are going to read some questions, and they should answer by standing in front of the appropriate expression of frequency.
- Have students stand, and ask a question: *How often do you get cash?* Encourage them to move to the correct sign.
- Call on a few students and ask the question, eliciting the response. This is a fast-paced activity, so continue asking questions and having students move.

LESSON 2: Giving Directions

OBJECTIVE
Giving directions

VOCABULARY

On a Map	Describing Location	Giving Directions
avenue	across from	go east
block	between	go north
boulevard	next to	go south
street	on the corner of	go straight
		go west
		take a left
		take a right

TARGET GRAMMAR
Prepositions of place and direction *page 152*

THINGS TO DO

1 Learn New Words 024

- Have students look at the map and ask: *What is this?* (*a city map*). Ask questions about the map: *What are the names of some streets on the map? What places do you see?*
- Have students listen and find the places on the map while you say the words or play the audio.
- Instruct students to circle the words that are new to them.
- Say the words or play the audio a second time. Pause after each word or phrase and ask the students to repeat.
- Ask students questions about the map using the new words: *What is between the hotel and the supermarket? What is across from the Grove Community Center? If you leave the restaurant and go east two blocks, what will you see?*

LISTENING SCRIPT

Lesson 2, Activity 1: Learn New Words

Listen to the words. Find the places on the map. Listen again and repeat.

On a map

1. avenue — The restaurant is on Central Avenue.
2. boulevard — The fire station is on Adams Boulevard.
3. block — The hotel and the shopping center are on the same block.
4. street — The library is on River Street.

Describing location

5. on the corner of — The park is on the corner of Grove and Bristol.
6. between — The library is between the park and the drugstore.
7. next to — The police station is next to the community center.
8. across from — The post office is across from the police station.

Giving directions

9. go north — Go north on Low Street.
10. go east — Go east on Adams Boulevard.
11. go south — Go south on Low Street.
12. go west — Go west on Adams Boulevard.
13. take a right — Take a right on Adams Boulevard.
14. take a left — Take a left on Scott Street.
15. go straight — Go straight on Diamond Street.

32 • UNIT 2 STUDENT BOOK PAGES 20-21

Unit 2: Lesson 2

 TARGET GRAMMAR

Prepositions of place and direction
The Target Grammar point is used in Activities 1, 2, 3, and 4. Presentation and practice of this grammar point appears on Student Book pages 152–153. Answer Keys appear on Teacher's Edition page 248.

EXPANSION ACTIVITY: Map It [Challenge]
- Have students work in pairs to draw a map of a multiple-block area around your school.
- Model the activity. Sketch a map of the school or neighborhood on the board. Label different places. Give directions to a volunteer: *Go out the front door of the building. Take a right. Go straight two blocks. Take a left on Smith Street. What building is on the corner?* Have the volunteer trace the path on the map.
- Have students take turns giving and following directions starting from one place on the map. Students should check to make sure their partners get to the right destination on the map.
- For variation, have students go in pairs to find the actual place, one partner following the directions and the other checking to make sure the directions are followed correctly.

2 Circle *True* or *False* 025
- Read the directions.
- Read the first question and answer from the script or play the audio. Elicit if the statement is *true* or *false* (*true*) and point out the fire station on the map.
- Play the audio and have students circle *True* or *False*.
- LOW LEVEL: Pause the audio between items so that students will have additional time to process what they hear.
- Have students check their answers in pairs.
- Go over the answers with the class. You may wish to have students correct the false statements.

LISTENING SCRIPT

Lesson 2, Activity 2: Circle *True* or *False*

Listen to the sentences. Look at the map. Circle True or False.

1. A: Excuse me. Where's the fire station?
   B: It's on Adams Boulevard.
2. A: Excuse me. Where's the library?
   B: It's next to the drugstore.
3. A: Excuse me. Where's the medical center?
   B: The medical center is between Central and Green.
4. A: Excuse me. Where is City Bank?
   B: City Bank is just north of the post office.
5. A: Excuse me. Where's the Community Center?
   B: It's across from the gas station.
6. Excuse me. Where's the hotel?
   B: It's on the corner of Green Avenue and Low Street.
7. A: Excuse me. Where's the train station?
   B: It's east of Diamond Street
8. A: Excuse me. Where's the shopping center?
   B: It's on Green Avenue between Elm Street and Low Street.

ANSWER KEY:
1. True; 2. True; 3. False; 4. False; 5. False; 6. True; 7. False; 8. True

Unit 2: Lesson 2

> **EXPANSION ACTIVITY: Growing City**
> - Tell students to imagine that there is new construction happening in the town shown on the map. Have each student write down one type of building or public place that they think the town should have (movie theater, gym, arcade, public pool, racecar track, church, etc.).
> - Have each student choose a location for the new building or place and write it down on a slip of paper in a sentence. (The movie theater is next to the train station on Francis Avenue and Diamond Street.) Direct them to be very specific in describing the location. Model a sentence if necessary.
> - Have students work with partners, and have partners ask each other true or false questions to determine the location of each other's new building or place. Model an example with a student as needed.
> - Students may change partners and complete the activity several times for additional practice.

❸ Practice the Conversation 026

- Read the conversation or play the audio as the students listen.
- Read or play the conversation again. Pause after each line and ask the students to repeat. Check comprehension by asking questions: *What place are they talking about? Which direction do you go on Elm?*
- Model the conversation with a student. Have the student read A's lines. Cue the student to ask about one of the places in a box below. Demonstrate how to substitute a different location in B's first line, and different directions in the second line.
- Have students work in pairs and practice the conversation asking about places in the boxes.
- Walk around the room to monitor the activity and provide help as needed.

> **LISTENING SCRIPT**
>
> **Lesson 2, Activity 3: Practice the Conversation**
> *Listen to the conversation. Listen again and repeat.*
>
> A: Excuse me. Where's the fire station?
> B: It's on Adams Boulevard between Diamond and Elm.
> A: How do I get there from the Medical Center?
> B: Just go north on Elm and take a left on Adams.
> A: Thank you!

> **EXPANSION ACTIVITY: Bingo [Low Level]**
> - Have students create a three by three grid.
> - Have them write the name of a place on the map in each of the squares. Remind them to choose nine places. They can write the places in any order they want.
> - Tell the students that you are going to read a series of statements. If the statement is true about a place, they should mark it off on their grid.
> - Tell them that they should call "Bingo" if they get three in a row.
> - Model the activity. Say a sentence: *This place is east of the hotel.* Elicit correct answers (*shopping center, medical center*). Tell students that if they have either of those places on their grid, they can mark off the square.
> - When a student calls "Bingo," the game is over.
> - For variation, you can continue reading sentences until all students have at least one bingo.

❹ Ask Questions

- Read the directions.
- Model the first example with a student. Have students confirm the locations on the map.
- Have two students model the second example and show the locations and route on the map.
- Have students work in pairs and practice asking and answering questions about the map.
- Have pairs present one question and answer each in front of the class.

Unit 2: Lesson 2

EXPANSION ACTIVITY: Find a Match

- Write questions and answers about places on the map on individual slips of paper, enough so each student has either a question or an answer. Create your own or use the ones below.

- Give each student a slip. Have them memorize the question or answer on their slips.

- Have students mingle, reciting their questions or answers. Tell them to stand in pairs when they find the question and answer that match.

- When everyone is matched, have them ask and answer the questions in front of the class.

Questions	Answers
Where's the medical center?	It's on Grove Boulevard, between Elm and Low.
Where's the gas station?	It's on Washington Boulevard between High and Market Streets.
Where's the supermarket?	It's on Central Avenue, two blocks west of the hotel.
Where's City Bank?	It's on Central Avenue between Bristol and River Streets.
Where's the restaurant?	It's on Central Avenue, two blocks west of City Bank.
Where's the library?	It's on River Street, next to the drugstore.
Where's the Community Center?	It's on Grand Avenue, next to the police station.
Where's the drugstore?	It's on the corner of Washington Boulevard and River Street, next to the library.
Where's the police station?	It's across from the post office, next to the community center.
Where's the post office?	It's across from the community center.
Where's the hotel?	It's east of the shopping center on Green Avenue.
Where's the shopping center?	It's on Green Avenue, next to the hotel.

LESSON 3  At a Train Station

OBJECTIVE
At a train station

VOCABULARY

baggage check
buy a ticket
information desk
make a phone call
newsstand
platform
read a train schedule
snack bar
ticket machine
ticket office
track
wait for a train
waiting area

⊙ TARGET GRAMMAR
Wh- questions review   *page 154*

THINGS TO DO

❶ Learn New Words 027

- Have students look at the Big Picture in their books (Student Book pages 22–23).
- To set the context, ask questions about the picture: *How many people do you see? Where are they? What are they doing? What words do you know?*
- Write the vocabulary that you have elicited on the board.
- Have students listen and find the places in the picture while you say the words or play the audio.
- Instruct students to circle the words that are new to them.
- Say the words or play the audio a second time. Pause after each word or phrase and ask the students to repeat and point to the correct part of the picture.
- Put students in pairs and have one say a word or phrase as the partner points to the correct picture. Reverse roles and repeat the activity.
- LITERACY: Help students identify compound nouns in the vocabulary list (*ticket machine, ticket office, snack bar, newsstand, information desk, waiting area, baggage check, phone call*). Point out that some compound nouns are two words joined together to form one new word, while other compound nouns are two separate words that express one idea. Have students scan the rest of the page and identify another compound noun (*newspaper*). Point out that when students read, they should use context clues to decide whether two words form a compound noun.

LISTENING SCRIPT

Lesson 3, Activity 1: Learn New Words

Look at the picture. Listen to the words. Listen again and repeat.

1. ticket machine		Where's the ticket machine?
2. ticket office		Where's the ticket office?
3. platform		Where's the platform?
4. track		Where's the track?
5. snack bar		Where's the snack bar?
6. newsstand		Where's the newsstand?
7. information desk		Where's the information desk?
8. waiting area		Where's the waiting area?
9. baggage check		Where's the baggage check?
10. buy a ticket		Who is buying a ticket?
11. wait for a train		Who is waiting for a train?
12. read a train schedule		Who is reading a train schedule?
13. make a phone call		Who is making a phone call?

⊙ TARGET GRAMMAR

Wh- questions review
The Target Grammar point is used in Activities 1, 2, and 3. Presentation and practice of this grammar point appears on Student Book page 154. Answer Keys appear on Teacher's Edition page 249.

36 • UNIT 2   STUDENT BOOK PAGES 22-23

Unit 2: Lesson 3

EXPANSION ACTIVITY: Word Scramble
[Literacy]

- Write the following three scrambled phrases on the board:

  > etcofeifiktc
  > ewtiarigana
  > kifsniodroemtan

- Have the students unscramble the words (ticket office, waiting area, information desk).
- Ask volunteers to write the correct phrases on the board.

❷ Talk About the Picture

- Go over the directions with students. Use the first example to model the exercise with a student. Then ask for two volunteers to model the second example for the class.
- Have students work in pairs to ask and answer questions about the picture.
- Walk around the room and provide help if needed.
- Call on a few students to share a question and answer with the class.

EXPANSION ACTIVITY: What's the Word?
[Multi-Level]

- Tell students that in this activity, you will give an answer based on the picture, and they must respond with the correct *Wh-* question word to match the answer. Briefly review the *Wh-* question words with students and elicit when each one is used.
- Model the activity. Call on a student and say: *Mrs. Hassan*. Elicit the question word that goes with this answer (*Who?*). Point out that sometimes more than one question word will work.
- Call on students and give answers based on the picture. Poll the class each time to see if everyone agrees. If not, discuss what other question word or words could match the prompt.

- With more advanced students, you can have them prepare "answers" and take turns prompting their classmates.
- For variation, have students work in small groups. Give each group a set of cards that has individual *Wh-* question words written on them. Members of each group take turns drawing a card and giving an answer based on that card and the Big Picture (Student Book pages 22–23). Another group member responds with the correct *Wh-* word.

❸ Practice the Conversation 028

- Read the conversation or play the audio as the students listen.
- Read or play the conversation again. Pause after each line and ask the students to repeat. Check comprehension by asking questions: *What does A want to do? Where can A do that?*
- Model the conversation with a student. Have the student read A's lines. Cue the student to ask about the idea in the first box below (get a train schedule). Demonstrate how to substitute a different place in B's first line (At the information desk), and a different location in the second line.
- Have students work in pairs and practice the conversation asking about ideas in the boxes.
- Walk around the room to monitor the activity and provide help as needed.

LISTENING SCRIPT

Lesson 3, Activity 3: Practice the Conversation

Listen to the conversation. Listen again and repeat.

A: Excuse me. Where can I buy a ticket?
B: At the ticket office.
A: Where's the ticket office?
B: It's over there, next to the ticket machine.

Unit 2: Lesson 3

EXPANSION ACTIVITY: Memory [Challenge]

- Divide the class into teams. Have each team write ten sentences about the picture, half of which are true and half false. Give an example if necessary.
- When the teams are finished writing their sentences, have everyone close their books. A member of one team will read a sentence. A member from another team should say if it is true or false. Each correct answer earns a point.
- Continue until all the students have read a sentence and have responded *true* or *false*.
- As a variation, have students correct the false statements to earn extra points.

BIG PICTURE EXPANSION ACTIVITY: SPEAKING—Creating Conversations

- Have students work in pairs to create a conversation for a situation in the picture (buying a ticket, making conversation while waiting for a train, asking about a train schedule, buying a magazine, buying some food, asking about a track, etc.).
- Walk around to monitor the activity and provide help as needed.
- Have volunteers role-play their conversation in front of the class.

BIG PICTURE EXPANSION ACTIVITY: GRAMMAR—*Wh-* Questions

- Make copies of Worksheet 3 (Teacher's Edition page 226) and distribute them to students.
- Have students look at the Big Picture in their books (Student Book pages 22–23).
- Instruct students to complete the activities and then check their answers with a partner.
- Go over the answers with the class.

ANSWER KEY:

Answers will vary. Possible answers include:
A. 1. It's in the middle of the station; 2. four; 3. David; 4. tickets, snacks and drinks, flowers, magazines; 5. Their trains are delayed; they are tired.
B. 1. How many people are there in the waiting area? 2. Where is the ticket office? 3. Why is Carmen standing on the platform? 4. What can you buy at the newsstand?

LESSON 4 Train Maps and Schedules

OBJECTIVE
Train maps and schedules

 TARGET GRAMMAR
Prepositions of time *page 155*

WINDOW ON MATH
Talking About Distance

THINGS TO DO

1 Check *True* or *False*
- Ask students how they get to school or work. Write their answers on the board.
- Have students look at the rail map. Check comprehension by asking questions: *What kind of map is this? How many train lines do you see? What are the end stops on the yellow line?*
- Read the first statement and elicit if it is true or false.
- Have students read the statements and check *True* or *False*.
- Go over the answers with the class.
- Have students correct the false statements. Go over the corrections.

ANSWER KEY:
1. True; 2. False. Covina is east of L.A.; 3. False. The San Bernadino Line runs both north and south and east and west; 4. False. El Monte is west of Baldwin Park; 5. True; 6. True

EXPANSION ACTIVITY: Another City
[Low-Level]
- Bring in a train or subway map for your city or town, or one nearby. You can go online and print copies or have students search online for maps.
- Have students work in pairs to write true and false statements about the map.
- Have pairs of students exchange statements and maps and write whether each statement is true or false.
- Have students correct false statements.

2 Read and Write
- Have students look at the train schedule. Ask questions: *What kind of information can we get from a train schedule?* Elicit that schedules often state the stops, the times the trains arrive and depart from the station, and sometimes the name or number of the train.
- Have students answer the questions and then check their answers in pairs.
- Go over the answers with the class.

ANSWER KEY:
1. 7:05; 2. between Anaheim and Fullerton; 3. 18 minutes; 4. almost 2 hours; 5. 605

TARGET GRAMMAR
Prepositions of time
The Target Grammar point is used in Activities 2 and 3. Presentation and practice of this grammar point appears on Student Book page 155. Answer Keys appear on Teacher's Edition page 249.

EXPANSION ACTIVITY: The Train Game
[Challenge]
- Create a set of questions or use the ones below. Write them in large letters on pieces of paper to show the students, or simply read them aloud when necessary.
- Write headings on the board: *What station? What train? What time? How long?* Under each heading write point values of 100, 200, 300, 400, and 500.

STUDENT BOOK PAGES 24-25

Unit 2: Lesson 4

- Divide the class into teams. Have teams take turns selecting a category and point value. The category and point values can be called in any order.
- Ask a question based on the corresponding square in the table below, and have the team that selected the square answer the question: *At what station is the 601 at 4:47 a.m.?*
- If the team that selects a question gives an incorrect answer, the other team has a chance to answer.
- Each correct answer earns the indicated point value.
- Once a question has been answered correctly, mark off the point value for that column so that it cannot be called again.
- Play until all questions have been asked and all point values have been marked off.

Points	What station?	What train?	What time?	How long? (minutes)
100	The 601 at 4:47	Oceanside at 5:56	The 605 at San Clemente	Oceanside to San Clemente on the 603
200	The 603 at 6:09	Tustin at 7:12	The 683 at Irvine	San Juan Capistrano to Irvine on 601
300	The 605 at 7:01	Fullerton at 7:35	The 603 at Santa Ana	Laguna Nigel to Orange on 603
400	The 683 at 7:12	Anaheim at 7:01	The 683 at Tustin	San Clemente to Fullerton on 605
500	The 683 at 7:27	Norwalk/ SF Springs at 7:18	The 601 at Anaheim	Tustin to L.A. on the 683

ANSWER KEY:

Points	What station?	What train?	What time?	How long? (minutes)
100	Oceanside	605	6:16	21 minutes
200	Irvine	683	7:05	17 minutes
300	Anaheim	683	6:22	28 minutes
400	Tustin	605	7:12	53 minutes
500	Anaheim	605	5:55	61 minutes (or 1 hour and 1 minute)

❸ Write

- Read the directions.
- Model the activity using the examples. If additional examples are needed, write a statement about the map (*Covina is east of L.A.*) and one about the schedule (*The 604 stops at Irvine at 5:59*). Elicit if the statements are true or false, and have students correct the false information.
- Have students write two true and two false statements about the map and schedule.
- Call on students to read sentences to the class. Elicit from the class whether each sentence is true or false, and have other students correct the false sentences.
- LOW LEVEL: Provide written true or false statements for lower level students, or have classmates write statements for them. Have partners read the statements and write *True* or *False*.

Unit 2: Lesson 4

EXPANSION ACTIVITY: Riddles

- Have the students use the information on the map or train schedule to write riddles.
- Model the activity. Read a riddle: Take the 603 train from Irvine. Stay on the train for 18 minutes. Get off at that stop. Where are you? Elicit the answer (*Orange*).
- Have students write their own riddles.
- Walk around the room to monitor the activity and provide help as needed.
- Collect the riddles and read them aloud, eliciting answers. Or, divide the class into teams and have teams take turns challenging their opponents with their riddles.

WINDOW ON MATH
Talking About Distance

A Read the information. Then write the answers on the lines.

- Go over the information in the box.
- Have the students complete the questions and check their answers in pairs.
- Go over the answers with the class.

B Read the sentences. Answer the questions.

- Have students answer the questions and check their answers in pairs.
- Go over the answers with the class.

ANSWER KEY:

A. 1. 2 feet; 2. 1 yard; 3. 10 inches; 4. 160 kilometers
B. 1. 31 miles; 2. 10 miles / 16 kilometers

EXPANSION ACTIVITY: The Train is Late

- Tell students that there was an accident on the 601 train today. The train is 25 minutes behind schedule. Have them work in pairs to write a new schedule that can be posted in the stations.
- Write the list of stations on the board. Have volunteers come to the board and write in the new train times.

BIG PICTURE EXPANSION ACTIVITY: READING—A Letter Home

- Make copies of Worksheet 4 (Teacher's Edition page 227) and distribute them to students.
- Have students look at the Big Picture in their books (Student Book pages 22–23).
- Have students read the letter or you can read the letter aloud line by line and have students repeat.
- Instruct students to complete the activities and then check their answers with a partner.
- Go over the answers with the class.

ANSWER KEY:

B. 1. B; 2. A; 3. A; 4. B; 5. B; 6. A

LESSON 5: Getting Travel Information

OBJECTIVE
Getting travel information

PRONUNCIATION
Word Stress

1 Practice Pronunciation: Word Stress 🎧 029

A. Listen to the words. Listen again and repeat.

- Go over the information with the class.
- Read the items or play the audio.
- Play the audio a second time and have students repeat the words.
- Have students practice saying the word pairs with a partner, circling each word they hear.
- Walk around to monitor the activity and help students stay on task.

B. Listen to the conversations. Circle the correct time or number. 🎧 030

- Read the directions.
- Read the items or play the audio and have students circle their answers.
- Go over the answers with the class, repeating each conversation as needed.

LISTENING SCRIPT

Lesson 5, Activity 1A: Practice Pronunciation: Word Stress

A. Listen to the words. Listen again and repeat.

1. thirty   thirteen
2. forty   fourteen
3. fifty   fifteen
4. sixty   sixteen
5. seventy   seventeen
6. eighty   eighteen
7. ninety   nineteen

Lesson 5, Activity 1B

B. Listen to the conversations. Circle the correct time or number.

1. A: What time is it?
   B: It's 10:15.
2. A: What time does the train leave?
   B: It leaves at 9:30.
3. A: What time is it?
   B: It's 12:40.
4. A: When's the next bus?
   B: 6:13.
5. A: How late is the bus to New York?
   B: 16 minutes.
6. A: When's the next train to Los Angeles?
   B: 8:50.
7. A: How old is Bob?
   B: Seventeen.
8. A: When's the next train?
   B: In 14 minutes.

ANSWER KEY:
1. a; 2. b; 3. b; 4. a; 5. a; 6. b; 7. a; 8. a

EXPANSION ACTIVITY: Listening Discrimination Practice

- Write pairs of numbers on the board (13, 30; 14, 40; 15, 50; 16, 60; 17, 70; 18, 80, 19, 90).
- Tell the students that you are going to say one of the numbers in each pair, and they should write down the number they hear.
- Dictate numbers.
- LITERACY: Have students write both the numerals they hear and the words that represent those numbers. For students who need further practice identifying number words with the corresponding numerals, have them create flash cards to practice each set of numbers.
- Go over the answers with the class.
- Alternatively, have the students take turns dictating numbers to partners.

Unit 2: Lesson 5

❷ Read and Write

- Read the lettered times on the left and have students repeat.
- Have the students look at the first clock. Ask what time it is (9:30). Point out the lettered times. Point out that 9:30 is written on the line.
- Have the students match the times with the clocks and write each answer on the correct line. Then have them check their answers in pairs.
- Go over the answers with the class.
- Call on students and ask about the times on the clocks. Correct pronunciation if necessary. Make sure they emphasize the second syllable in *fifteen* and the first syllable in *thirty*.

ANSWER KEY:

1. 9:30; 2. 6:10; 3. 11:45; 4. 5:15; 5. 3:20; 6. 1:10

EXPANSION ACTIVITY: Television Schedule [Multi-Level]

- Make copies of a television program schedule from a newspaper or other source.
- Have students write questions based on the schedule, asking when programs begin and end. You may wish to review verbs that could be helpful in this activity, such as *begin, start, come on, end,* and so on. Have more advanced students write questions that give clues about the shows but that don't reveal the shows' names. For example: *Which show that starts at 8:00 is about a police officer in New York City?* Have students answer with the name of the show and another fact about the show, such as who it stars.
- Have students switch papers with a partner and answer each other's questions.
- Have partners check each other's questions.
- Go over some of the questions and answers as a class, allowing each pair to read one or two of their examples.

❸ Practice the Conversation: Buying a Ticket 🎧 031

- Set the context for the conversation by having students look at the picture and asking them questions: *Where are they? Who do you see?*
- Have students look at the boxes on the right. Make sure they understand the meanings of *round-trip* and *one-way*.
- Read the conversation or play the audio.
- Check comprehension by asking questions: *What kind of ticket does the customer want? To where? What time is the next train?*
- Read or play the conversation again. Pause after each sentence and ask students to repeat.
- Divide the class in half. Have half the class read A's part, and half the class read B's part. Then have them cover the conversation in their books and say it again. Switch parts and do it again.
- Model substituting items with a more proficient student. You read A's part. Demonstrate how to substitute *a round-trip ticket to Chicago* from the first box below. Have the student read B's lines. Cue the student to substitute *$14.50* and *3:13* by pointing to the box below.
- Put students in pairs and have them practice the conversation, making substitutions from the boxes and using their own ideas. Have students take turns playing both parts. Then have them close their books and practice again.

LISTENING SCRIPT

Lesson 5, Activity 3: Practice the Conversation: Buying a Ticket

Listen to the conversation. Listen again and repeat.

A: I'd like a one-way ticket to Irvine, please.
B: Did you say one-way?
A: Yes, that's right.
B: That's $12.50, please.
A: Okay. When's the next train?
B: 5:15.
A: 5:50?
B: No. 5:15.
A: Okay. Thanks.

Unit 2: Lesson 5

EXPANSION ACTIVITY: Wrong Ticket!

- After students have finished practicing the conversations in Activity 3, have partners work together to write a new dialogue that takes place at the ticket counter. Allow students to use their own ideas, or suggest this scenario: you've purchased your ticket and are ready to board the train when you realize you've been given the wrong ticket. You go back to the ticket office to exchange your ticket.
- Have partners role-play their dialogues for the class. Discuss any similarities and differences that come up during the presentations.
- Take notes of important errors in the students' dialogues and use them to give a brief review of grammar or pronunciation points after the role-plays have been finished.

4 Practice the Conversation: Asking for Travel Information 032

- Have students look at the box on the right. Make sure they understand the meanings of each column's header.
- To set the context, ask questions: *What is this chart? Where do you usually see schedules? Have you ever transferred between buses or trains? Was it easy or difficult? Why?*
- Read the conversation or play the audio.
- Check comprehension by asking questions: *Is the bus on time? Where will the bus arrive?*
- Read or play the conversation again. Pause after each sentence and ask students to repeat.
- Divide the class in half. Have half the class read A's part, and half the class read B's part. Then have them cover the conversation in their books and say it again. Switch parts and do it again.
- Have students continue practicing the conversation, making substitutions from the boxes and using their own ideas. Model substituting information as needed.

LISTENING SCRIPT

Lesson 5, Activity 4: Practice the Conversation: Asking for Travel Information

Listen to the conversation. Listen again and repeat.

A: Is the 9 o'clock bus on time?
B: No, it's about 15 minutes late.
A: How late?
B: 15 minutes.
A: Okay. Which platform will it be on?
B: Number 5.
A: Okay, thanks.
B: You're welcome.

EXPANSION ACTIVITY: Information Mingle

- Write questions and answers about a schedule on separate slips of paper. Write one question and one answer for every student. For example: *Is the 10:30 bus on time? Yes, the 10:30 bus is on time. When does the next bus to Phoenix leave? The next bus to Phoenix leaves at 1:15.*
- Randomly distribute the questions and answers, making sure no student receives the answer to the question he or she already has.
- Have students mingle, asking their questions to try to find the answer and giving the answer when asked the correct question (*or saying "I don't know," "I'm sorry,"* or some other such polite conversational reply).
- You may need to model this activity once or twice before beginning.
- CHALLENGE: Have students create their own questions and answers and then proceed with the activity.

LESSON 6: Locating Community Agencies

OBJECTIVE
Locating community agencies

1 Answer the Questions

- Have students look at the page from the telephone directory on page 29. Ask questions: *What is this? What city is it? What places do you see listed? What is the telephone number for _____? Do you ever call these places in our town/city?*
- Have students look at the first picture and ask: *What place is this?* (a library).
- Read the first question and elicit the answer (2258 N. Main Street). Have students write the information on the line.
- Have students answer the questions.
- Have students check their answers in pairs.
- Go over the answers with the class.
- LOW LEVEL Help students identify and interpret abbreviations used in the telephone directory, such as *N., St., Ave., Dept.*, and so on. Go over the information about abbreviations in the box. Have students write each abbreviation and the word it corresponds to in a list.

ANSWER KEY:
1. 2258 N. Main Street; 2. 718-555-9347; 3. 718-555-9887 (Bus Travel); 4. the Licensing Exam Office; also acceptable: the Department of Motor Vehicles, or 601 Oak Street; 5. 911; 6. 718-555-5746 (Dog Officer); also acceptable: 911; 7. 718-555-9445; 8. 718-555-9685

Civics Note:
- Some students may not know the answer to question 8 if they are unfamiliar with the idea of citizen complaint lines. Explain to students or have them find out the purpose of such complaint lines, as well as typical complaints that may be registered.

EXPANSION ACTIVITY: Create Questions
- Divide the class into teams, mixing ability levels on each team.
- Have each team create questions based on the telephone directory on page 45 (one per team member).
- Have the teams take turns asking questions of the other team(s). Each correct answer earns a point.
- You may wish to have lower-level students listen to the questions asked and point to the topic of each question on the telephone directory. Have more advanced students confirm whether they are correct, and if not, help them find the topic.

2 Write

- Have students look in a local telephone directory and find the telephone numbers of the places indicated.
- Call on students to share the information they found with the class.

EXPANSION ACTIVITY: Telephone Directory Scavenger Hunt
- Have students bring in copies of a local telephone directory. Give each student three index cards, each with a unique number on the back. If the class has 12 students, the cards will be numbered 1–36.
- Have each student write one question on the front of each index card that can be answered using the directory. Have students write the answers on the backs of the cards.
- Place each directory on a separate table with its matching three questions, face up. You may wish to tape down the cards so that students cannot check the answers.
- Have students number a piece of paper with the number of questions written. Instruct students that they will have two minutes at each table to answer the three questions using the directory. At the end of the two minutes, they must move to the next table. Remind them to be sure they write their

Unit 2: Lesson 6

answers next to the correct numbers on their papers.
- Begin the activity, keeping strictly to the time limit. You may wish to ring a bell to alert students when it is time to move to the next table.
- When students have finished one complete rotation of the tables, collect all of the cards and review the answers. Students may check their own answers, or you may have them trade papers to check each other's answers.

LESSON 7 — What Do You Know?

1 Listening Review 033

- Read the directions with the class. Read the items or play the audio and have the students mark their answers on the Answer Sheet.
- Walk around to monitor the activity and help students stay on task.
- Have students check their answers with a partner.
- Go over the answers with the class.

LISTENING SCRIPT

Lesson 7, Activity 1: Listening Review

Look at the pictures and listen. Choose the correct answer: A, B, or C. Use the Answer Sheet.

1. A: Where's Donna?
   B: She's at the medical center. She's seeing a doctor.
2. Tony is mailing a package.
3. Go north and take a left on Park Street.
4. A: When's the next bus?
   B: 5:50.
5. A: Excuse me. Where can I get a train schedule?
   B: At the information desk.

ANSWER KEY:
1. B; 2. C; 3. B; 4. C; 5. A

TESTING FOCUS: Completing Answer Sheets

- Copy the Answer Sheet on the board.
- Read item 1 from the Listening Script aloud. Ask the students which answer is correct (*B*).
- Show them how to color in circle *B* on the answer sheet on the board.
- Point out the Answer Sheet box in the book for the Listening Review.
- After students have answered the first question, walk around to make sure all the students have marked the answer box correctly. Note that they may have marked the wrong answer, but they should have correctly colored in the corresponding circle.

2 Listening Dictation 034

- Copy the numbers and lines from the Listening Dictation section on the board.
- Read the first item. Have a more advanced student write the missing sentence on the board. Have students copy the sentence in their books.
- Play the audio and have students write the sentences they hear. Repeat as many times as necessary.
- Put students in pairs to compare answers.
- Have volunteers write the sentences on the board.

LISTENING SCRIPT

Lesson 7, Activity 2: Listening Dictation

Listen. Write the words you hear.

1. A: Excuse me, where's the bank?
   B: It's on Main Street.
2. A: Where's Tina?
   B: She's at the library. She's studying.
3. A: What time does the train arrive in New York?
   B: It arrives at 4:50.
4. A: Can I help you?
   B: Yes, I'd like a one-way ticket to San Diego, please.
5. A: Excuse me, how do I get to the drugstore?
   B: Just go south on Elm St. and take a left on Center St.

Unit 2: Lesson 7

❸ Grammar Review

- Go over the directions.
- Read the first sentence. Elicit the appropriate completion. Have students circle C for item 1.
- Have students answer the rest of the questions.
- Put students in pairs to compare answers.
- Go over the answers with the class.

ANSWER KEY:

1. C; 2. B; 3. A; 4. A; 5. B; 6. C

LEARNING LOG

- Point out the four sections of the Learning Log: *I know these words, I can ask, I can say,* and *I can write*.
- Have students check what they know and what they can do.
- Walk around to note what students don't know or can't do. Use this information to review areas of difficulty.

BIG PICTURE EXPANSION ACTIVITY:
SPEAKING—Assessment: Talking about the Picture

- You can use the Big Picture on Student Book pages 22–23 as an individual assessment to place new students in open entry classes, to diagnose difficulties, or to measure progress.
- Work with one student. Show the Big Picture to the student. Ask: *What do you see in the picture?* or say: *Tell me about the picture*. Tell the student you want him or her to speak for as long as possible. Wait a moment for the student to prepare to answer.
- If the student has difficulty, you can use prompts: *What do you see in the train station? What are the people doing?*
- You can use a rubric like the one below to rate beginning speakers.
- Review areas of difficulty.

4	Exhibits confidence, begins speaking without prompting Uses some complex sentences, although may make mistakes with irregular forms Can use more than one tense
3	Uses sentences, although form may be incorrect Can speak for a sustained length of time Responds to prompts, but doesn't need them to begin speaking
2	Can use nouns and verbs Uses phrases Answers informational questions
1	Can name objects Uses single words Can answer *yes/no* questions
0	Cannot say anything independently May be able to point to objects when prompted

Unit 2: Lesson 7

BIG PICTURE EXPANSION ACTIVITY: WRITING—Describing Activities and Locations

- Have students look at the Big Picture in their books (Student Book pages 22–23).
- Have the students write a paragraph about the picture. Remind them to use the present continuous to describe what the people are doing.
- Walk around to monitor the activity and provide help as needed.
- Have students read their paragraphs to a partner.
- Have a few volunteers read their paragraphs to the class.

TEACHER'S NOTES:

Things that students are doing well:
_____
_____
_____
_____

Things students need additional help with:
_____
_____
_____
_____

Ideas for further practice or for the next class:
_____
_____
_____
_____

UNIT 3: DOLLARS AND CENTS

UNIT OVERVIEW

LESSON	STUDENT BOOK PAGE	TEACHER'S EDITION PAGE
1. Living Expenses	32	51
2. Using Coins and Bills	34	54
3. Activities at a Bank	36	57
4. Completing a Check Register	38	61
5. Talking About Money	40	64
6. Understanding a Pay Stub	42	67
7. What Do You Know?	44	69

Big Picture Expansion Activities

FOCUS	TITLE	SUGGESTED USE
Grammar	*Yes/No* Questions + Simple Past	Lesson 3
Reading	Ali's Day	Lesson 3
Speaking	Nonsense!	Lesson 3
Writing	Describing What People Did	Lesson 6
Speaking	Assessment: Talking about the Big Picture	Lesson 7

Big Picture Expansion Activity Worksheets

FOCUS	TITLE	TEACHER'S EDITION PAGE
5. Grammar	*Yes/No* Questions + Simple Past	228
6. Reading	Ali's Day	229

LESSON 1: Living Expenses

OBJECTIVE
Living expenses

VOCABULARY

bus fare	electricity	personal check
car payments	electronic debit	recreation
car repairs	gas	rent
cash	groceries	toiletries
credit card	money order	utilities

 TARGET GRAMMAR

Simple past, statements *page 156*

THINGS TO DO

1 Learn New Words 035

- Have students look at the pictures and elicit the words they know.
- Have students listen and look at the pictures while you say the words or play the audio.
- Instruct students to circle the words that are new to them.
- Say the words or play the audio a second time. Pause after each word or phrase and ask the students to repeat and point to the correct picture.
- Put students in pairs and have one say a word or phrase as the partner points to the correct picture. Reverse roles and repeat the activity.

LISTENING SCRIPT

Lesson 1, Activity 1: Learn New Words

Look at the pictures. Listen to the words. Listen again and repeat.

1. groceries — How much do you spend on groceries?
2. recreation — How much do you spend on recreation?
3. toiletries — How much do you spend on toiletries?
4. bus fare — How much do you spend on bus fare?
5. car repairs — How much do you spend on car repairs?
6. car payments — How much do you spend on car payments?
7. rent — How much do you spend on rent?
8. utilities — How much do you spend on utilities?
9. gas — How much do you spend on gas?
10. electricity — How much do you spend on electricity?
11. cash — Do you pay your rent by cash?
12. credit card — Do you pay your rent by credit card?
13. personal check — Do you pay your rent by personal check?
14. money order — Do you pay your rent by money order?
15. electronic debit — Do you pay your rent by electronic debit?

Unit 3: Lesson 1

EXPANSION ACTIVITY:
Flashcard Concentration [Low-Level]

- Distribute 20 index cards to pairs of students. Have them choose ten words from the new words list.
- Have students write one word on each of ten cards and draw pictures of those words on the other ten cards. At the end of the activity, each pair of students should have 20 cards (ten words matched with ten pictures).
- Have students shuffle the cards and lay them out so the pictures and words are face down.
- Have each pair of students take turns turning over two cards at a time. If the two cards show a matching word and picture, the student who chose them keeps the matching pair and has another turn. If the two cards don't match, the student turns the cards back over and the turn passes to the other player. The player with the most matches wins.

❷ Listen and Write 036

- Go over the directions and the chart.
- Play the audio and have students mark their answers in the chart.
- Put students in pairs to compare answers. Play the audio again if necessary to have students confirm their answers.
- Go over the answers with the class.
- CHALLENGE: Have advanced students work in pairs or groups to try to reconstruct the conversation they heard, including as much information and exact wording as possible. Allow them to listen to the audio one additional time and have them take notes while they are listening. When they are finished, have them read back their version of the conversation to the class, one line at a time. Check each line by playing the audio after students have read the line.

LISTENING SCRIPT

Lesson 1, Activity 2: Listen and Write

Listen. How much did Lei spend last month? Fill in the chart.

Man:	How much did you spend on groceries last month?
Woman:	Last month? Let's see . . . My family visited me, so I spent a lot on groceries.
Man:	How much did you spend on recreation?
Woman:	Oh . . . not very much. Maybe ten dollars.
Man:	How much did you spend on toiletries?
Woman:	I spent an average amount.
Man:	Okay. And how much did you spend on bus fare?
Woman:	I took the train last month, so not very much.
Man:	What about rent? How much did you spend on rent last month?
Woman:	Our rent is very expensive, so I spent a lot on rent.

ANSWER KEY:

groceries (a lot); recreation (not very much); toiletries (an average amount); bus fare (not very much; rent (a lot)

🎯 TARGET GRAMMAR

Simple past, statements
The Target Grammar point is used in Activities 2 and 3. Presentation and practice of this grammar point appears on Student Book pages 156–157. Answer Keys appear on Teacher's Edition page 250.

Unit 3: Lesson 1

EXPANSION ACTIVITY:
How much is a lot? [Multi-Level]

- Put students in small groups. Have them decide how much money is a lot, an average amount, and not very much to spend on each item in Activity 2.
- Call on representatives from each group to share their ideas with the class.

3 Interview

- Model the activity. Write the first question and answers on the board.

- Call on a student and ask the question. Check the box that indicates his or her answer.
- Have students work in pairs to ask and answer the questions. Have them check the box that indicates their partners' answers.
- When students are finished, call on a few students to tell about their partners.

EXPANSION ACTIVITY: Category Sort

- Have students stand. Tell them they are going to sort themselves by category.
- Give an example. Say: *Sort yourselves by the type of credit card you use most often.* Encourage students to move and stand next to those classmates that are in the same category. Have someone from each group name the category (Visa, no credit card, MasterCard etc.).
- Create your own categories or use the ones below:
  - *How you pay your rent*
  - *How you pay for groceries*
  - *When your rent is due*
  - *When you pay your bills*
  - *What utilities you pay for*

LESSON 2 Using Coins and Bills

OBJECTIVE
Using coins and bills

VOCABULARY

dime (10¢)	razor
dollar ($1.00)	shampoo
fifty dollars ($50.00)	shaving cream
five dollars ($5.00)	ten dollars ($10.00)
nickel (5¢)	toothbrush
penny (1¢)	toothpaste
quarter (25¢)	twenty dollars ($20.00)

TARGET GRAMMAR

Simple past of *be*, Statements *page 158*

THINGS TO DO

1 Learn New Words 037

- Have students look at the pictures and elicit the words they know. Make sure students understand that people are buying items and getting change.
- Have students listen and look at the pictures while you say the words or play the audio.
- Say the words or play the audio a second time. Pause after each word or phrase and ask the students to repeat and point to the correct picture.
- Put students in pairs and have one say a word or phrase as the partner points to the correct picture. Reverse roles and repeat the activity.

LISTENING SCRIPT

Lesson 2, Activity 1: Learn New Words

Look at the pictures. Listen to the words. Listen again and repeat.

1. toothbrush	Dana bought a toothbrush yesterday.
2. razor	Sam bought a razor yesterday.
3. shaving cream	Sam bought some shaving cream yesterday.
4. shampoo	Jim bought some shampoo yesterday.
5. toothpaste	Jim bought some toothpaste yesterday.
6. penny	The customer's change was a penny.
7. nickel	The customer's change was a nickel.
8. dime	The customer's change was a dime.
9. quarter	The customer's change was a quarter.
10. dollar	The customer's change was a dollar.
11. five dollars	The customer's change was five dollars.
12. ten dollars	The customer's change was ten dollars.
13. twenty dollars	The customer's change was twenty dollars.
14. fifty dollars	The customer gave the cashier fifty dollars.

EXPANSION ACTIVITY:
At the Five and Dime [Multi-Level]

- Bring in realia or pictures of the toiletries listed in the new vocabulary. Display each one prominently with a sign that tells its price.
- On index cards, write different amounts of money, using the remaining vocabulary words. For example: *four dimes and one quarter; five dollars and three pennies.* Write one slip of paper for each student in the class. You may wish to include extra cards for students who finish early.

54 • UNIT 3

STUDENT BOOK PAGES 34-35

Unit 3: Lesson 2

- Have each student draw a card and look at the amount of money listed. Have the student list on the card how many of each toiletry item can be purchased for that amount of money. Then have them list combinations of products they can buy. Have advanced students write in full sentences.
- Have volunteers share their "purchases" with the class.

Culture Note:

- You may wish to tell students about stores known as "five and dimes" in American history, as well as discuss the myths and realities of "small town America." Explain that many people today have a strong nostalgia for Americana and for times past. If desired, introduce conversational phrases such as *the good old days, back when I was a kid,* and *in my day.*

TARGET GRAMMAR

Simple past of *be*, statements

The Target Grammar point is used in Activities 1–4. Presentation and practice of this grammar point appears on Student Book page 158. Answer Keys appear on Teacher's Edition page 250.

❷ Check *True* or *False* 038

- Go over the directions.
- Read the listening script or play the audio for the class. Have students mark the answer to each question.
- Have students check their answers in pairs. Reread each item or replay the audio to help students check their answers.
- Go over the answers with the class. Have students correct each false statement to make it true.

LISTENING SCRIPT

Lesson 2, Activity 2: Check *True* or *False*

Listen to the sentences. Look at the pictures. Check True or False.

1. Dana bought a toothbrush.
2. Dana gave the cashier $20.
3. Sam gave the cashier $50.
4. Sam's change was 30 cents.
5. Jim bought a razor and shaving cream.
6. Jim's change was 50 cents.

ANSWER KEY:

1. True; 2. False; she gave the cashier $10; 3. True; 4. False; his change was $30; 5. False; he bought toothpaste and shampoo; 6. False; he didn't get any change

EXPANSION ACTIVITY: Meet Your Match

- Give each student an index card.
- Have students work in pairs. Have them write a monetary amount and a price on one card ($15.00/$8.99). Have them write the correct change on the other card. Collect all the cards and shuffle them.
- Give one card to each student. Have the students with the "amount/price" cards figure out how much change they should get. Have them walk around the room, show their cards to other students, and ask "How much change should I get?" until they find the student with the correct "change" card.
- Have the partners stand together and tell the class the information: amount, price, and change.
- LOW LEVEL: Remind lower level students how to read numerical values aloud. For example, *$8.99* can be read as *eight dollars and ninety-nine cents* or as *eight ninety-nine*.

STUDENT BOOK PAGES 34–35

Unit 3: Lesson 2

3 Talk About the Picture

- Ask students questions about the pictures using the new vocabulary words: *Who bought toothpaste? Who paid ten dollars?*
- Have students write five sentences about the pictures. Remind them to use the words in Activity 1.
- Walk around the room and provide help if needed.
- Call on a few students to read their sentences to the class.

> **EXPANSION ACTIVITY: Dictation [Challenge]**
> - Tell the students that you are going to dictate some sentences. Have them get out paper and pencils.
> - Dictate sentences. Create your own or use these: *Dana gave the clerk $30 for a bill of $24.78. Sam paid for a toothbrush that cost $1.99 with $10. Jim spent $53.25 on groceries. He gave the cashier $60.*
> - Have students compare their sentences in pairs.
> - Have volunteers write the sentences on the board.
> - Have students figure out the change for each situation.

4 Practice the Conversation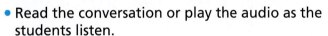

- Read the conversation or play the audio as the students listen.
- Read or play the conversation again. Pause after each line and ask the students to repeat. Check comprehension by asking: *How much is it? What does the customer give the cashier?*
- Model the conversation with a student. Have the student read B's lines. Demonstrate how to substitute a different price in A's first line, and different change in the second line.
- Cue the student to ask about the amount in a box below.
- Have students work in pairs and practice the conversation, making substitutions from the numbered items and using their own ideas.
- Walk around the room to monitor the activity and provide help as needed.

> **LISTENING SCRIPT**
>
> **Lesson 2, Activity 4: Practice the Conversation**
>
> *Listen to the conversation in a store. Listen again and repeat.*
>
> A: The total is $1.25.
> B: Can you change a twenty?
> A: Sure. Your change is $17.75.
> B: I thought it was $18.75.
> A: Oh, sorry. You're right.

> **EXPANSION ACTIVITY: Stand and Deliver**
> - Give the students three minutes to remember as much of the conversation as they can.
> - Write single words or phrases from the conversation on index cards (*The total is / You're right. / a twenty?*) Write one card for each student or make multiple sets of cards if needed for larger classes.
> - Divide students into groups if you are using multiple sets of cards. Shuffle the cards and distribute one to each student. Have the students reconstruct the conversation by ordering themselves according to the words on their cards.
> - When the students have the conversation all assembled, have them each recite the word or phrase on their card in order of the conversation.

LESSON 3 Activities at a Bank

OBJECTIVE
Activities at a bank

VOCABULARY

ATM	make a deposit
bank officer	make a withdrawal
bank teller	monthly statement
check register	open a checking account
checkbook	paycheck
debit card	safe-deposit box
deposit slip	savings account
endorse a check	withdrawal slip

TARGET GRAMMAR

Simple past, yes/no questions *page 159*

THINGS TO DO

1 Learn New Words 040

- Have students look at the Big Picture in their books (Student Book pages 36–37). Elicit the words they know.
- Have students listen and look at the pictures while you say the words or play the audio.
- Instruct students to circle the words that are new to them.
- Say the words or play the audio a second time. Pause after each word or phrase and ask the students to repeat and point to the correct part of the picture.
- Put students in pairs and have one say a word or phrase as the partner points to the correct part of the picture. Reverse roles and repeat the activity.

LISTENING SCRIPT

Lesson 3, Activity 1: Learn New Words

Look at the picture. Listen to the words. Listen again and repeat.

1.	bank officer	The bank officer's name is Marie.
2.	bank teller	Ali is a bank teller.
3.	safe-deposit box	The safe-deposit boxes are near the exit.
4.	ATM	There is an ATM at the front door of the bank.
5.	check register	It's a check register.
6.	checkbook	It's a checkbook.
7.	deposit slip	It's a deposit slip.
8.	withdrawal slip	It's a withdrawal slip.
9.	savings account	She has a savings account.
10.	debit card	He has a debit card.
11.	monthly statement	It's a monthly statement.
12.	paycheck	It's her paycheck.
13.	endorse a check	You need to endorse a check to cash it.
14.	make a deposit	He wants to make a deposit.
15.	make a withdrawal	She wants to make a withdrawal.
16.	open a checking account	He wants to open a checking account.

Unit 3: Lesson 3

> **EXPANSION ACTIVITY: Twenty Questions**
>
> - Model how to play Twenty Questions. Secretly choose an object or person from the picture and have students ask *yes/no* questions to discover its identity. Keep track of the number of questions they ask, up to 20. If students haven't guessed by the 20th question, give them clues until they guess the correct answer.
> - Continue playing by having volunteers choose an object or person, then repeating the game.

❷ Talk About the Picture

- Go over the directions. Have students write five statements about the picture. Remind them to use the words in Activity 1.
- Have partners share their ideas with each other.
- Walk around the room and provide help if needed.
- Call on students to share their ideas with the class.

> **EXPANSION ACTIVITY: Riddles [Challenge]**
>
> - Have partners expand on the previous activity by writing riddles to describe two different people in the picture.
> - Write a model on the board for students to follow, including two negative statements and one positive statement. For example: *She doesn't have dark hair. She isn't standing in line. She has a necklace she wants to keep safe. Who is she?* (Lea)
> - Have students share their riddles with the class or in small groups.

❸ Practice the Conversation 041

- Read the conversation or play the audio as the students listen.
- Read or play the conversation again. Pause after each line and ask the students to repeat.
- Check comprehension by asking: *What does the customer want to do? What does the customer need?*
- Model the conversation with a student. Have the student read A's lines. Cue the student to substitute an action from the items below. Demonstrate how to substitute a different question in B's first line.
- Have students work in pairs and practice the conversation, making substitutions from the numbered items.
- Walk around the room to monitor the activity and provide help as needed.

> **LISTENING SCRIPT**
>
> **Lesson 3, Activity 3: Practice the Conversation**
>
> *Listen to the conversation. Listen again and repeat.*
>
> A: I'd like to make a deposit.
> B: Did you fill out a deposit slip?
> A: A deposit slip?
> B: Yes. You can get one by the front door.

> ### ⊙ TARGET GRAMMAR
>
> **Simple past, *yes/no* questions**
> The Target Grammar point is used in Activity 3. Presentation and practice of this grammar point appears on Student Book pages 159–160. Answer Keys appear on Teacher's Edition page 250.

Unit 3: Lesson 3

EXPANSION ACTIVITY: SPEAKING— Inside/Outside Circles [Low-Level]

- Have the students review the options for the first two lines of the conversation (*I'd like to _____ / Did you _____*).
- Have the students stand and form two circles: an inner circle facing out and an outer circle facing in. Each student should be aligned with a partner.
- Have the students in the inner circle play the customer and state a desire to the bank teller. Have the students in the outer circle play the role of the bank teller, who asks an appropriate question.
- Once the partners have exchanged lines, ask the inner circle to rotate counterclockwise one position. Now everyone should be facing a new partner. Have them practice the conversation again, and then rotate. Switch roles. Continue until everyone has practiced both roles several times.
- CHALLENGE: Have students practice the conversation substituting different requests and simple past questions.

BIG PICTURE EXPANSION ACTIVITY: GRAMMAR—*Yes/No* Questions + Simple Past

- Make copies of Worksheet 5 (Teacher's Edition page 228) and distribute them to students.
- Have students look at the Big Picture in their books (Student Book pages 36–37).
- Instruct students to complete the activities and then check their answers with a partner.
- Go over the answers with the class. Have students restate each *no* answer to tell the correct facts.

ANSWER KEY:

A. 1. Yes, he did. 2. No, she didn't. (A man filled out a deposit slip.) 3. No, they didn't. (A woman put something in a safe-deposit box.) 4. Yes, they did. 5. No, she didn't. (No one used the ATM.) 6. No, she didn't. (No one endorsed a check.)

B. Answers may vary slightly. Possible answers include: 1. Did Dan deposit a check? 2. Did Lea put papers in her safe-deposit box? 3. Did Al fill out a withdrawal slip? 4. Did the bank tellers stop working at 2 P.M.? 5. Did the people wait in line for the teller?

Unit 3: Lesson 3

 BIG PICTURE EXPANSION ACTIVITY:
READING—Ali's Day

- Make copies of Worksheet 6 (Teacher's Edition page 229) and distribute them to students.
- Have students look at the Big Picture in their books (Student Book pages 36–37).
- Instruct students to complete the activities and then check their answers with a partner.
- Go over the answers with the class.

ANSWER KEY:

A: 1 – I went to work; 2 – The bank opened; 3 – I worked at the drive-through window; 4 – I had lunch; 5 – A woman went to her safe-deposit box; 6 – A boy brought in some cash; 7 – The bank closed.

B: 1. He went to work. 2. (He left) at 5:30. 3. (He's) a bank teller. 4. (He was at work for) 8 hours. 5. (He took) an hour. 6. (He worked) at the regular teller window. 7. (The bank closed) at 5.

 BIG PICTURE EXPANSION ACTIVITY:
SPEAKING—Nonsense!

- Have students look at the Big Picture in their books (Student Book pages 36–37).
- Tell students that they are going to work in teams to create some sentences about the picture. Some of the sentences will make sense and some will not. Write the words *sense* and *nonsense* on the board. Explain what these two words mean.
- Explain that for each sentence, students from the opposing team must decide if it makes sense or not.
- Model the activity. Say two sentences, one of which makes sense: *The man is filling out a deposit slip*; and another that does not: *The woman is endorsing a safe-deposit box*. If the sentence makes sense, students should say, "That makes sense." If it does not make sense, they should say, "Nonsense" and then correct the sentence (*The woman is putting something in a safe-deposit box*).
- Divide the class into teams. Give the teams five minutes to create enough sentences about the picture so that each team member will say one sentence.
- Have the teams take turns saying a sentence to the other team and getting their response. Each correct answer earns the guessing team a point.

LESSON 4: Completing a Check Register

OBJECTIVE
Completing a check register

VOCABULARY
balance
check number
check register
transaction amount

TARGET GRAMMAR
Simple past, Wh- questions *page 161*

THINGS TO DO

1 Learn New Words 042

- Have students listen and look at the pictures while you say the words or play the audio.
- Say the words or play the audio a second time. Pause after each word and ask the students to repeat.
- Answer any questions that students may have about the words, giving further examples as needed.

LISTENING SCRIPT
Lesson 4, Activity 1: Learn New Words

Look at the pictures. Listen to the words. Listen again and repeat.

1.	check register	It's a check register.
2.	transaction amount	The transaction amount is $60.
3.	balance	The balance is $385.89.
4.	check number	The check number is 326.

EXPANSION ACTIVITY: "In the Hole" [Challenge]

- Explain to students the idiom *in the hole* (to be short on money). Tell students that if the balance in their checking account falls below zero, they are "in the hole." Ask students what they think might be the consequences if this happened. Point out that many banks charge fees for overdrafts, which is why it's important to balance your checkbook.
- Have students practice the idiom by writing word problems that tell about spending. Write an example on the board, such as *Ryan had $86 in his account. He wrote check number 177 for $112 to buy new video games. Now he is in the hole by–!*
- Have students share their word problems with the class, withholding the answer. Have the class figure out by how much each person is "in the hole."

2 Answer the Questions

- Go over the directions.
- Read the questions aloud and have students repeat.
- Have the students answer the questions and then compare answers in pairs.
- Go over the answers with the class.

ANSWER KEY:
1. Bank Two; 2. September 4; 3. Veritas Telephone Company; 4. two; 5. $385.89

STUDENT BOOK PAGES 38-39

Unit 3: Lesson 4

EXPANSION ACTIVITY: Create Questions

- Have students work in pairs to write three new questions about Al's check register.
- Walk around the room to monitor the activity and provide help as needed.
- Have each pair exchange and answer questions with another pair. Have them check their answers with each other.
- LOW LEVEL: Have lower level students work in pairs to write three *True* or *False* statements about Al's check register. Have pairs exchange papers and answer each others' questions.

TARGET GRAMMAR

Simple past, *Wh-* questions

The Target Grammar point is used in Activity 2. Presentation and practice of this grammar point appears on Student Book page 161. Answer Keys appear on Teacher's Edition page 250.

3 Read and Take Notes 043

- Have students look at the check register. Ask them questions about it: *What do you write in the first column? What goes in the second column? Do you write the amount of a check in the fourth or fifth column?*
- Have students look at the documents below the check register (personal checks and deposit slips) and complete the register. Remind them to write the information in chronological order.
- Have the students check their work in pairs.
- Read the check register or play the audio. Have the students check their work.

LISTENING SCRIPT

Lesson 4, Activity 3: Read and Take Notes

Read the personal checks and deposit slips and complete Al's check register on page 39. Listen again and check your work.

- Check number: 326. Date: 9/16. Description: Veritas Telephone Company. Transaction amount: $42.76. Balance: $228.38.
- Date: 9/17. Description: deposit. Deposit amount: $312.00. Balance: $540.38.
- Check number: 327. Date: 9/18. Description: Bank Two. Transaction amount: $356.76. Balance: $183.62.
- Date: 9/26. Description: Cash withdrawal. Transaction amount: $50.00. Balance: $133.62.
- Date: 9/30. Description: deposit. Deposit amount: $850.00. Balance: $983.62.

ANSWER KEY:

Missing information by line entry: line 3, balance $228.38; line 4, 9/17 / balance $540.38; line 5, check number 327 / transaction amount 356.76 / balance $183.62; line 6, cash withdrawal / transaction amount $50.00 / balance $133.62; line 7, deposit amount $850.00 / balance $983.62

Unit 3: Lesson 4

EXPANSION ACTIVITY:
What's Missing? [Literacy]

- Tell students that you are going to give two pieces of information from the check register. These two items will be from the same column and separated by another item that you will not say. For example, you might choose August 30th and September 16th. Elicit that the missing information is *September 4th* because it is the item on the register between the other two.
- Call on a volunteer and give two other pieces of information (*$60.00* and *$42.76*). Elicit the answer from the student (*$114.75*). Have that student call on another student and give two pieces of information. Remind the student to choose items that are in the same column and are on either side of a missing item.
- Continue until everyone has had a chance to participate.

ANSWER KEY:

Date: 9/4; Pay to the order of: Jon's Garage; Amount: $114.75; One-hundred fourteen and 75/100 [dollars]

EXPANSION ACTIVITY: The Real Thing

- Bring in deposit and withdrawal slips from a local bank.
- Have students practice completing the slips with information that you give them.

4 Write

- Have students look at the information in the check register for check #325. Ask questions: *What is the date? Who is the check to? How much is it?* Explain what the memo line is, and point out that students may leave it blank on Al's check.
- Have students complete the check with the information. Have them compare their checks in pairs.
- Draw check #325 on the board and have students complete it with the correct information.

LESSON 5: Talking About Money

> **OBJECTIVE**
> Talking about money

> **PRONUNCIATION**
> Ng versus Nk

1 Practice Pronunciation: Ng versus Nk 🎧 044

A. Listen to the words. Listen again and repeat.

- Go over the information in the first box. Point out that the sounds *ng* and *nk* are never at the beginning of words, although they can be in the middle or at the end of words.
- Write *-ing* and *-ink* on the board. Say the sounds several times as you point to each. Exaggerate the sounds.
- Have students look at the words. Read the words or play the audio.
- Read or play the audio a second time. Pause and have students repeat.

LISTENING SCRIPT

Lesson 5, Activity 1: Practice Pronunciation: Ng versus Nk

A. Listen to the words. Listen again and repeat.

bank	bang	saving	sink	think
thank	thing	sing	nothing	checking
ink	drink	long	wondering	young

B. Listen to the questions and answers. Listen again and repeat. 🎧 045

- Read the sentences or play the audio.
- Read the sentences or play the audio a second time. Pause and have students repeat.

LISTENING SCRIPT

Lesson 5, Activity 1: Practice Pronunciation: Ng versus Nk

B. Listen to the questions and answers. Listen again and repeat.

Questions	Answers
1. What is that bank?	a. First National Bank.
What is that bang?	b. Something fell in the kitchen.
2. Do you have a sink?	a. Yes, in the bathroom.
Do you have to sing?	b. No, I can tell a story.
3. Now think. What do you want?	a. I can't. I'm too tired.
Nothing. What do you want?	b. I don't want anything either.

C. Now listen again. You will hear one question from each pair in Activity B. Circle the correct answer. 🎧 046

- Point out that the questions are very similar.
- Read the questions or play the audio. Have students circle the answers to the questions they hear.
- Read the questions or play the audio a second time so students can check their answers.
- Go over the answers with the class.

LISTENING SCRIPT

Lesson 5, Activity 1: Practice Pronunciation: Ng versus Nk

C. Now listen again. You will hear one question from each pair in Activity B. Circle the correct answer.

1. What is that bang?
2. Do you have a sink?
3. Now think. What do you want?

> **ANSWER KEY:**
>
> 1. b; 2. a; 3. a

Unit 3: Lesson 5

EXPANSION ACTIVITY:
Distinguishing Sounds [Low-Level]

- Write these pairs on the board: *thing/think; checking/check ink; wondering/one drink; sing/sink.*
- Have a volunteer come to the board. Say a word from one of the pairs and have the student point to the word on the board.
- Have the class confirm whether or not the answer is correct. Repeat with other volunteers.

❷ Listen and Write: Listening to an Automated Phone System 🎧 047

- Have students read the text in the box. Point out that they will write the missing numbers and words as they listen.
- Read the script or play the audio. If necessary, read the script or play the audio again. Have students check their answers in pairs.
- Go over the answers with the class.

LISTENING SCRIPT

Lesson 5, Activity 2: Listen and write. Listening to an Automated Phone System

Listen and write the missing words. Listen again and check your answers.

Thank you for calling Horizon Bank. For existing account information, press 1. For all other services, press 2. To speak to a customer service specialist at any time, press 0.
For checking accounts, press 1. For savings, press 2. For credit cards, press 3.
Please enter your checking account number followed by the pound sign.
For personal accounts, please enter the last four digits of your Social Security number followed by the pound sign.
Your available balance is $886.59.

ANSWER KEY:

Thank; Bank; one; two; zero; one; savings; two; three; checking; balance; $886.59

EXPANSION ACTIVITY: You Make the Call

- Call a local bank or credit union and listen to the automated system. Write down what you hear.
- Have students call the same number to listen to the automated system.
- Have them write down what they hear and share it with the class.
- LOW LEVEL: Provide lower level students with a cloze of the recording. Have them fill in the missing words they hear as they listen.

❸ Practice the Conversation: Buying a Money Order 🎧 048

- Set the context for the conversation by having students look at the picture and asking them questions: *Where is it? Who do you see?*
- Read the conversation or play the audio.
- Check comprehension by asking questions: *What does the customer want? For how much? How much does the post office charge to provide a money order?*
- Read or play the conversation again. Pause after each sentence and ask students to repeat.
- Divide the class in half. Have half the class read A's part, and half the class read B's part.
- Have students cover the conversation in their books and say it again. Switch parts and repeat.
- Model substituting items with a more proficient student. You read A's part. Demonstrate how to substitute a different amount from the items below. Have the student read B's lines. Cue the student to substitute the correct amount.
- Tell students to write down their own ideas.
- Put students in pairs and have them practice the conversation, making substitutions from the numbered items and using their own ideas. Have them take turns playing both parts. Then have them close their books and practice again.

Unit 3: Lesson 5

> **LISTENING SCRIPT**
>
> **Lesson 5, Activity 3: Practice the Conversation: Buying a Money Order**
>
> *Listen to the conversation. Listen again and repeat.*
>
> A: Welcome to Horizon Bank.
>
> B: Thank you.
>
> A: How can I help you?
>
> B: I'd like to buy a money order.
>
> A: How much do you want it for?
>
> B: Two hundred dollars.
>
> A: Anything else?
>
> B: No, that's all.
>
> A: Okay. Your total is $205.00.

> **Culture Notes:**
>
> Your students may not know about various methods of payment commonly used in the United States. Discuss the topic with students, reviewing these points and others:
> - Although we can use cash for many purposes, it is not safe to send cash through the mail.
> - Money orders are an alternative to personal or bank checks.
> - For people who do not have checking accounts, money orders can be a relatively inexpensive way to send money.
> - Personal checks usually have to clear before they can be cashed. Money orders can be cashed immediately.
> - Money orders can be purchased at post offices and some stores.

❹ Practice the Conversation: Asking for Change 049

- Repeat the basic procedure from Activity 3.
- To set the context, ask questions: *Who is in the picture? What is their relationship?*
- After students have listened to and repeated the conversation, check comprehension by asking more questions: *What are they talking about?*
- Have students continue practicing the conversation, making substitutions from the numbered items and using their own ideas.

> **LISTENING SCRIPT**
>
> **Lesson 5, Activity 4: Practice the Conversation: Asking for Change**
>
> *Listen to the conversation. Listen again and repeat.*
>
> A: Do you have change for a twenty?
>
> B: I think so. How do you want it?
>
> A: Do you have 2 tens?
>
> B: Sure. Here you are—ten, twenty.
>
> A: Thanks.

> **Vocabulary Note:**
> - When we talk about paper money, we often use just the number of the denomination without the word *dollar* or *bill*. We can make the number singular or plural (*I have a twenty. Do you have two tens?*).

LESSON 6 — Understanding a Pay Stub

OBJECTIVE
Understanding a pay stub

WINDOW ON MATH
Computing Deductions

VOCABULARY
deducts salary
employee

1 Learn New Words

- Tell students that *context* is the words and ideas around the word.
- Point out that they can use context to figure out the meaning of words.
- Have students look at the first sentence. Read the sentence aloud or have a volunteer read it. Ask students what they think an employee is. Elicit words in the sentence that help students figure out the meaning: *He works as a bank teller.*
- Have students complete the questions and then check their answers in pairs.
- Go over the answers with the class.

ANSWER KEY:
1. B; 2. C; 3. B

EXPANSION ACTIVITY: Guess the Meaning [Challenge]

- Have students bring in various short texts in English or provide them yourself.
- Have the students work in pairs to read the text and circle the words that are new to them.
- Have each pair choose two new words to define by using context. Have them make notes about what each word means and then check their guesses by using a dictionary.
- Have students tell the class their words, meanings, and what context clues helped them guess the meanings.

2 Answer the Questions

- Have students look at the pay stub and ask: *What is this? Who gets this? When?*
- Have the students read the questions, or read the questions aloud and have students repeat. Have students answer the questions and check their answers in pairs.
- Go over the answers with the class.

ANSWER KEY:
1. His pay is $20 per hour. 2. He worked 80 hours. 3. It is two weeks. 4. It was $1,128.00. 5. $40.00 was deducted.

EXPANSION ACTIVITY: Find Someone Who

- Write the following "Find Someone Who" activity on the board and have students copy it.

Find someone who:
- earns more than $10 per hour
- gets paid every two weeks
- gets paid every month
- gets paid every week
- works 80 hours in a pay period
- has health insurance deducted from his or her paycheck

- Have students stand and walk around the room, asking each other questions. Remind them to write a name next to each item and to use each name only once.
- Have students share what they learned after the activity concludes.

Culture/Civics Note:

- Your students may not understand all the deductions on their pay stubs. Point out that Federal taxes, state taxes, and FICA deductions are usually indicated on the pay stub. FICA includes payments made for Social Security and Medicare.

STUDENT BOOK PAGES 42–43

Unit 3: Lesson 6

③ Write

- Have students complete the paragraph about Andy, using the information from Activity 2.
- Have students check their answers in pairs.
- Go over the answers with the class.
- Have students complete the deposit slip.
- Walk around the room to monitor the activity and provide help as needed.

ANSWER KEY:

Andy Kalish works <u>40</u> hours a week. He earns <u>$20</u> an hour or <u>$800</u> a week. Every <u>two</u> weeks he gets a paycheck. In the last pay period his earnings were <u>$1,600</u>, but he got a paycheck for <u>$1,128</u>. That's because the company <u>deducts</u> some money for taxes and health insurance. Andy deposited his $1,128 paycheck in his checking account. He took out $200 in cash. Complete his deposit slip.

NOTE:

Have students sign Andy's name on the deposit slip for cash back.

WINDOW ON MATH

Computing Deductions

A Read the information below.

- Have the students read the information silently, or read it aloud and have them follow along silently.
- Ask comprehension questions: *What do employers deduct? How much is deducted for taxes? Are deductions for health insurance always the same?*
- Go over the example.

B Answer the word problems.

- Have students solve the word problems and check their answers in pairs.
- MULTI LEVEL: Pair advanced students with lower level students who speak their native language. Have partners work through the math content in English and their native language as necessary. Then, have the lower level student write an answer for each question. Have the advanced student check the answers.
- Go over the answers with the class.

ANSWER KEY:

1. 40 hours x $20/hour = $800. 30% of $800 = $240. $800 - $240 - $40 = $520
2. 40 x $15 = $600. 25% of $600 = $150. $600 - $150 - $35 = $415

BIG PICTURE EXPANSION ACTIVITY:
WRITING—Describing What People Did

- Have students look at the Big Picture in their books (Student Book pages 36–37).
- Have the students write a paragraph about the picture. Suggest they use the simple past to describe what the people did.
- Walk around to monitor the activity and provide help as needed.
- Have students read their paragraphs to a partner.
- Have a few volunteers read their paragraphs to the class.

LESSON 7: What Do You Know?

1 Listening Review 050

- Go over the directions with the class.
- Read the items or play the audio and have the students mark their answers on the Answer Sheet.
- Walk around to monitor the activity and help students stay on task.
- Have students check their answers with a partner.
- Go over the answers with the class.

LISTENING SCRIPT

Lesson 7, Activity 1: Listening Review

You will hear a question. Listen to the conversation. You will hear the question again. Choose the correct answer: A, B, or C. Use the Answer Sheet.

1. How did the person pay the bill?
   A. What are you doing?
   B. I'm paying the electric bill.
   A. I paid it yesterday with a check.
   How did the person pay the bill?
   A. the electric bill
   B. with a check
   C. with a money order

2. How much money did she spend on groceries?
   A: How much money did you spend on bus fare last month?
   B: A lot. How much money did you spend on groceries last month?
   A: Not much.
   How much money did she spend on groceries?
   A. A lot.
   B. An average amount
   C. Not much.

3. What was the correct amount of change?
   A: Your change is $12.25.
   B: Hmmm. I thought it was $12.50.
   A: Oh, sorry. You're right.
   What was the correct amount of change?
   A. $12.15
   B. $12.25
   C. $12.50

4. Where can you get a withdrawal slip?
   A: Did you fill out a withdrawal slip?
   B: A withdrawal slip?
   C: Yes. You can get one from a teller.
   Where can you get a withdrawal slip?
   A. a withdrawal slip
   B. from a teller
   C. from an ATM

5. How much is the money order worth?
   A: I'd like to buy a money order.
   B: How much do you want it for?
   A: Two hundred fifty dollars.
   B: Okay. Your total is two hundred fifty-five dollars.
   How much is the money order worth?
   A. $215
   B. $250
   C. $255

ANSWER KEY:
1. B; 2. C; 3. C; 4. B; 5. B

2 Listening Dictation 051

- Copy the numbers and lines from the Listening Dictation section on the board.
- Read the first item. Have a more advanced student write the missing sentence on the board. Have students copy the sentence in their books.
- Play the audio and have students write the sentences they hear. Repeat as many times as necessary.
- Put students in pairs to compare answers.
- Have volunteers write the sentences on the board.

STUDENT BOOK PAGES 44-45   DOLLARS AND CENTS • 69

Unit 3: Lesson 7

LISTENING SCRIPT

Lesson 7, Activity 2: Listening Dictation

Listen and write the sentences you hear.

1. A: How much did you spend on recreation last month?
   B: I didn't spend very much.
2. A: How did you pay the gas bill last month?
   B: I paid with a money order.
3. A: The total is $8.95.
   B: Can you change a fifty?
   A: Sure. Your change is $41.05.
4. A: I'd like to make a withdrawal.
   B: Did you fill out a withdrawal slip?
   A: Yes, I did.
5. A: I'd like to buy a money order.
   B: How much do you want it for?
   A: Four hundred fifty dollars.

❸ Grammar Review

- Go over the directions with the class.
- Read the first sentence. Elicit the appropriate completion. Have students circle C for item 1.
- Have students answer the rest of the questions.
- Put students in pairs to compare answers.
- Go over the answers with the class.

ANSWER KEY:

1. C; 2. A; 3. C; 4. A; 5. B; 6. C

LEARNING LOG

- Point out the four sections of the Learning Log: *I know these words; I can ask; I can say;* and *I can write.*
- Have students check what they know and what they can do.
- Walk around to note what they don't know or can't do. Use this information to review areas of difficulty.

TESTING FOCUS: Remembering Vocabulary

- After students have completed the Learning Log, review with them strategies for remembering difficult vocabulary words.
- Write the word toiletries on the board. Have students give suggestions on how they can remember the word. Elicit or explain the following possibilities: writing the word several times or on a flashcard, with its definition and/or with the equivalent word in the student's native language; writing sentences using the word in context and reading them aloud; making a word web about the term to understand it better.
- Have students try one of the techniques mentioned with a word or phrase from the Learning Log that they have trouble remembering.

Unit 3: Lesson 7

 BIG PICTURE EXPANSION ACTIVITY:
SPEAKING—Assessment: Talking about the Picture

- You can use the Big Picture in Unit 3, Lesson 3 (Student Book pages 36–37) to place new students in open entry classes, to diagnose difficulties, or to measure progress.

- Work with one student at a time and show the Big Picture. Ask: *What do you see in the picture? Tell me about the picture.* Tell the student you want him or her to speak for as long as possible. Wait a moment for the student to prepare to answer. If the student has difficulty, you can use prompts: *Where are the people in the picture? Who do you see in the picture? What are they doing?*

- You can use a rubric like the one below to rate beginning speakers.

4	Exhibits confidence, begins speaking without prompting Uses some complex sentences, although may make mistakes with irregular forms Can use more than one tense
3	Uses sentences, although form may be incorrect Can speak for a sustained length of time Responds to prompts, but doesn't need them to begin speaking
2	Can use nouns and verbs Uses phrases Answers informational questions
1	Can name objects Uses single words Can answer *yes/no* questions
0	Cannot say anything independently May be able to point to objects when prompted

TEACHER'S NOTES:

Things that students are doing well:
_____
_____
_____

Things students need additional help with:
_____
_____
_____

Ideas for further practice or for the next class:
_____
_____
_____

UNIT 4 PLANS AND GOALS

UNIT OVERVIEW

LESSON	STUDENT BOOK PAGE	TEACHER'S EDITION PAGE
1. Identifying Goals	46	73
2. Making Plans	48	76
3. On the Job	50	79
4. A Success Story	52	83
5. Asking for and Giving Advice	54	86
6. Help Your Child Succeed in School!	56	89
7. What Do You Know?	58	91

Big Picture Expansion Activities

FOCUS	TITLE	SUGGESTED USE
Grammar	Future with *be going to*	Lesson 2
Reading	Memo on Policies	Lesson 3
Speaking	Chain Story	Lesson 3
Speaking	Assessment: Talking about the Big Picture	Lesson 7
Writing	The Day's Events	Lesson 7

Big Picture Expansion Activity Worksheets

FOCUS	TITLE	TEACHER'S EDITION PAGE
7. Grammar	Future with *be going to*	230
8. Reading	Memo on Policies	231

LESSON 1  Identifying Goals

OBJECTIVE
Identifying goals

VOCABULARY

be a good citizen	get good grades
be a good parent	get married
become a U.S. citizen	get vocational training
buy a house	graduate from a university
get a GED	learn something new
get a job	start a business
get a promotion	win an award
get a raise	

TARGET GRAMMAR

Want to, like to, would like to   page 162

THINGS TO DO

1 Learn New Words 052

- Have students look at the pictures, and elicit the words they know.
- Have students listen and look at the pictures while you say the words or play the audio.
- Instruct students to circle the words that are new to them.
- Say the words or play the audio a second time. Pause after each word or phrase and ask the students to repeat and point to the correct picture.
- Put students in pairs and have one say a word or phrase as the partner points to the correct picture. Reverse roles and repeat the activity.
- Call on students and ask questions: *Would you like to get a job? Do you want to be a good parent? Would you like to start a business?*

LISTENING SCRIPT

Lesson 1, Activity 1: Learn New Words

Look at the pictures. Listen to the words. Listen again and repeat.

Personal Goals
1. become a U.S. citizen — He would like to become a U.S. citizen.
2. get married — They would like to get married.
3. buy a house — She would like to buy a house.
4. be a good parent — She would like to be a good parent.
5. be a good citizen — He would like to be a good citizen.

Educational Goals
6. get good grades — He would like to get good grades.
7. get vocational training — They would like to get vocational training.
8. graduate from a university — She would like to graduate from a university.
9. get a GED — He would like to get a GED.
10. learn something new — She would like to learn something new.

Work Goals
11. get a job — He would like to get a job.
12. get a raise — She would like to get a raise.
13. get a promotion — He would like to get a promotion.
14. start a business — She would like to start a business.
15. win an award — He would like to win an award.

STUDENT BOOK PAGES 46-47

Unit 4: Lesson 1

 TARGET GRAMMAR

Want to, like to, would like to
The Target Grammar point is used in Activities 1, 2 and 4. Presentation and practice of this grammar point appears on Student Book page 162. Answer Keys appear on Teacher's Edition page 251.

EXPANSION ACTIVITY: Vote with Your Feet

- Tell students that you will give them two goals and they must decide which one is more important to them as individuals. They will move to the side of the room that indicates their choice.

- Have students or a group of students come to the front of the room. Ask: *Which is more important to you, being a good parent or getting good grades?* Point to one side of the room to indicate one choice and the other side of the room to indicate the other. Remind the students to "vote with their feet," or move, to show their goals.

- Give several more choices. If you have a large class, repeat with other groups of students.

 Culture/Civics Note:

- Students may be unfamiliar with the educational system in this country. You may want to explain our levels of schooling (primary or elementary school, middle school or junior high, high school, vocational school, community college, college or university, graduate school, continuing education). You may also want to point out that many people continue their education well into adulthood.

 Grammar Note:

- The vocabulary for this lesson includes a number of phrases beginning with *get*. In almost all cases here, *get* means "to obtain or acquire"—you don't have something and then you do. When used in the expression *get married*, *get* means "to become."

❷ Listen and Write 053

- Go over the directions.
- Play the audio. Pause after each statement and have students write the number of the picture that corresponds to it correctly.
- Put students in pairs to compare answers. Play the audio again if necessary to have students confirm their answers.
- Go over the answers with the class.

LISTENING SCRIPT

Lesson 1, Activity 2: Listen and Write

Listen to people talk about goals. Look at the pictures. Write the correct number.

  a. Carla would like to graduate from a university.
  b. Sonia would like to be a good parent.
  c. I would like to win an award at work.
  d. Bob would like to learn something new.
  e. José would like to get married.
  f. John would like to get a job.

ANSWER KEY:

a. 8; b. 4; c. 15; d. 10; e. 2; f. 11

Unit 4: Lesson 1

EXPANSION ACTIVITY:
Creative Writing [Challenge]

- Have students imagine that they are one of the people illustrated in the Big Picture on pages 50–51.
- Have students write about what they are doing. On the board, write prompts to help them such as: *Why did you decide to do this? How did you achieve this? What do you want to gain from this?*
- LOW LEVEL: Have lower level students write three to five sentences in their native language about the person they chose. Then have them work with a more advanced partner to translate the sentences, using a bilingual dictionary and grammar reference guides as necessary.
- Have students in small groups share what they wrote. Have one member of each group present his or her writing to the class.

❸ Write

- Have students look at the chart. Point out that we often have different kinds of goals. The categories listed here are *Personal Goals, Educational Goals,* and *Work Goals.*
- Have students list their goals on the chart.
- Go over the example for sharing information.
- Have students share three of their goals in pairs.
- Call on volunteers to tell the class about one of their partner's goals.

EXPANSION ACTIVITY:
Picture it! [Multi-Level]

- Bring in magazines or have students bring some in. You will also need glue or tape, and large pieces of paper.
- Have students find pictures in the magazines that represent their goals.
- Have students make a collage of their goals. Have lower level students label their collage with words or phrases to describe the pictures and their goals. Have more advanced students explain their collages to the class. Encourage students to ask each other questions about their goals.
- Display the collages around the room.

❹ Find Someone Who

- Go over the directions. Encourage students to write a different name next to each goal as they complete the chart.
- Have students move around the room to talk to classmates and fill out the chart.
- Call on students to tell about a classmate's goal.

EXPANSION ACTIVITY: Compare and Contrast

- Draw a Venn Diagram on the board, titled "Goals." Label the left circle with your name and the right circle with a student's name.

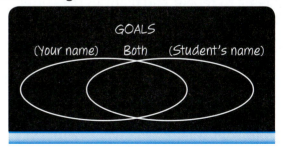

- Model the activity by comparing yourself to the student listed in the diagram. Compare and contrast your goals.
- Have students work in pairs to create Venn Diagrams about themselves and their partners.
- Have students use the ideas on the Venn Diagram to write sentences.
- Call on students to tell the class about their diagrams.

STUDENT BOOK PAGES 46-47

LESSON 2: Making Plans

OBJECTIVE
Making plans

VOCABULARY

do volunteer work
go back to school
learn more English
learn to use a computer
read to your children
save money
spend time with your children
take a business course
take a writing course
vote

TARGET GRAMMAR

Future with *be going to*   page 163

THINGS TO DO

1 Learn New Words 054

- Have students look at the pictures and elicit the words they know.
- Have students listen and look at the pictures while you say the words or play the audio.
- Instruct students to circle the words that are new to them.
- Say the words or play the audio a second time. Pause after each word or phrase and ask the students to repeat and point to the correct picture.
- Put students in pairs and have one say a word or phrase as the partner points to the correct picture. Reverse roles and repeat the activity.
- Call on students and ask questions: *Are you going to learn more English? Are you going to read to your children this week? Are you going to learn to use a computer?*

LISTENING SCRIPT

Lesson 2, Activity 1: Learn New Words

Look at the pictures. Listen to the words. Listen again and repeat.

1. go back to school — She is going to go back to school.
2. take a business course — She is going to take a business course.
3. save money — She is going to save money.
4. learn to use a computer — She is going to learn to use a computer.
5. take a writing course — She is going to take a writing course.
6. learn more English — He is going to learn more English.
7. vote — He is going to vote.
8. do volunteer work — He is going to do volunteer work.
9. read to your children — Are you going to read to your children?
10. spend time with your children — Are you going to spend time with your children?

TARGET GRAMMAR

Future with *be going to*

The Target Grammar point is used in Activities 1–3. Presentation and practice of this grammar point appears on Student Book pages 163–164. Answer Keys appear on Teacher's Edition page 251.

76 • UNIT 4

STUDENT BOOK PAGES 48-49

Unit 4: Lesson 2

EXPANSION ACTIVITY: Rank It

- Have students rank the activities from Activity 1 in order of importance. Tell them to write a *1* next to the activity that they think is most important.
- Have students share their ideas in pairs.
- LOW LEVEL: Have students choose three of the activities and complete the following sentence frame: *It is (not important, somewhat important, important, very important) for me to (insert activity).* If possible, have students use the word *because* to add a reason that tells why they think the activity is important or not. Have students share their sentences with a partner or the class.
- Ask questions: *Who ranked reading to children as number 1? Who thinks taking a business course is most important? What did you rank as number 10?*

Culture Note:

- You may wish to lead a discussion on the priorities that people from different cultures assign to the actions in Activity 1. For example, point out that volunteer work is important to many Americans. Ask students whether volunteer work is important in their own cultures, or whether they prioritize other ways to help people (such as family and friends) or to spend their time.

❷ Practice the Conversation 🎧 055

- Have students listen and look at the conversation while you read it or play the audio.
- Say the words or play the audio a second time. Pause after each line and have the students repeat.
- Model the conversation with a student. Have the student read B's lines. Demonstrate how to substitute from the boxes below. Cue the student to make the appropriate substitutions.
- Have students work in pairs to practice the conversation, making substitutions from the boxes.
- Walk around to make sure students understand the activity and provide help if needed.

LISTENING SCRIPT

Lesson 2, Activity 2: Practice the Conversation

Listen to the conversation. Listen again and repeat.

A: What is your goal?

B: My goal is to start my own business, so I'm going to take a writing course. How about you?

A: My goal is to get a raise, so I'm going to learn to use a computer.

B: That's great. Good luck!

EXPANSION ACTIVITY: Famous Goal-Setters [Challenge]

- Have students brainstorm the names of famous people who achieved difficult goals. Write their ideas on the board. Ask students what goal or goals each person achieved, and if they know, how the person accomplished each goal. If students have trouble thinking of people, suggest famous sports stars, politicians, business people, or celebrities and ask leading questions about each one to elicit information.
- Have partners or groups each choose one of the famous people to research. Have them find out about the person's goals and how he or she achieved each one.
- Have each pair or group report back to the class what they discovered. Have the class vote on the most accomplished goal-setter of the famous people chosen.

Unit 4: Lesson 2

Academic Notes:

- Point out to students that they should think critically about the information they find on the Internet. Encourage them to think about the person or group that wrote or posted information to determine whether it shows any bias or special interest on the subject. Give students pointers about various kinds of websites, such as these:
- A **.com** or **.net** address tells users that the information most likely comes from a for-profit organization or private party. Such information may be trying to sell a product or service or promote a certain point of view.
- A **.org** address represents a non-profit organization.
- A **.gov** address represents an official government agency.
- A **.edu** address represents a school, college, or university.

3 Write

- Go over the directions.
- Model the activity by telling about one of your goals or use the example in the activity. Write it on the board. Elicit ideas for ways that you can reach that goal. Write the ideas on the board in a cluster diagram.
- Have students create cluster diagrams for their goals and how to reach them.
- Have students share their ideas in pairs.
- Have volunteers report what they learned about their partners to the class.

EXPANSION ACTIVITY: Timeline [Multi-Level]

- Have students list the ideas they included in their cluster diagrams.
- Next to each idea, have them write a suggested time frame. For example, if someone wants to improve his or her English and listed *take a class, study hard,* and *make English-speaking friends* as ideas, the student should write when these could happen *(take a class—next term)*. Have lower level students use the sentence frame *I'm going to (activity) (time frame)*. For example, *I'm going to study hard this semester.*
- Have students share their ideas in pairs.
- Have volunteers outline their goals for the class, explaining their timelines. Encourage more advanced students to provide details about how they plan to achieve their goals.

BIG PICTURE EXPANSION ACTIVITY: GRAMMAR—Future with *be going to*

- Make copies of Worksheet 7 (Teacher's Edition page 230) and distribute them to students.
- Have students look at the Big Picture in their books (Student Book pages 50–51).
- Instruct students to complete the activities and then check their answers with a partner.
- Go over the answers with the class.

ANSWER KEY:

A. 1. is going to change; 2. is going to greet; 3. is going to lose; 4. is going to get; 5. is going to fall; 6. are going to buy; 7. is going to wake

B. 1. He's not going to sleep at work; 2. He's going to come on time; 3. He's going to be organized; 4. She's going to work hard; 5. He's going to have a good attitude.

LESSON 3 — On the Job

OBJECTIVE
On the job

VOCABULARY

bad attitude	hardworking	on time
bookkeeper	late	organized
designer	lazy	salesperson
disorganized	mechanic	supervisor
good attitude	office manager	
good with people	office worker	

TARGET GRAMMAR

Future with *will* *page 165*

THINGS TO DO

① Learn New Words 056

- Have students look at the Big Picture in their books (Student Book pages 50–51). Elicit the words they know.
- Have students listen and look at the pictures while you say the words or play the audio.
- Instruct students to circle the words that are new to them.
- Say the words or play the audio a second time. Pause after each word or phrase and ask the students to repeat and point to the correct part of the picture.
- Put students in pairs and have them take turns saying the words as their partners point to the correct parts of the picture.

LISTENING SCRIPT

Lesson 3, Activity 1: Learn New Words

Look at the picture. Listen to the words. Listen again and repeat.

1. office manager	He is an office manager.
2. office worker	He is an office worker.
3. designer	He is a designer.
4. bookkeeper	She is a bookkeeper.
5. salesperson	He is a salesperson.
6. supervisor	He is a supervisor.
7. mechanic	She is a mechanic.
8. late	He is late.
9. on time	He is on time.
10. organized	He is organized.
11. disorganized	He is disorganized.
12. good with people	He is good with people.
13. hardworking	He is hardworking.
14. lazy	He is lazy.
15. bad attitude	He has a bad attitude.
16. good attitude	She has a good attitude.

EXPANSION ACTIVITY:
Opposite Toss [Low-Level]

- Point out that there are four sets of opposites in Activity 1. Elicit them by saying a word: *hardworking* and asking for its opposite: *lazy*. (Other pairs: *late/on time, organized/disorganized, good attitude/bad attitude*)
- Brainstorm a list of opposites students know from previous units or elsewhere and write them on the board (*heavy/light, tall/short, married/single,* etc.).
- Explain that you are going to toss the beanbag or ball to a student and say a word. They should respond with the correct opposite.
- Demonstrate with a student. After the student responds, have him or her toss the beanbag back to you.
- Continue tossing the beanbag until all students have had a chance to respond. If possible, have students toss the object to a classmate while saying a word and eliciting its opposite.

Unit 4: Lesson 3

❷ Talk About the Picture

- Have students look at the Big Picture in their books (Student Book pages 50–51).
- To set the context, ask questions about the picture: *How many people do you see? Where are they? What are they doing?*
- Write the vocabulary elicited from students on the board.
- Go over the directions and the example, having a student role-play with you if necessary.
- Put students in pairs. Have partners talk about the picture, using the example as a model. Remind them to use the words on the board or from Activity 1.
- Walk around the room and provide help as needed.
- Call on a few pairs to reenact their descriptions for the class.

EXPANSION ACTIVITY: Role-Play [Multi-Level]

- On pieces of paper, write the names of two people that are interacting in the Big Picture, such as Ken and the female customer. Fold up the papers and place them in a bag.
- Have two students come to the front of the class and have each one draw one of the pieces of paper. Have them improvise a dialogue between the two characters based on the picture. Tell students that each character must speak at least three times before they may finish their dialogue.
- For lower level students, have pairs write a dialogue first and then perform it for the class.

BIG PICTURE EXPANSION ACTIVITY: SPEAKING—Chain Story

- Explain that the class is going to tell a chain story. Arrange students in a circle.
- Begin the story by saying a sentence about the Big Picture (Student Book pages 50–51). Call on the student next to you in the circle. Have him or her repeat your sentence and add a new one.
- The next student in the circle should then repeat the previous student's sentence—not yours also—and add a new one.
- Continue the activity until the story has gone around the circle and everyone has added a sentence.
- CHALLENGE Have more advanced students repeat all of the sentences that were said up to their turn, not just the sentence from the previous student.

❸ Practice the Conversation 057

- Have students listen and look at the conversation while you read it or play the audio.
- Say the words or play the audio a second time. Pause after each line and ask the students to repeat.
- Check comprehension by asking questions: *Who is having this conversation? What do you think their relationship is?*
- Model the conversation with a student. Have the student read B's lines. Demonstrate how to substitute from the boxes below. Cue the student to make the appropriate substitutions.
- Have students work in pairs to practice the conversation, making substitutions from the boxes.
- Walk around to make sure students understand the activity and provide help if needed.

Unit 4: Lesson 3

LISTENING SCRIPT

Lesson 3, Activity 3: Practice the Conversation

Listen to the conversation. Listen again and repeat.

A: Who will get the job as the new bookkeeper?
B: I think Jon will get the job. He's organized.
A: Yes, and he is always on time.

EXPANSION ACTIVITY: Evaluate Yourself

- Have students write items 8–16 from Activity 1 on a piece of paper *(late, on time, organized, disorganized, good with people, hardworking, lazy, bad attitude, good attitude)*
- Ask them to evaluate themselves on each quality from 1 to 5 (1 – never, 2 – rarely, 3 – sometimes, 4 – often, 5 – always).
- Have them share their evaluations in pairs, telling about each quality in a sentence that uses the adverb they chose. Model an example, such as: *I am sometimes disorganized.*
- Have volunteers report to the class on their best qualities.

Culture Notes:

- Point out that the conversations in Activity 3 could be considered typical topics of workplace chitchat or gossip. Introduce the idiom "around the water cooler" and lead a discussion on the kinds of things people talk about (or avoid discussing) with co-workers in the United States. Point out that it is common to speculate about who may get a certain job, and that people sometimes comment on the work habits of their coworkers in certain situations. In Activity 3, all of the possible conversations mention positive characteristics of the people being discussed, though this is not always the case.
- You may wish to discuss topics that are considered inappropriate for the workplace in terms of current business standards. Have students share their ideas about how American standards compare with the norms of their own cultures or countries.
- Be aware that students from various cultures may not feel comfortable "bragging" about themselves, so they may have trouble discussing their strengths. Explain to students that in the United States, job candidates or workers looking for a promotion or pay raise are often expected to "sell themselves" by telling reasons why they are the best person for the job.

TARGET GRAMMAR

Future with *will*

The Target Grammar point is used in Activity 3. Presentation and practice of this grammar point appears on Student Book page 165. Answer Keys appear on Teacher's Edition page 252.

4 Find Someone Who

- Go over the directions.
- Have students stand and move around the classroom in order to talk to their classmates. Have them write one classmate's name next to each item.
- Have partners discuss the results they found. You may wish to have students tell their results, taking care not to allow the conversation to turn critical when discussing negative qualities such as disorganization.

EXPANSION ACTIVITY: Pair Evaluation

- Explain to students that people are often asked to write recommendations for co-workers, friends, and employees. In recommendations, we usually describe someone's good qualities.
- Put students in pairs and have them describe their good qualities to each other.
- Have the students write a paragraph about their partners' good qualities and then read them in pairs.
- Have volunteers read their paragraphs to the class.

Unit 4: Lesson 3

Culture Note:
- Emphasize that when giving recommendations, it is important to be truthful. Explain to students that if they do not feel comfortable recommending someone, they should not agree to give a recommendation. In addition, point out that employers usually will not accept recommendations from relatives.

BIG PICTURE EXPANSION ACTIVITY:
READING—Memo on Policies

- Make copies of Worksheet 8 (Teacher's Edition page 231) and distribute them to students.
- Have students look at the Big Picture in their books (Student Book pages 50–51).
- Instruct students to complete the activities and then check their answers with a partner.
- Go over the answers with the class. Have students correct each statement to make it true.

ANSWER KEY:

A: 1. False. It is not okay to wear a T-shirt and jeans. You should look professional at all times; 2. True.; 3. False. Being on time and a good attitude are both important; 4. False. The president of the company is going to visit; 5. True.; 6. False. The memo is from Donna Tate; 7. False. The memo is about work policies.

B: Possible answers:
1. Ken: He is dressed appropriately and professionally.
2. Tim: He has a good attitude.
3. Laura: She is hardworking.
4. Mike: He does not treat customers as if they are important.

LESSON 4 — A Success Story

OBJECTIVE
A success story

VOCABULARY
coach gymnastics
gold medal

TARGET GRAMMAR
Because and *to* for reasons page 166

THINGS TO DO

1 Learn New Words 058

- Point to each picture that illustrates the words.
- Have students listen and look at the pictures while you say the words or play the audio.
- Say the words or play the audio a second time. Pause after each word and ask the students to repeat.
- Say the words in random order and have students point to the item in the picture.

LISTENING SCRIPT

Lesson 4, Activity 1: Learn New Words

Look at the pictures and photos. Listen to the words. Listen again and repeat.

1. gymnastics — She is doing gymnastics.
2. gold medal — She won a gold medal.
3. coach — She likes to coach.

EXPANSION ACTIVITY: Pros and Cons

- Explain to students the terms *pros* and *cons*.
- Have students imagine that they are Olympic gymnasts.
- Divide the class into three groups and assign each group one vocabulary word. Have each group discuss and make notes about the pros and cons associated with their word. If necessary, write a guiding question for each group: *What are the pros and cons of competing in gymnastics? What are the pros and cons of trying to win a gold medal? What are the pros and cons of having a coach?*
- Have each group report to the class what they listed as the pros and cons of each item. Encourage students to discuss any interesting or arguable ideas.

2 Preview

- Have students look at the pictures and read the title.
- Have them check the box or boxes to indicate what the story is about.
- Elicit students' ideas and have them give reasons to support each one (*It says "Olympic gymnast" in the title*).

ANSWER KEY:
Students should check: a gymnast; an important person

Unit 4: Lesson 4

EXPANSION ACTIVITY: Previewing Practice: "On the Right Track" [Multi-Level]

- Collect several one-page articles from popular magazines. Be sure that each article includes photographs, captions, diagrams, and other text features. Be prepared to summarize each article for the class.

- Tape construction paper over the main text of each article so that students cannot read it. Be sure to leave any headings or titles visible, along with illustrations, captions, and so forth.

- Give small groups one article each. Have students use only the information visible to make predictions of what the article is about. Have lower level students give words and phrases to describe the picture and their ideas. Circulate and offer each group hints about whether they are "on the right track." Explain the idiom as needed.

- Have groups check how accurate their predictions were by summarizing each article for them. Have them identify which predictions they got right, and which ones were "on the wrong track."

- You may wish to have more advanced students uncover the text, read the article, and discover for themselves whether or not they were on the right track.

Grammar Note:

- The biography in this lesson contains many phrases related to time. Students may be confused about the use of prepositions (*in, on, at*) in time expressions. Point out that *in* is used with years and months (*in 1951, in July*), *on* is used with dates and days (*on April 13, 1933, on Tuesday*), and *at* is used with times on the clock (*at 3:15*).

Academic Notes:

- You may want to stress the importance of previewing. Previewing is an important reading skill and will help students if they take academic courses. Comprehension improves if readers have a general idea of what a reading is about. Then they can activate prior knowledge as they begin to read.

- Explain to students that when they preview, they should look at any visuals (pictures, photos, graphics), special formatting (boldfaced, italics, headings, and subheadings), and the first and last sentences of paragraphs.

❸ Read and Underline

- Have students look at the reading and ask what a biography is. Elicit that it is a story about someone's life. Point out that in biographies, we pay special attention to the dates and times of events.

- Have students read and underline the important events and time information in the story.

- Have students answer the questions and fill in the timeline. Then check their answers in pairs.

- Go over the answers with the class.

ANSWER KEY:

1. 1961; 2. 7; 3. 1976; 4. 1989; 5. 1996; 6. 2006

TARGET GRAMMAR

Because and *to* for reasons

The Target Grammar point is used in Activity 3. Presentation and practice of this grammar point appears on Student Book pages 166–167. Answer Keys appear on Teacher's Edition page 252.

Unit 4: Lesson 4

> **EXPANSION ACTIVITY: Memory Test**
> **[Challenge]**
> - Give students five minutes to study the information on Nadia Comaneci.
> - Divide the class into teams. Have each team create ten questions about the information in the reading.
> - Have the teams take turns posing questions to the members of another team. Both teams should have their books closed. Each correct answer earns a point for the answering team.

❹ Write

- Brainstorm a list of important events and write the ideas on the board. They may include birth, graduations, weddings, deaths, moves, sports events, and so on.
- Have students write five or more events in the left column of the chart and the year of each event in the right column.
- Instruct students to use the information in the chart to make timelines of their lives.
- Have students share their timelines in pairs.

> **EXPANSION ACTIVITY: Interview**
> - Explain to students that they are going to interview each other to write a short biography.
> - Brainstorm questions to ask in the interview and write them on the board.
> - Put students in pairs and have them take turns interviewing each other. Remind them to use the questions on the board and their timelines and to take notes about what their partner says.
> - CHALLENGE: Encourage advanced students to ask follow-up questions and to elaborate on the events they describe when responding to a question.
> - Have students write a biographical paragraph about their partners.
> - Call on students to read their paragraphs to the class.

LESSON 5: Asking for and Giving Advice

OBJECTIVE
Asking for and giving advice

PRONUNCIATION
Past endings

1 Practice Pronunciation: Past Endings 059

A. Listen to the words. Listen again and repeat.

- Go over the information in the box. Explain to students that the regular past tense ending (-ed) can have different sounds, like a t, like a d, and as a separate syllable -id. Encourage them to pay attention to this ending sound as they listen to the words.
- Have students look at the words while you say the words or play the audio.
- Say the words or play the audio a second time, pausing after each word to have students repeat.
- Call on a few students to read a word and help them pronounce the correct ending for each one.

LISTENING SCRIPT

Lesson 5, Activity 1: Practice Pronunciation: Past Endings

A. Listen to the words. Listen again and repeat.

1. married		9. immigrated
2. wanted		10. studied
3. volunteered		11. graduated
4. relaxed		12. learned
5. liked		13. practiced
6. helped		14. saved
7. cashed		15. promoted
8. voted			

B. Write the words from the list above in the correct place in the chart.

- Have students look at the chart. Go over the examples in each column.
- Have students write the words from Activity A in the correct place in the chart.
- Go over the answers with the class.

ANSWER KEY:

Ending sounds like t: relaxed, cashed, practiced, liked, helped
Ending sounds like d: married, studied, saved, volunteered, learned
Ending sounds like id: wanted, voted, graduated, immigrated, promoted

C. Work with a partner. Ask and answer the questions. Use complete sentences.

- Go over the directions. Read each question and have students repeat. Remind them to use the past tense with the correct ending in their answers. You may wish to elicit example answers for each question, writing starters on the board such as I liked to, I wanted to, and I learned.
- Walk around to monitor the activity and provide help as needed.
- Call on students to answer the questions.

EXPANSION ACTIVITY: Dictation

- Write headings on the board: Sounds like t, Sounds like d, Sounds like id.
- Dictate a list of ten verbs (e.g., ask, decide, live, need, order, shop, work, report, talk, open).
- LOW LEVEL: For lower level students, write the list of verbs on the board and have them copy it. Have them work with a partner to complete the activity.
- Have students write the verbs in the simple past and then sort the verbs by the past tense sound.
- Have students compare their answers in pairs.
- Ask volunteers to write the verbs in the chart on the board.

Unit 4: Lesson 5

❷ Listen and Write: Listening to a Recorded Message 🎧 060

- Have students look at the picture in the book for Activity 2. To set the context, ask questions about the picture: *What is he doing? What do you think he is listening to?*
- Read the script or play the audio. Have the students write the missing information.
- Read or play the message again. Pause after each sentence and have students check their answers.
- Go over the answers with the class.

LISTENING SCRIPT

Lesson 5, Activity 2: Listen and Write: Listening to a Recorded Message

Listen and write the missing words. Listen again and check your answers.

Welcome to Westville Adult School. Sorry we missed your call. For information about adult ESL classes, press 1. For information about vocational training, press 2. For information about the computer classes, press 3. To register for a class, press 4. To hear this message again, press 5.

ANSWER KEY:

Answers are underlined:
Welcome to Westville Adult School. Sorry we <u>missed</u> your call. For information about adult ESL classes, press 1. For information about <u>vocational training</u>, press 2. For information about <u>the computer classes</u>, press 3. To register for <u>a class</u>, press 4. To hear this message again, press <u>5</u>.

❸ Practice the Conversation: Asking for Advice 🎧 061

- Have students look at the picture of the two men passing each other on page 55. To set the context, ask questions about the picture: *Who do you see? How do they feel?*
- Read the conversation or play the audio.
- Read or play the conversation again. Pause after each sentence and ask students to repeat.
- To confirm understanding, ask comprehension questions about the conversation: *Why is B happy? How did B get the raise?*
- Point out that there are three pieces of scripted information in the conversation that can be substituted with information from the boxes: the initial action *(got a raise)*, a goal *(get a raise)*, and a strategy *(worked hard and was always on time)*. Model the conversation with a student. Have the student read B's lines. Demonstrate how to substitute *got a promotion* for the scripted action. Cue the student to respond with the goal *(get a promotion)*. Substitute *graduated from a good university* for the scripted strategy.
- Put students in pairs to practice the conversation, making substitutions from the boxes.
- Walk around to monitor the activity and provide help as needed.

LISTENING SCRIPT

Lesson 5, Activity 3: Practice the Conversation: Asking for Advice

Listen to the conversation. Listen again and repeat.

A: You look happy. What's up?

B: I just got a raise.

A: That's great. I want to get a raise, too. How did you do it?

B: I worked hard and was always on time.

A: That's good advice.

Unit 4: Lesson 5

EXPANSION ACTIVITY: Radio Talk Show Host [Challenge]

- Discuss radio call-in advice shows with students. Have students brainstorm the kinds of questions listeners ask. If students have trouble, point out that many callers ask for advice on relationships, finances, or even hobbies such as gardening.
- Put students in small groups. On an index card, have each group write a scenario or question from a listener to a radio talk show host. Have the group specify at the top of the card what kind of talk show it is (a show about relationships, pets, parenting, etc.). Be sure that the students write the question or scenario as if it is being asked or spoken by a real person.
- Preview each group's question as you circulate to monitor progress.
- If groups have written easy or moderately difficult questions, call on volunteers to role-play the radio talk show host and answer each question. If groups have written questions that are difficult to answer due to advanced language or concepts, have them ask the questions to you, then role-play the answer for the class.
- Each question may lead to open discussion if desired. Did students agree with the advice given? Do they have other suggestions or answers for each question?

4 Practice the Conversation: Giving Advice 062

- Repeat the basic procedure from Activity 3.
- To set the context, ask questions about the picture: *Who is in the picture? Where are they?*
- After students have listened to and repeated the conversation line by line, check comprehension by asking questions: *What kind of course are they talking about? What does B want to do?*
- Point out that there are three pieces of scripted information in the conversation that can be substituted: the initial action (*take a writing course next term*), the shortened form of that action (*take one*), and a goal (*getting a GED*). Model the conversation with a student. Have the student read B's lines. Demonstrate how to substitute *vote in the next election* for the scripted action. Cue the student to ask about the action in a shortened form (*vote*). Substitute *be a good citizen* for the scripted goal.
- Have students continue practicing the conversation, making substitutions from the boxes and using their own ideas.

LISTENING SCRIPT

Lesson 5, Activity 4: Practice the Conversation: Giving Advice

Listen to the conversation. Listen again and repeat.

A: Are you going to take a writing course next term?

B: No, I'm not going to take one.

A: I think you should.

B: Really? Why?

A: Because it will help you meet your goal of getting a GED.

B: Maybe you're right. I think I will take one.

Culture/Civics Note:

- Some students may be unfamiliar with the concept of volunteer work. You may want to point out that many people in this country do volunteer work for different reasons: to help the community, to get valuable experience, or to learn about a particular field.

LESSON 6 Help Your Child Succeed in School!

OBJECTIVE
Help your child succeed in school!

WINDOW ON MATH
Calculating a Grade Point Average

❶ Before You Read

- Read aloud or have volunteers read aloud each statement.
- Answer questions students may have about unknown words or concepts.
- Have students work independently to check the boxes of the statements with which they agree.
- Have partners compare their answers and discuss their opinions.
- Lead a class discussion about each statement. You may wish to take a survey to see who agreed and who disagreed with each one.

❷ Read

- Go over the directions and the question asked.
- Have students read the text or read it aloud as a class. Allow students to ask questions about unfamiliar words or concepts.
- Have students choose the three tips they think are most important.
- Have partners compare the tips they chose.
- Take a class poll to determine which tips, if any, were more popular than others. Lead a discussion about the results.

EXPANSION ACTIVITY:
Promotional Posters [Literacy]

- Divide the class into five groups.
- Assign each group one main idea from the webpage shown in Activity 2, such as *Encourage your child to read* or *Use the library*.
- Have groups design a poster that tells in pictures and simple words the advice given for each idea. Tell groups to imagine they are designing the poster for an audience that is just learning to read English. For example, for the main idea *Help with homework,* students may draw a picture of a television with a red X crossing it out, labeled *Turn off the TV.*
- Have groups display their posters around the room. Have the class circulate to look at each poster.
- Discuss the positive ways in which each poster portrayed its message. Have students give suggestions for things they might change or do to improve each poster.

❸ Check *True* or *False*

- Go over the directions.
- Have students complete the questions.
- Have partners compare their answers.
- Go over the answers with the class. Have students show where they found the answer to each question on the website.
- As an added challenge, you may wish to have students correct each false statement to make it true.

ANSWER KEY:
1. False; 2. True; 3. True; 4. False; 5. False; 6. False

Unit 4: Lesson 6

EXPANSION ACTIVITY: Homework is Hard!

- Have students brainstorm reasons why homework can be difficult. List their ideas on the board. For example, students may cite factors such as these: lack of study time, nobody to ask questions to, did not receive adequate instruction to understand the material in class, dislike for the subject, and so on.

- Discuss strategies that students can use to overcome each factor. For example, if students say that lack of time to study is a major problem, challenge them to keep a one-week diary of how they spend their time. Have them analyze their diaries for "lost" time that might be used for study, such as time spent surfing the Internet or watching television.

- **LOW LEVEL:** Have lower level students copy the reasons from the board. Help them write each reason as a statement. For example, *lack of study time = I don't have time to study*. Then, have them write an *I can* statement about how they can overcome each problem.

④ Interview

- Go over the directions and the questions in the chart. For students who do not have children, have them tell what they would do if they did have children or if they were a teacher of young children.

- Have partners interview each other.

- Call on volunteers to present information about their partner to the class.

WINDOW ON MATH

Calculating a Grade Point Average

A Read the information below.

- Have students read the information in the paragraph.
- Review the example GPA calculation with the class.
- Answer any questions students may have.
- To test comprehension, have partners change the grades that Lily got and recalculate her GPA. Have volunteers present their math to the class on the board.

B Answer these word problems.

- Have students read and solve the word problems, showing their work on paper.
- Have partners compare answers.
- Go over the answers with the class.

ANSWER KEY:

B. 1. 3.2 GPA; 2. 3.4 GPA

LESSON 7 — What Do You Know?

1 Listening Review 063

- Go over the directions with the class.
- Read the items or play the audio and have the students mark their answers on the Answer Sheet.
- Walk around to monitor the activity and help students stay on task.
- Have students check their answers with a partner.
- Go over the answers with the class.

LISTENING SCRIPT

Lesson 7, Activity 1: Listening Review

Look at the pictures and listen. Choose the correct answer: A, B, or C. Use the Answer Sheet.

1. A: What's your goal?
   B: I would like to get a raise.
2. A: What's your goal?
   B: I have a personal goal. I would like to buy a house.
3. A: What's your goal?
   B: My goal is to be a good parent, so I'm going to read to my children every day.
4. A: Who do you think will get the new job as a salesperson?
   B: I think Liz will. She's good with people.
5. A: You look happy. What's up?
   B: I just got a promotion.

TESTING FOCUS: Previewing the Answers

- Tell students that before they listen to each conversation, they should look at the pictures for each answer. Then, when they listen, they can be alert for words that relate to the pictures.
- Look at question 1 as an example. Have a student look at the picture for answer C. Have students suggest words they might hear that would relate to this topic, such as job, money, and work.
- Play question 1 and have students tell which words they heard that relate to one of the answers. Have them correctly identify C as the answer, eliciting that *get a raise* relates to work.

ANSWER KEY:

1. C; 2. A; 3. C; 4. A; 5. B

2 Listening Dictation 064

- Copy the numbers and lines from the Listening Dictation section on the board.
- Read the first item. Have a more advanced student write the sentence on the board. Have students copy the sentence in their books.
- Play the audio and have students write the sentences they hear. Repeat as many times as necessary.
- Put students in pair to compare answers.
- Have volunteers write the sentences on the board.

Unit 4: Lesson 7

LISTENING SCRIPT

Lesson 7, Activity 2: Listening Dictation

Listen. Write the words you hear.

1. A: What are your goals?
   B: I would like to become a U.S. citizen.
2. A: What is your goal?
   B: I have a work goal. I would like to start a business.
3. A: What is your goal?
   B: I would like to get a promotion, so I'm going to go back to school.
4. A: Who do you think will get the job as the new office worker?
   B: I think Sara will get it. She's hardworking.
5. A: You look happy. What's up?
   B: I just learned to use a computer.

❸ Grammar Review

- Go over the directions.
- Read the first sentence. Elicit the appropriate completion. Have students circle A for item 1.
- Have students answer the rest of the questions.
- Put students in pairs to compare answers.
- Go over the answers with the class.

ANSWER KEY:

1. A; 2. C; 3. B; 4. B; 5. B; 6. B

LEARNING LOG

- Point out the four sections of the Learning Log: *I know these words; I can ask; I can say;* and *I can write.*
- Have students check what they know and what they can do.
- Walk around to note what they don't know or can't do. Use this information to review areas of difficulty.

BIG PICTURE EXPANSION ACTIVITY:
SPEAKING—Assessment: Talking about the Picture

- You can use the Big Picture on Student Book Pages 50–51 to place new students in open entry classes, to diagnose difficulties, or to measure progress.
- Work with one student at a time and show them the Big Picture. Ask: *What do you see in the picture? Tell me about the picture.* Tell the student you want him or her to speak for as long as possible. Wait a moment for the student to prepare to answer. If the student has difficulty, use prompts: *What do you see in the picture? Who do you see in the picture? What are the people doing?*
- You can use a rubric like the one below to rate beginning speakers.

4	Exhibits confidence, begins speaking without prompting
	Uses some complex sentences, although may make mistakes with irregular forms
	Can use more than one tense
3	Uses sentences, although form may be incorrect
	Can speak for sustained length of time
	Responds to prompts, but doesn't need them to begin speaking
2	Can use nouns and verbs
	Uses phrases
	Answers informational questions
1	Can name objects
	Uses single words
	Can answer *yes/no* questions
0	Cannot say anything independently
	May be able to point to objects when prompted

Unit 4: Lesson 7

 BIG PICTURE EXPANSION ACTIVITY:
WRITING—The Day's Events

- Have students look at the Big Picture in their books (Student Book pages 50–51).
- Ask the class: *What do you see in the car dealership? What are the people doing? What has happened?* Call on a few students to share their observations with the class.
- Read the following paragraph as a model: *My name is Ken. I work at Allen Motors. I am a salesperson. I wore a blue suit and blue tie today. I showed many people our new cars. I talked to one woman about a dealer rebate. She liked the car, and she bought it. I sold two other cars. Today was a good day for me.*
- Tell the students to write a paragraph about what happened at the car dealership from the point of view of one of the people in the picture. Remind them to look at the Big Picture for ideas. Remind them to use the past tense and words from the unit.
- Put students in pairs to read their paragraphs.
- Have volunteers read their paragraphs to the class.

TEACHER'S NOTES:

Things that students are doing well:
_____
_____
_____
_____

Things students need additional help with:
_____
_____
_____
_____

Ideas for further practice or for the next class:
_____
_____
_____
_____

UNIT 5: SMART SHOPPING

UNIT OVERVIEW

LESSON	STUDENT BOOK PAGE	TEACHER'S EDITION PAGE
1. Identifying Common Purchases	60	95
2. Activities at a Mall	62	99
3. Reading Ads	64	102
4. A Shopper's Calendar	66	105
5. Making Exchanges, Returns, and Purchases	68	108
6. Shopping Tips	70	111
7. What Do You Know?	72	113

Big Picture Expansion Activities

FOCUS	TITLE	SUGGESTED USE
Speaking	Guess Who's Talking	Lesson 2
Reading	Mall Information	Lesson 3
Grammar	Which One is the Cheapest?	Lesson 4
Speaking	Assessment: Talking about the Big Picture	Lesson 7
Writing	Comparing Stores	Lesson 7

Big Picture Expansion Activity Worksheets

FOCUS	TITLE	TEACHER'S EDITION PAGE
9. Reading	Mall Information	232
10. Grammar	Which one is the cheapest?	233

LESSON 1 Identifying Common Purchases

OBJECTIVE
Identifying common purchases

VOCABULARY

blender	dishwasher	pair of boots
broom	dryer	peeler
bucket	heavy coat	refrigerator
can opener	jacket	stove
coffeemaker	mop	toaster
cutting board	pair of athletic	vacuum cleaner
dish soap	shoes	washing machine

TARGET GRAMMAR

Go + verb *-ing*   page 168

THINGS TO DO

1 Learn New Words 065

- Have students look at the pictures and elicit the words they know.
- Have students listen and look at the pictures while you say the words or play the audio.
- Instruct students to circle the words that are new to them.
- Say the words or play the audio a second time. Pause after each word or phrase and ask the students to repeat and point to the correct picture.
- Put students in pairs and have one say a word or phrase as the partner points to the correct picture. Reverse roles and repeat the activity.
- Call on students and ask questions: *Do you have a heavy coat? Do you need a broom?*

LISTENING SCRIPT

Lesson 1, Activity 1: Learn New Words

Look at the pictures. Listen to the words. Listen again and repeat. Which words or phrases are new to you? Circle them.

1. pair of athletic shoes — I need to get a pair of athletic shoes.
2. jacket — I need to get a jacket.
3. heavy coat — I need to get a heavy coat.
4. pair of boots — I need to get a pair of boots.
5. washing machine — I need to get a washing machine.
6. dryer — I need to get a dryer.
7. refrigerator — I need to get a refrigerator.
8. stove — I need to get a stove.
9. dishwasher — I need to get a dishwasher.
10. dish soap — I need to get some dish soap.
11. broom — I need to get a broom.
12. mop — I need to get a mop.
13. bucket — I need to get a bucket.
14. vacuum cleaner — I need to get a vacuum cleaner.
15. coffeemaker — I need to get a coffeemaker.
16. blender — I need to get a blender.
17. toaster — I need to get a toaster.
18. can opener — I need to get a can opener.
19. peeler — I need to get a peeler.
20. cutting board — I need to get a cutting board.

EXPANSION ACTIVITY: Draw the Item [Low-Level]

- Divide the class into two teams. Ask a volunteer from each team to come to the board.
- Whisper the name of one of the items (*a pair of boots*) to both students and instruct

Unit 5: Lesson 1

them to draw the object on the board. As they draw, the rest of the class should try to guess what it is.
- The first student to correctly name the article of clothing earns a point for his or her team.
- Invite new students to the board and continue playing until all the objects have been illustrated and named.
- The team with the most points wins. Small prizes for the winning team may increase enthusiasm for the game and raise the energy level in the classroom.

Pronunciation Note:
- Many of the new vocabulary items are compound nouns (cutting board, coffeemaker, can opener, dish soap). Point out to students that the first word in the compound noun usually receives the main stress.

2 Practice the Conversation 066

- Have students listen and look at the conversation while you read it or play the audio.
- Say the lines or play the audio a second time. Pause after each line and have the students repeat.
- Model the conversation with a student. Have the student read A's lines. Demonstrate how to substitute from the boxes below. Cue the student to make the appropriate substitution.
- Have students work in pairs to practice the conversation, making substitutions from the boxes and using their own ideas.
- Walk around to make sure students understand the activity and provide help if needed.

LISTENING SCRIPT

Lesson 1, Activity 2: Practice the Conversation

Listen to the conversation. Listen again and repeat.

A: Where are you going?
B: I'm going shopping. I need to get a heavy coat.
A: Can I come with you? I want to get a coffeemaker.
B: Sure. Let's go!

TARGET GRAMMAR

Go + verb -ing
The Target Grammar point is used in Activities 2 and 3. Presentation and practice of this grammar point appears on Student Book page 168. Answer Keys appear on Teacher's Edition page 253.

EXPANSION ACTIVITY: What Happened to the Old One? [Challenge]

- Write the first three lines of the conversation from Activity 2 on the board. For the fourth line, model person B asking a question about why person A needs to replace or get a new one of the item named. For example: *What happened to your old one(s)?* (heavy coat, refrigerator, boots) *You just bought* (a pair of boots, dish soap).
- Model writing an appropriate response from person A. For example: *I know, but my old one is worn out/broken; I did, but they're too big* (boots); or *I was going to, but I forgot* (dish soap).
- Have partners or groups work to write a new dialogue based on your model. Have students present their work to the class.

Unit 5: Lesson 1

③ Listen and Take Notes 067

- Go over the directions and review the chart with students.
- Read the conversation or play the audio as the students listen. Have students mark their answers in the chart.
- Read or play the conversation again. Have students check their work.
- Go over the answers with the class.

LISTENING SCRIPT

Lesson 1, Activity 3: Listen and Take Notes

Amanda is moving into a new apartment. Listen to her talk about what she has and what she wants to buy. Complete the chart.

A: Hi, Amanda. Do you want to go shopping together for your new apartment?

B: Sure! That sounds like fun!

A: What do you need to get?

B: Well, let's see. There is already a refrigerator and a stove, but I need to get a washing machine.

A: Okay. Do you have a toaster and a coffeemaker?

B: I have a toaster, but I don't have a coffeemaker. I want to buy one.

A: Do you have a blender?

B: No, I don't, but I don't use blenders, so I don't want to buy one.

ANSWER KEY:

Students should check the following items.
Has it: refrigerator, toaster
Doesn't have it: washing machine, blender, coffeemaker
Wants to buy it: washing machine, coffeemaker

EXPANSION ACTIVITY: Bargain Hunting

- Have students look at the list of items in Activity 3 and name common places in your area to buy each one.
- Have students research alternative places or ways to buy each item, either in your community or otherwise. For example, you might point out that there are often community websites where people sell, trade, or give away used appliances. Ask students to find out about local resale shops, swap meets, or flea markets where such items can be purchased at reduced prices. Have students complete this activity outside of class.
- CHALLENGE: Have more advanced students compare prices on two or three items at various bargain websites or shops. Ask them to find out whether they can negotiate the price of the item, or whether the prices are fixed. Have them evaluate which website or shop offers the best prices on the items chosen.
- Have students report back their findings to the class, including the URLs of websites, names and contact information for resale shops, and so on.

Culture Note:

- Explain to students that many people in America love to bargain hunt at places like thrift shops, swap meets, garage or yard sales, and flea markets. Present the proverb: *One man's trash is another man's treasure*; ask students what they think it means. Have students tell what they think a *curb alert* is, then explain the term. Students may also be interested in researching resources on frugal living, a cultural trend that has become popular again in recent years.

Unit 5: Lesson 1

4 Interview

- Go over the directions and review the chart with students. Point out that they should write in an item of their choice for question 5.
- Put students in pairs and have them ask and answer questions to complete the chart.
- Have each student tell one or two facts about what their partner has or doesn't have. Tell students to pay close attention to the information if you wish to do the Expansion Activity afterwards.
- You may wish to survey the class to find out what item they chose to ask about for question 5.

EXPANSION ACTIVITY: True or False Elimination

- Have all pairs of students from Activity 4 stand up.
- Call on a pair of students randomly.
- Have the pair choose one student (student A) in the class and give a true statement about what he or she has or doesn't have, based on what they heard in Activity 4. Student A's partner (Student B) should confirm that the statement is true or should correct the statement if it's false. If the statement is false, the pair who guessed is eliminated.
- Students A and B now become the guessing pair. Have them choose another pair and continue the game.
- Play continues until only one pair is left standing.

LESSON 2: Activities at a Mall

OBJECTIVE
Activities at a mall

VOCABULARY

appliance store	go into	push a stroller
carry	go out of business	sale
demonstrate	jewelry store	take a break
furniture store	mall directory	toy store

TARGET GRAMMAR
Comparative adjectives *page 169*

THINGS TO DO

1 Learn New Words 068

- Have students look at the Big Picture in their books (Student Book pages 62–63). Ask questions: *Where is this? How often do you go to a shopping mall? What kind of stores are there?*
- Have students listen and look at the picture while you say the words or play the audio.
- Instruct students to circle the words that are new to them.
- Say the words or play the audio a second time. Pause after each word or phrase and ask the students to repeat the word and point to the correct part of the picture.
- Put students in pairs and have one say a word or phrase as the partner points to the correct part of the picture. Reverse roles and repeat the activity.

LISTENING SCRIPT

Lesson 2, Activity 1: Learn New Words

Look at the pictures. Listen to the words. Listen again and repeat.

1. carry — What is Jim carrying?
2. take a break — Who is taking a break?
3. go out of business — Which store is going out of business?
4. jewelry store — Where's the jewelry store?
5. go into — Which store is Carla going into?
6. toy store — Where's the toy store?
7. push a stroller — Who is pushing a stroller?
8. furniture store — Where's the furniture store?
9. sale — What's on sale at Arches Shoe Store?
10. demonstrate — What is Lola demonstrating?
11. mall directory — Where's the mall directory?
12. appliance store — Where's the appliance store?

EXPANSION ACTIVITY: Picture It [Low-Level]

- Have students find pictures in magazines to represent each vocabulary word from Activity 1. Help students find examples of more difficult concepts such as *demonstrate*. For example, you might find a photo of a teacher showing a student how to do a math problem or a veterinarian showing a child how to care for a puppy.
- Have students use the pictures they found to create mini-posters on construction paper or poster board to represent each word. Students should label each poster with the word, but may also include phrases and sentences using the word in context for each picture.
- Display the completed mini-posters around the room. Have volunteers answer *yes/no* questions about the posters or describe individual pictures using simple sentences.

Unit 5: Lesson 2

2 Check *True* or *False*

- Go over the directions.
- Read the listening script or play the audio for the class. Have students mark the answer to each question after checking the picture.
- Have students check their answers in pairs. Reread each item or replay the audio to help students check their answers.
- Go over the answers with the class. Have students correct each false statement to make it true.

LISTENING SCRIPT

Lesson 2, Activity 2: Check *True* or *False*

Listen to the sentences about the mall. Look at the picture. Check (√) True or False.

1. Le Chic Clothing is busier than Gemma's Jewels.
2. A lot of people are buying hot dogs.
3. Frank is pushing a stroller.
4. Don bought a bike for his son.
5. Arches is bigger than May's.
6. The mall opens earlier on Sunday than it does on Saturday.

ANSWER KEY:

1. True; 2. False; nobody is buying hot dogs; 3. True; 4. True; 5. False; Arches is smaller than May's; 6. False; the mall opens later on Sunday than it does on Saturday.

TARGET GRAMMAR

Comparative adjectives
The Target Grammar point is used in Activities 2 and 4. Presentation and practice of this grammar point appears on Student Book pages 169–170. Answer Keys appear on Teacher's Edition page 253.

EXPANSION ACTIVITY: Creative Writing

- Divide the class into small groups.
- Assign each group one of the named or unnamed characters from the Big Picture on pages 62–63.
- Have the group imagine they are the assigned character. Have students brainstorm why the person is at the mall, what he or she wants to do or buy there, how he or she feels, and so on. You may wish to have students give unnamed characters a name.
- Have groups write a paragraph telling about the person or a dialogue between the person and somebody else. Students should include the information they brainstormed.
- MULTI-LEVEL: Have lower level students suggest ideas using single words or phrases. You may want to allow them to use their native language as a last resort to explain more difficult ideas if others in the group speak the same language. Have more advanced students help lower level students put their ideas into English.
- Have groups present their paragraphs or dialogues to the class.

3 Talk About the Picture

- Go over the directions and the example sentences.
- Have students write three true and three false statements about the picture.
- Call on students to read sentences aloud and have the rest of the class say if the sentences are true or false.

EXPANSION ACTIVITY: Team Challenge [Multi-Level]

- Instead of calling on individual students to read sentences aloud, divide the class into two teams.
- Give students a minute to study the picture and then close their books.
- Have members from opposing teams take turns saying a sentence to the other team. The other team must say if the sentence is true or false. Each correct answer earns a point. Have lower level students tell whether the sentence is true or false and more advanced students correct false sentences.

Unit 5: Lesson 2

❹ Practice the Conversation 070

- Have students listen and look at the conversation while you read it or play the audio.
- Say the lines or play the audio a second time. Pause after each line and have the students repeat.
- Model the conversation with a student. Have the student read A's lines. Demonstrate how to substitute from the boxes below. Cue the student to make the appropriate substitution.
- Have students work in pairs to practice the conversation, making substitutions from the boxes and using their own ideas.
- Walk around to make sure students understand the activity and provide help if needed.

LISTENING SCRIPT

Lesson 2, Activity 4: Practice the Conversation

Listen to the conversation. Listen again and repeat.

A: Where do you buy shoes?

B: I like May's Department Store.

A: Is May's better than Arches?

B: I think so. It has a bigger selection.

Language Note:

- Point out that *I like May's Department store* is not really a direct answer to the question *Where do you buy shoes?* It is a way of stating a preference: *I like May's as a place to buy shoes.*

EXPANSION ACTIVITY: Pair Interview

- Write questions on the board: *When did you go to a mall? Who did you go with? Did you get anything to eat? How long did you spend at the mall? Were there any sales? What kind of store(s) did you visit?*
- Put students in pairs to practice asking and answering the questions.
- Call on students to tell the class about their partners' trips to the mall.

BIG PICTURE EXPANSION ACTIVITY: SPEAKING—Guess Who's Talking

- Have students look at the Big Picture in their books (Student Book pages 62–63).
- Ask students who they see having conversations in the picture. Tell students that they will create conversations for characters in the picture.
- Put students in pairs. Walk around the room and point to the characters in the picture that you want each pair to create a conversation for. Examples could include the couple in front of the men's store, the mother and child at Jingle's Toys, the two women walking in the foreground, the customers at Kitchens Galore, and people seated in the food court.
- Have each pair write a conversation for their characters and then practice saying the lines to each other.
- Walk around the room to monitor the activity and provide help as needed.
- Have volunteers act out the conversation in front of the class.
- Have their classmates guess who is talking.

LESSON 3 Reading Ads

OBJECTIVE
Reading ads

VOCABULARY

20 percent off	marked down 50 percent
clearance sale	receipt
exchange	refund
half price	regular price

TARGET GRAMMAR

There was and *there were*   page 171

1 Learn New Words 071

- Have students look at the ads and ask questions: *What are these? Where do you see them?*
- Have students look at the pictures and listen while you say the words or play the audio.
- Say the words or play the audio a second time. Pause after each phrase and ask the students to repeat the phrase and point to the correct picture.
- Put students in pairs and have one say a phrase as the partner points to the correct advertisement. Reverse roles and repeat the activity.

LISTENING SCRIPT

Lesson 3, Activity 1: Learn New Words

Look at the picture. Listen to the words. Listen again and repeat.

1. refund	He got a refund for the toy.
2. exchange	He exchanged the jacket for another one.
3. receipt	You need a receipt to make an exchange.
4. regular price	The regular price of the coffeemaker is $24.99.
5. marked down 50 percent	Whirley vacuum cleaners are marked down 50 percent at Al's Superstore.
6. half price	Sierra Stoves are half price at Al's Superstore.
7. 20 percent off	Ovay coffeemakers are now 20 percent off.
8. clearance sale	There was a clearance sale.

TARGET GRAMMAR

There was/there were

The Target Grammar point is used in Activities 1 and 3. Presentation and practice of this grammar point appears on Student Book page 171. Answer Keys appear on Teacher's Edition page 253.

EXPANSION ACTIVITY: Realia Hunt [Low-Level]

- Have students bring in ads and flyers from local stores, or bring ads in yourself.
- Have students work with the ads or flyers in pairs to find and list words related to prices and sales.
- Elicit examples and write them on the board. Go over the meaning of any unfamiliar words.

BIG PICTURE EXPANSION ACTIVITY:
READING—Mall Information

- Make copies of Worksheet 9 (Teacher's Edition page 232) and distribute them to students.
- Have students look at the Big Picture in their books (Student Book pages 62–63).
- Instruct students to complete the activities and then check their answers with a partner.
- Go over the answers with the class.

Unit 5: Lesson 3

ANSWER KEY:

A. 1. Le Chic Clothing; 2. Sam's Appliances and Goods; 3. Kitchens Galore; 4. Arches
B. 1. Sam's Appliances and Goods; 2. Arches; 3. Kitchens Galore; 4. Le Chic Clothing; 5. two days

❷ Compare

- Have students look at the ad for the coffeemaker at Al's Superstore. Ask: *What's the regular price? What is the sale price? How much is the savings?*
- Have students tell where they would write this information in the comparison chart (on the first line about Al's Superstore).
- Have students read the ads and write the information in the appropriate places. Make sure students understand how to compute the savings.
- Have students check their answers in pairs, then go over the answers with the class.
- Have partners discuss where they would buy each item and why.

ANSWER KEY:

Al's Superstore			
Item	Regular Price	Sale Price	Savings
coffeemakers	$24.99	$17.99	$7.00
vacuum cleaners	$69.98	$34.99	$34.99
blenders	$39.99	$29.99	$10.00

Barb's Discount House			
Item	Regular Price	Sale Price	Savings
coffeemakers	$28.99	$23.19	$5.80
vacuum cleaners	$89.98	$31.48	$58.50
blenders	$33.94	$27.15	$6.79

EXPANSION ACTIVITY: Consider the Factors [Challenge]

- Put students in small groups. Have them brainstorm the factors that affect their decisions about where to buy different items.
- Elicit factors and write them on the board. Ideas might include: price, location of store, convenience, credit cards the store accepts, quality of items, selection.
- Write five items on the board from Lesson 1. Have students choose the most important factor for each item (coffeemaker—quality).
- Call on students to share their ideas with the class.

Unit 5: Lesson 3

③ Practice the Conversation 072

- Have students listen and look at the conversation while you read it or play the audio.
- Say the lines or play the audio a second time. Pause after each line and have the students repeat.
- Check comprehension by asking questions: *What item are they talking about? How much did A save?*
- Model the conversation with a student. Have the student read A's lines. Demonstrate how to substitute from the ideas in the boxes below. Cue the student to make the appropriate substitution.
- Have students work in pairs to practice the conversation, making substitutions from the boxes and using their own ideas.
- Walk around to make sure students understand the activity. Provide help if needed.

EXPANSION ACTIVITY: Dictation

- Have students take out paper and pencils for a dictation.
- Dictate several sentences that are similar to the lines in the conversation. Create your own or use these:

    Did you buy a new jacket?

    Yes, I got one for half-price at Barb's.

    Is that a good deal?

    I think so. I saved 30 dollars.

- Have volunteers write the sentences on the board. You may wish to look at their work before they write the sentences on the board, or to have students peer-correct each other's work.
- LOW-LEVEL: Use this dictation activity as an opportunity to review common problems that lower level students may have, such as missed capitalization, punctuation, misspellings, or grammar.

LISTENING SCRIPT

Lesson 3, Activity 3: Practice the Conversation

Listen to the conversation. Listen again and repeat.

A: There was a big sale at Al's yesterday.

B: Really? Was there a sale on toasters?

A: No, but there were great prices on blenders. I got one for only $29.99!

B: That's a good deal. How much did you save?

A: I saved $10.00.

LESSON 4 A Shopper's Calendar

OBJECTIVE
A shopper's calendar

 TARGET GRAMMAR

Superlative adjectives *page 172*

THINGS TO DO

1 Preview
- Have students look at the article. Remind students how to preview: look at the title, visuals, headings, and words in special format.
- Read the items in Activity 1. Remind students that scanning is reading quickly to find specific information. Have students scan the article and check the information they find.
- Ask students what they checked and why.

ANSWER KEY:

Students should check: the best times to get sales; what you should buy in the winter

 TARGET GRAMMAR

Superlative adjectives
The Target Grammar point is used in Activities 1, 2, and 3. Presentation and practice of this grammar point appears on Student Book pages 172–173. Answer Keys appear on Teacher's Edition page 253.

EXPANSION ACTIVITY: Bingo [Multi-Level]
- Write 15 words or phrases from the reading on the board (*January, June, September, shopping, new clothes, sheets, garden supplies, markdowns, original, Cyber Monday, plants, leftovers, outdoor furniture*).
- Have students make a 3 x 3 grid on a piece of paper and write a different word or phrase from the list in each box. Tell them to write in the words in a random order so that their grids are different from other students' grids.
- Tell the students to cross off a word when they hear it. Remind them to yell "Bingo" when they have marked off three in a row.
- Read sentences from the article aloud and have students mark off words as they hear them. Choose sentences at random. You may wish to stop after each sentence to ask students what word(s), if any, they heard in the sentence. Put a check next to each word on the board once students have correctly confirmed that they heard it in a sentence.

2 Read and Take Notes
- Read the list of items students will take notes about.
- Have students read the article and take notes in the chart about the best time to buy each item.
- Have students compare notes in pairs.
- Go over the answers with the class.

ANSWER KEY:

ITEM	THE BEST TIME TO BUY
summer clothes	in August
outdoor furniture	in September
fall clothes	in January
a DVD player	in June, July, and November
spring clothes	in August
sheets and towels	in January
a laptop computer	in June and July

Unit 5: Lesson 4

EXPANSION ACTIVITY: Born to Shop?

- Brainstorm a list of questions about shopping and write them on the board. For example: *Do you like to shop? Do you like sales? What kind of things do you love to shop for? What kind of things do you hate to shop for? Do you shop on certain days or at certain times of the year?*

- Have partners discuss the questions, telling their reasons for each answer. Students should tell why or why not for each question. Have each student take notes about his or her partner.

- When partners have finished discussing the questions, lead a group discussion by asking questions such as: *Who hates to shop? Why?* Have students tell about their partner's responses rather than answer for themselves.

❸ Talk

- Go over the directions and questions with the class.
- Have students write answers to each question and then share their answers with a partner.
- Have volunteers share what they learned with the class.

EXPANSION ACTIVITY: It's Worth the Money!
[Multi-Level]

- Have students think about something that they pay full price for or buy even though it is expensive. If students have trouble thinking of an item, give examples such as foods, cars, designer clothing, and so on.

- Have students make notes about why they decided to buy the full-price or expensive item, listing the reasons why it was worth the money for them.

- Put students into small groups to share their items and reasons. Point out that students do not have to tell how much they paid for an item.

- Lead a class discussion on the reasons people buy full-price or expensive items. Have volunteers tell about the items they purchased as examples to illustrate important points.

❹ Write

- Assign this as an out-of-class activity, or bring in newspapers for students to use.
- Go over the example.
- Have students look at newspapers and write several sentences about the sales that interest them.
- LOW-LEVEL: Have students write simple sentences describing items on sale. Provide models, such as: *The shirt costs $20* and *The shoes cost $35.*
- Put students in pairs and have them take turns reading their sentences and sharing where they found the information in their newspapers.
- Call on volunteers to read their sentences aloud to the class.

Unit 5: Lesson 4

EXPANSION ACTIVITY: True or False

- Have students rewrite some of their sentences from Activity 4 to make them false.
- Have students exchange their sentences (both true and false) and their newspapers with a partner.
- Have students write *True* or *False* next to each of their partners' sentences, and correct the false ones.

BIG PICTURE EXPANSION ACTIVITY: GRAMMAR—Which One is the Cheapest?

- Make copies of Worksheet 10 (Teacher's Edition p. 233) and distribute them to students.
- Have students look at the Big Picture in their books (Student Book pages 62–63).
- Instruct students to complete the activities and then check their answers with a partner.
- Go over the answers with the class.

ANSWER KEY:

A: 1. bigger; 2. smaller; 3. cheaper; 4. more expensive; 5. more useful

B: Today I went to the mall. First I went to May's Department Store because it is the <u>biggest</u> store at the mall and has the <u>best</u> selection. Then I went to Arches because it has the <u>cheapest</u> shoes. After Arches, I went to Jingle's Toys. It has the <u>most interesting</u> toys. I wanted to go to Le Chic because it had the <u>lowest</u> prices on women's clothing, but it was the <u>busiest</u> store in the mall. It was the <u>worst</u> time to go because so many people were there. So I decided to eat lunch. I got something at the bagel place. I think the food there is the <u>healthiest</u>.

LESSON 5 Making Exchanges, Returns, and Purchases

OBJECTIVE
Making exchanges, returns, and purchases

PRONUNCIATION
Stress

1 Practice Pronunciation: Stress 073

A. Listen to the stress in these conversations. Listen again and repeat.

- Explain that we sometimes stress words in a sentence to show what is most important.
- Have students look at the conversations while you read them or play the audio.
- Say the words or play the audio a second time, pausing after each line to have students repeat.
- Read the conversations or play the audio a third time and have students circle the stressed word in each one.
- Point out that in conversations 1 and 3, the stressed word is about the quality (tight, softer), whereas in conversations 2 and 4, the stressed word is about the degree (too, much).
- Explain that the questions in 1 and 3 are more general, and that those in 2 and 4 ask more specifically about the degree of a quality.
- Have students practice the conversations in pairs.
- Walk around to monitor the activity and correct stress patterns if necessary.

LISTENING SCRIPT

Lesson 5, Activity 1: Practice Pronunciation: Stress

A. Listen to the stress in these conversations. Listen again and repeat.

1. A: What's wrong with it?   B: It's too **tight**.
2. A: Is it tight enough?   B: It's **too** tight.
3. A: How is that one?   B: It's much **softer**.
4. A: Is it softer?   B: Yes, it's **much** softer.

Listen to the conversations again. Circle the stressed words.

ANSWER KEY:
1. tight; 2. too; 3. softer; 4. much

B. Work with a partner. Practice the conversations. Stress the important words. Circle the stressed word in each conversation.

- Have students look at the questions in each conversation. Elicit which questions are more general, and which ones focus on a specific quality.
- Put students in pairs and have them practice the conversations, switching roles to play both parts. Remind students to stress the key words.
- Walk around to monitor the activity and provide help as needed.

ANSWER KEY:
1. small; 2. too; 3. much; 4. cheaper

EXPANSION ACTIVITY: Conversation Circle [Low-Level]

- To give students additional practice with intonation, have the class stand in a circle with you. Use the conversations from Activity 1 or create new conversations using similar ideas.
- Turn to the first student on your left and say the first line of a conversation, using correct intonation.
- Have the student turn to the student on his or her left and repeat the first line, using the same intonation you used.
- Continue around the circle to the left until the line has made it all the way back around to you. Encourage students to say the line quickly, using a natural rate of speech.
- Reverse directions. Turn to the first student on your right and say the second line of the conversation, having him or her repeat it to the person on the right.
- Continue reversing directions with each line until the conversation is finished, or begin new conversations as needed.

108 • UNIT 5   STUDENT BOOK PAGES 68-69

Unit 5: Lesson 5

❷ Practice the Conversation: Exchanging Something 🎧 074

- Have students look at the picture in the book for Activity 2. To set the context, ask questions about the picture: *Who is in the picture? Where are they?*
- Read the conversation or play the audio.
- Read or play the conversation again. Pause after each sentence and ask students to repeat.
- To confirm understanding, ask comprehension questions about the conversation: *What does B want to return? What's the problem? What does B want to do?*
- Point out that there are three pieces of scripted information in the conversation that can be substituted: the item, the problem, and type of exchange.
- Model the conversation with a student. Have the student read A's lines. Demonstrate how to substitute *vacuum cleaner* for the scripted item and *It's too heavy* for the scripted problem. Cue the student to suggest a *lighter* one.
- Have students work in pairs to practice the conversation, making substitutions from the boxes and using their own ideas.
- Walk around to monitor the activity and provide help as needed.

LISTENING SCRIPT

Lesson 5, Activity 2: Practice the Conversation: Exchanging Something

Listen to the conversation. Listen again and repeat.

A: Can I help you?
B: Yes. I want to return this jacket.
A: Okay. Was there something wrong with it?
B: Yes. It's too tight.
A: Do you want to exchange it for a bigger one?
B: Yes, I do.
A: Okay. I'll be right with you.

> **Vocabulary Notes:**
> - Some students may confuse *too* with *very*. Point out that when we use *too*, we are indicating that there is a problem with the degree. For example, if something is *too tight*, it is a problem for us.
> - Explain that *I'll be right with you* means I'll be able to help you very soon.

EXPANSION ACTIVITY: Store Policies

- Have each student choose a store in your area, making sure that no students have the same store. Be sure students choose a variety of stores such as clothing stores, grocery stores, music stores, and so on.
- Outside of class, have students research the return and exchange policies of the store they selected. Point out that students should ask specifically about returning or exchanging items that have been used, opened, worn, and so on. If stores have multiple policies depending on the type of item sold, have students choose one or two items and learn about the policies for each one.
- LOW-LEVEL: Print out a copy of a simple store return or exchange policy. Review it with students, allowing them to ask questions. You may want to let them use a bilingual dictionary as necessary to look up unfamiliar words.
- Have students report back what they learned to the class. Some students may also share written return and exchange policies that they received from their store.
- Lead a discussion about any unusual rules or prohibitions on returns and exchanges.

❸ Practice the Conversation: Asking for a Refund 🎧 075

- Repeat the basic procedure from Activity 2, having students look at the picture at the top of page 69.
- To set the context, ask questions about the picture: *Who do you see? What are they talking about?*

Unit 5: Lesson 5

- After students have listened to and repeated the conversation line by line, check comprehension by asking more questions; *What does B want to do? Why? What does B want?*
- Have students continue practicing the conversation, making substitutions from the boxes and using their own ideas.

LISTENING SCRIPT

Lesson 5, Activity 3: Practice the Conversation: Asking for a Refund

Listen to the conversation. Listen again and repeat.

A: Can I help you?

B: Yes, I want to return these toys. They're just too noisy.

A: Do you want some quieter ones?

B: No, thank you. I just want a refund.

A: Do you have your receipt?

B: Yes, I have it right here.

EXPANSION ACTIVITY: Refund Rejection
[Multi-Level]

- Brainstorm reasons why a store might refuse to refund money for an item. For example, clothing that has been worn, stained, or had the tags removed; new CDs or DVDs that have been opened or scratched; food products that have been partially or mostly consumed; and so on.
- Have mixed-level groups of students write a dialogue between a customer service worker at a store and a person trying to get a refund for one of the items from the brainstorm. The representative should refuse to give a refund for the item. If students need help, model an example conversation on the board.
- Have groups present their dialogues to the class.
- Lead a discussion about how each customer reacted to being refused a refund. Was the reaction reasonable? Was it culturally appropriate in the United States? Have students give their opinions.

4 Practice the Conversation: Comparing Price and Quality 076

- Repeat the basic procedure from Activity 2, having students look at the picture in the middle of page 69.
- To set the context, ask questions about the picture: *Who do you see? What are they looking at?*
- After students have listened to and repeated the conversation line by line, check comprehension by asking more questions: *Why does B like the item? How much more does it cost?*
- Have students continue practicing the conversation, making substitutions from the boxes and using their own ideas.

LISTENING SCRIPT

Lesson 5, Activity 4: Practice the Conversation: Comparing Price and Quality

Listen to the conversation. Listen again and repeat.

A: Which coat do you like better?

B: This one. It's much softer.

A: Yes, but it's a lot more expensive, too.

B: How much more expensive?

A: Fifty dollars.

B: It's a little nicer, but fifty dollars is a lot more expensive. I'll get the other one.

LESSON 6: Shopping Tips

OBJECTIVE
Shopping tips

WINDOW ON MATH
Percentages

1 Check *True* or *False*

- Have students look at the graphics and ask them questions to test their comprehension: *What do you see in Tip #1? What store is it for? How much is the discount? What do you see in Tip #2? What information does the picture tell you? What do you see in Tip #3? What product is the warranty for?*
- Have students read the shopping tips and check *True* or *False*.
- Have students check their answers in pairs.
- Go over the answers with the class.

ANSWER KEY:

1. True; 2. False; 3. True; 4. True; 5. False; 6. False; 7. False

2 Answer the Questions

- Go over the directions. If necessary, complete the first question orally with the class as an example.
- Have students read and answer the questions, then compare answers in pairs.
- Go over the answers with the class.

ANSWER KEY:

Possible answers include: 1. Camera.com; it has the best rating and it is cheaper than some of the others; 2. He should call Shark Customer Service; 3. $70

EXPANSION ACTIVITY: Coupon Clipping [Literacy]

- Have students bring in coupons or bring some in yourself.
- Distribute one or more coupons to each student. Put students in small groups.
- Write a chart on the board with each of the following words at the top of a column: *Product name; How many items; How much off; Expiration date.*
- Have students copy the chart.
- Have students work in their groups to complete the chart. Have each student describe his or her coupon or coupons to the group.
- Lead a discussion on what students learned about coupons: *What kinds of products have coupons? How much can you save? How long are the coupons valid?*

3 Write

- Read the directions. Have students look at the tips on page 71.
- Elicit the forms we use in tips (imperatives: *Check the date*; modals *can* and *should*; *You can save money; You should keep the warranty*). Remind students to use these forms in their tips.
- Have students write their shopping tips.
- Call on volunteers to read their tips to the class.

Unit 5: Lesson 6

EXPANSION ACTIVITY: Poster Tips

- Put students in small groups. Distribute large sheets of paper or poster board.
- Have students work in groups to create posters with several shopping tips. Encourage them to use visuals to illustrate the tips.
- MULTI-LEVEL: Have lower level students label their posters with appropriate words or phrases. Have more advanced students use complete sentences to label their posters, or have them write an explanatory paragraph about the poster.
- Ask a representative from each group to present their poster to the class.
- Display the posters around the classroom.

ANSWER KEY:
B. 1. $100; 2. $45; 3. $30

EXPANSION ACTIVITY: Bean Bag Toss [Challenge]

- Explain that you are going to toss the beanbag to a student and say the name of a coin or an amount of money. That person will have to respond with the appropriate percentage of a dollar. For example, if you say *one quarter*, the student should say *25%*. You can help students review money amounts by listing more than one coin (*a quarter, two pennies and a dime*).
- Continue tossing the beanbag until all students have had a chance to respond.

WINDOW ON MATH
Percentages

A Read the sentences.

- Write the numbers (*10%, 10/100, .10, 50%, 50/100, .50*) on the board. Say each one and have students repeat.
- Read the sentences aloud and have students repeat.
- Ask comprehension questions to make sure students understand the equivalent expressions.

B Answer the questions.

- Have the students read the problems or read the problems aloud line by line and have students repeat.
- Have students answer the questions and then check their answers with a partner.
- Go over the answers with the class.

LESSON 7 — What Do You Know?

1. Listening Review 077

- Go over the directions with the class.
- Read the items or play the audio and have the students mark their answers in the Answer Sheet box.
- Walk around to monitor the activity and help students stay on task.
- Have students check their answers with a partner.
- Go over the answers with the class.

LISTENING SCRIPT

Lesson 7, Activity 1: Listening Review

You will hear a question. Listen to the conversation. You will hear the question again. Choose the correct answer: A, B, or C. Use the Answer Sheet.

1. What does the woman need to buy?
   - A: Where are you going?
   - B: I'm going shopping. I need to get a washing machine.

   What does the woman need to buy?
   A. She's going shopping
   B. a washing machine
   C. a dishwasher

2. How much was the discount on the toaster?
   - A: Did you get a new toaster?
   - B: Yes, I got one on sale at Kitchens Galore. It was 15 percent off.
   - A: That's great!

   How much was the discount on the toaster?
   A. 15 percent off
   B. 50 percent off
   C. half price

3. What's wrong with the athletic shoes?
   - A: Can I help you?
   - B: Yes, I want to return these athletic shoes.
   - A: Is there something wrong with them?
   - B: Yes, they are too small.

   What's wrong with the athletic shoes?
   A. athletic shoes
   B. They are too small.
   C. They are too big.

4. What does the woman want?
   - A: Can I help you?
   - B: I want to return this coat. It's too small.
   - A: Do you want to exchange it for a bigger one?
   - B: No, thank you. I just want a refund.

   What does the woman want?
   A. to buy a jacket
   B. to exchange a jacket
   C. to get a refund for a jacket

5. Where does the man usually shop?
   - A: Where do you buy furniture?
   - B: I like Ben's Furniture Store.
   - A: Is Ben's better than May's?
   - B: I think so. They have nicer salespeople.

   Where does the man usually shop?
   A. furniture
   B. Ben's
   C. May's

ANSWER KEY:

1. B; 2. A; 3. B; 4. C; 5. B

2. Listening Dictation 078

- Copy the numbers and lines from the Listening Dictation section on the board.
- Read the first item. Have a more advanced student write the sentence on the board. Have students copy the sentence in their books.
- Play the audio and have students write the sentences they hear. Repeat as many times as necessary.
- Put students in pairs to compare answers.
- Have volunteers write the sentences on the board.

STUDENT BOOK PAGES 72-73

Unit 5: Lesson 7

LISTENING SCRIPT

Lesson 7, Activity 2: Listening Dictation

Listen. Write the sentences you hear.

1. A: Where are you going?
   B: I'm going shopping. I want to get a new heavy coat.
2. A: Where did you buy your vacuum cleaner?
   B: At May's Department Store. There was a sale.
3. A: Were they having a sale at Jingle's?
   B: No, but there were a lot of people there!
4. A: Is CompWorld better than ElecUSA?
   B: I think so. They have cheaper prices.
5. A: Why do you always shop at May's?
   B: I like shopping at May's because they have the biggest selection.

TESTING FOCUS: Predicting

- Tell students that before they listen, it is a good idea to scan each question for information. Based on the written question or statement provided, students can predict what kind of information they might expect to hear.
- As an example, have students look at question 1, covering part B. Read the question: *Where are you going?* Have students tell what kind of answers they might expect to hear, such as the names of places. Then have them tell grammatical structures they might hear, such as: *I'm going to* or *I'm going* (verb)*ing*.
- Have students uncover line B to check their prediction.

❸ Grammar Review

- Go over the directions.
- Read the first sentence. Elicit the appropriate completion. Have students circle *B* for item 1.
- Have students answer the rest of the questions.
- Put students in pairs to compare answers.
- Go over the answers with the class.

ANSWER KEY:

1. B; 2. C; 3. B; 4. B; 5. A; 6. C

LEARNING LOG

- Point out the four sections of the Learning Log: *I know these words; I can ask; I can say;* and *I can write*.
- Have students check what they know and what they can do.
- Walk around to note what they don't know or can't do. Use this information to review areas of difficulty.

BIG PICTURE EXPANSION ACTIVITY:
SPEAKING—Assessment: Talking about the Picture

- You can use the Big Picture on Student Book pages 62–63 to place new students in open entry classes, to diagnose difficulties, or to measure progress.
- Work with one student at a time and show him or her the Big Picture. Ask: *What do you see in the picture? Tell me about the picture.* Tell the student you want him or her to speak for as long as possible. Wait a moment for the student to prepare to answer. If the student has difficulty, use prompts: *Who do you see in the picture? What are the people doing?*
- Use a rubric like the one below to rate beginning speakers.

4	Exhibits confidence, begins speaking without prompting Uses some complex sentences, although may make mistakes with irregular forms Can use more than one tense
3	Uses sentences, although form may be incorrect Can speak for a sustained length of time Responds to prompts, but doesn't need them to begin speaking
2	Can use nouns and verbs Uses phrases Answers informational questions

Unit 5: Lesson 7

1	Can name objects Uses single words Can answer *yes/no* questions
0	Cannot say anything independently May be able to point to objects when prompted

BIG PICTURE EXPANSION ACTIVITY:
WRITING—Comparing Stores

- Have students look at the Big Picture in their books (Student Book pages 62–63).

- Draw a Venn diagram on the board to compare Le Chic and May's Department Store. Elicit ideas from the students for an example of what to write in each section of the diagram (Le Chic: *cheap prices*, both: *sell clothing*; May's: *bigger selection*). Point out that it is all right for students to imagine details.

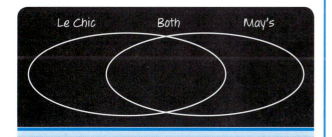

- Write two sentences on the board comparing Le Chic and May's (*Le Chic has cheaper prices; May's has a bigger selection*).

- Tell the students to write a paragraph comparing two stores at City Mall. Remind them to look at the Big Picture for ideas. Remind them to use comparative forms and words from the unit.

- Put students in pairs to read their paragraphs.

- Have volunteers read their paragraphs to the class.

TEACHER'S NOTES:

Things that students are doing well:
_____
_____
_____
_____

Things students need additional help with:
_____
_____
_____
_____
_____

Ideas for further practice or for the next class:
_____
_____
_____
_____
_____

UNIT 6 FOOD

UNIT OVERVIEW

LESSON	STUDENT BOOK PAGE	TEACHER'S EDITION PAGE
1. Identifying Foods	74	117
2. Activities at a Restaurant	76	120
3. Ordering from a Menu	78	123
4. Cooking at Home: Thanksgiving	80	128
5. Ordering at a Deli	82	130
6. Food Groups	84	133
7. What Do You Know?	86	135

Big Picture Expansion Activities

FOCUS	TITLE	SUGGESTED USE
Speaking	What's Happening?	Lesson 2
Reading	Sam's Family Restaurant	Lesson 3
Grammar	Quantifiers	Lesson 3
Writing	Describing the Restaurant	Lesson 7
Speaking	Assessment: Talking about the Big Picture	Lesson 7

Big Picture Expansion Activity Worksheets

FOCUS	TITLE	TEACHER'S EDITION PAGE
11. Reading	Sam's Family Restaurant	234
12. Grammar	Quantifiers	235

LESSON 1: Identifying Foods

OBJECTIVE
Identifying foods

VOCABULARY
cereal	fish	milk	red meat
cheese	flour	oil	soft drinks
coffee	fruit	peanuts	sugar
eggs	ice cream	poultry	vegetables

TARGET GRAMMAR
Count and noncount nouns *page 174*

THINGS TO DO

1 Learn New Words 079

- Have students look at the pictures and graph and elicit the words they know.
- Have students listen and look at the pictures while you say the words or play the audio.
- Instruct students to circle the words that are new to them.
- Say the words or play the audio a second time. Pause after each word or phrase and ask the students to repeat and point to the correct picture.
- Put students in pairs and have one say a word or phrase as the partner points to the correct picture. Reverse roles and repeat the activity.
- Call on students and ask questions: *Do you like cheese? How often do you eat fruit?*

LISTENING SCRIPT

Lesson 1, Activity 1: Learn New Words

Look at the pictures. Listen to the words. Listen again and repeat. Which words are new to you? Circle them.

1.	red meat	Did you eat any red meat yesterday?
2.	poultry	Did you eat any poultry yesterday?
3.	fish	Did you eat any fish yesterday?
4.	eggs	Did you eat any eggs yesterday?
5.	milk	Did you drink any milk yesterday?
6.	ice cream	Did you eat any ice cream yesterday?
7.	cheese	Did you eat any cheese yesterday?
8.	oil	Did you eat anything with oil in it yesterday?
9.	fruit	Did you eat any fruit yesterday?
10.	peanuts	Did you eat any peanuts yesterday?
11.	vegetables	Did you eat any vegetables yesterday?
12.	sugar	Did you eat any sugar yesterday?
13.	flour	Did you eat anything with flour in it yesterday?
14.	cereal	Did you eat any cereal yesterday?
15.	soft drinks	Did you drink any soft drinks yesterday?
16.	coffee	Did you drink any coffee yesterday?

TARGET GRAMMAR

Count and noncount nouns
The Target Grammar point is used in Activities 1–4. Presentation and practice of this grammar point appears on Student Book pages 174–175. Answer Keys appear on Teacher's Edition page 254.

EXPANSION ACTIVITY: Category Words [Multi-Level]

- Point out that some of the new words in Activity 1 are category words—nouns that refer to a group of things. Help the students identify those words: *red meat, poultry, fish, fruit, vegetables, cereal, soft drinks*. More advanced students may recognize that cheese is also a category noun: *Swiss, American, Gouda, feta*. Write the category words on the board as headings.

STUDENT BOOK PAGES 74–75

Unit 6: Lesson 1

- Put the students in small groups and have them list as many examples of each category as they can.
- Call on each group in turn to name a food for a given category. List the words on the board. A group earns a point for every new word its members can name after the other groups have exhausted their lists.
- Continue the activity with the other categories.

❷ Read and Write

- Have students look at the bar graph and ask questions: *How many pounds of red meat do people in the United States eat a year? How much oil do they use? Do they eat more than 10 pounds of sugar a year?* Make sure students understand how to read the graph.
- Have students complete the questions. Then, have them check their answers with a partner.
- Go over the answers with the class.

> **ANSWER KEY:**
>
> 1. flour; 2. soft drinks; 3. sugar, oil, and poultry; 4. vegetables; 5. ice cream and peanuts

EXPANSION ACTIVITY: Class Graph

- Assign each student a countable food item to survey the class about: *apples, oranges, bananas, carrots, eggs, potatoes, onions, cookies.*
- Write the question: *How many _____ did you eat in the last week?* on the board.
- Have students stand and move around the room, asking their classmates the question about their particular food item and tally the results. Remind them to make a tally mark for each item eaten, rather than for each person. For example, if one classmate ate five apples, the student would mark five tally marks.
- Ask the students to write the name of the item and the total count for that item on the board: *apples: 21*

- Distribute graph paper and have students create bar graphs about the data on the board.
- As an alternate, put the students in groups of four. Assign each group the same four items. Have them tally the results for their group and make bar graphs. Ask representatives of each group to present their bar graph to the class.

❸ Talk About the Picture

- Go over the directions and the examples.
- Have students make three true and false statements about the bar graph.
- Call on students to repeat their sentences and have the class say whether the sentences are true or false.

EXPANSION ACTIVITY: Nutrition Facts [Challenge]

- Have partners choose one of the foods from the bar graph.
- Have partners research their food to find out about the nutritional benefits and/or potential health hazards it offers.
- Have each pair report their findings to the class.

❹ Interview

- Have students look at the survey. Point out the possible answers.
- Copy part of the survey on the board: *Did you eat any fish yesterday? Yes I did. I had _____ for _____. / No, I didn't.* Under *Yes, I did. I had _____ for _____,* copy the options: *breakfast, lunch, dinner, a snack.*
- Read each line in the sample conversation and have students repeat.
- Model the activity with a student. Ask: *Did you eat any fish yesterday?* Mark the answer on the board.
- Have students work in pairs to ask and answer the questions, asking about all the items in the list. Tell them to think of their own type of food for the last question.

Unit 6: Lesson 1

- Call on a few students to tell the class about their partners: *Sonia ate fish for breakfast yesterday*.

EXPANSION ACTIVITY: Compare and Contrast

- Draw a Venn Diagram on the board.

- Model the activity by comparing yourself to one of the students in terms of what you ate yesterday. Instead of Person A and Person B, use your name and the student's name. Label the circle with your name, the student's name, and the word *Both* in the center section.

- Ask the student about the foods he or she ate yesterday and provide information about what you ate. Write the foods in the appropriate places on the diagram.

- Have students work in pairs to create Venn Diagrams about themselves. Have them use the ideas on the Venn Diagram to write sentences.

- LOW-LEVEL: Provide question prompts for students to ask each other, such as: *What did you (eat/drink) yesterday for (breakfast/lunch/dinner/a snack)?* Have partners ask each other the questions, then answer using a sentence frame such as: *I (ate/drank) _____ for (breakfast/lunch/dinner) yesterday*.

- Call on students to tell the class about their diagrams and read their sentences.

STUDENT BOOK PAGES 74-75

LESSON 2: Activities at a Restaurant

OBJECTIVE
Activities at a restaurant

VOCABULARY

booth	hostess	set the table
bowl	menu	spill
check	napkin	take an order
clear the table	plate	tray
counter	pour	trip over
fall off	serve food	waiter

TARGET GRAMMAR

One, each, some, another, and *the other(s)*   page 176

THINGS TO DO

1 Learn New Words 080

- Have students look at the Big Picture in their books (Student Book pages 76–77). Elicit the words they know.
- Have students listen and look at the pictures while you say the words or play the audio.
- Instruct students to circle the words that are new to them.
- Say the words or play the audio a second time. Pause after each word or phrase and ask the students to repeat and point to the correct part of the picture.
- Put students in pairs and have one say a word or phrase as the partner points to the correct part of the picture. Reverse roles and repeat the activity.
- Call on students and ask questions: Who takes the order? Can you eat at the counter?

LISTENING SCRIPT

Lesson 2, Activity 1: Learn New Words

Look at the picture. Listen to the words. Listen again and repeat.

1. counter	They are sitting at the counter.
2. menu	She is looking at a menu.
3. waiter	The waiter is wearing a white shirt.
4. check	The waiter is giving her the check.
5. booth	They are sitting in a booth.
6. hostess	The hostess is seating them at a table.
7. tray	He is carrying a tray.
8. plate	There is a plate on the table.
9. bowl	There is a bowl on the table.
10. napkin	There is a napkin on the table.
11. serve food	She is serving food.
12. take an order	She is taking an order.
13. pour	She is pouring water.
14. trip over	He tripped over a purse.
15. fall off	The glass is falling off his tray.
16. set the table	He is setting the table.
17. clear the table	She is clearing the table.
18. spill	He is spilling his milk.

EXPANSION ACTIVITY: Twenty Questions

- Put students in pairs.
- Have the first student choose a word or phrase from the vocabulary list.
- Have the second student ask up to twenty questions to discover which word or phrase their partner chose.
- MULTI-LEVEL: For lower level students, provide models of questions they might ask, such as: *Is it a thing? Is it an action? Who uses it? Who does the action?* If pairing lower level students with more advanced students, have the more advanced students ask *yes/no* questions.
- Have partners switch roles and play again.

Unit 6: Lesson 2

2 Write the Names 🎧 081

- Go over the directions. Have students identify the named people in the picture.
- Play the audio and have students write the name of each person described.
- Play the audio a second time and have students check their answers.
- Go over the answers as a class.

LISTENING SCRIPT

Lesson 2, Activity 2: Write the Names

Listen to the sentences about the picture. Write the person's name.

1. A: Have you seen our waiter?
   B: She's over there. She's clearing a table.
2. A: Have you seen our waiter?
   B: She's over there. She's taking an order.
3. A: Have you seen our waiter?
   B: He's over there. He just tripped over a bag.
4. A: Have you seen our waiter?
   B: She's over there. She's pouring water.
5. A: Have you seen our waiter?
   B: She's over there. She's serving food.
6. A: Have you seen our waiter?
   B: He's over there. He's setting the table.

ANSWER KEY:

1. Janet; 2. Lucy; 3. David; 4. Anna; 5. Lisa; 6. Max

EXPANSION ACTIVITY: Who Is It? [Multi-Level]

- Have students work in pairs to choose a named person from the picture. Have them write five clues about the person, ranging from broader clues at first: *Is it a woman?* to more specific clues last: *She has blonde hair and wears glasses.*
- Put two pairs together to form small groups. Have pairs take turns giving clues about their mystery person and having the other pair guess who it is.
- The pair who guesses the person using the fewest clues wins the round.
- Put pairs in new groups and have students repeat the exercise with a different pair. Continue pairing up new groups as desired, or have students write new clues and begin again.

3 Talk About the Picture

- Have students look at the Big Picture in their books (Student Book pages 76–77).
- To set the context, ask questions about the picture: *How many people do you see? Where are they? What are they doing?* Write the vocabulary that you have elicited from students on the board.
- Ask students to write five questions about the picture. Remind them to use the words on the board or in Activity 1 if they need help.
- Walk around the room and provide help as needed.
- Put students in pairs. Have them take turns asking and answering their questions.

EXPANSION ACTIVITY: Team Challenge

- Have students study the Big Picture for one minute and then close their books.
- Divide the class into teams.
- Have teams take turns asking a question about the picture. Each correct answer earns the team a point.

BIG PICTURE EXPANSION ACTIVITY: SPEAKING—What's Happening?

- Have students look at the Big Picture in their books (Student Book pages 76–77).
- Tell students that you are going to assign them each an unnamed character in the picture. In small groups, they will tell what is happening from that character's point of view.

Unit 6: Lesson 2

- Model the activity. Choose a character and tell what is happening: *I am a young woman having dinner with my husband. Our baby just knocked over a glass of milk. Our waitress Lisa is delivering our order now.*
- Have a student identify which character you are describing in the book.
- Put students in groups of four. Point to a character in the picture as you pass each student. Don't let the other students in the group hear or see which characters you've chosen. Remind students to use count and noncount nouns in the story.
- After each student has described what is happening to the character, call on a few volunteers to repeat their stories to the class. Have the class guess who is being described.

4 Practice the Conversation 082

- Have students listen and look at the conversation while you read it or play the audio.
- Say the words or play the audio a second time. Pause after each line and ask the students to repeat.
- Check comprehension by asking questions: *Who is having a conversation? What does the customer want?*
- Model the conversation with a student. Have the student read B's lines. Demonstrate how to substitute from the ideas in the boxes below. Cue the student to make the appropriate substitutions.
- Have students work in pairs to practice the conversation, making substitutions from the boxes and using their own ideas.
- Walk around to make sure students understand the activity and provide help if needed.

LISTENING SCRIPT

Lesson 2, Activity 4: Practice the Conversation

Listen to the conversation. Listen again and repeat.

A: Excuse me.

B: Yes. Can I help you?

A: Yes. Can you bring me a menu, please?

B: Sure. I'll get one right away.

Grammar Note:

- You may want to point out that singular count nouns are replaced by *one* in the sentence: *I'll get one for you right away.* Noncount nouns or plural count nouns can be replaced with *some*: *I'll get some for you right away.*

EXPANSION ACTIVITY: Substitute a Pronoun [Low-Level]

- Explain that in this activity the students will practice making the appropriate substitutions of *one* or *some* in small groups. The first student will make a request: *Can you bring me a bowl please?* The next student responds with the appropriate substitution: *Sure. I'll get one right away.* That student makes a request of a third student and so on until everyone in the group has made a request and responded.
- Put the students in groups of four. Have them practice making and responding to requests with count and noncount nouns.
- Walk around the room to monitor the activity and provide help as needed.

TARGET GRAMMAR

One, each, some, another, and *the other(s)*
The Target Grammar point is used in Activity 4. Presentation and practice of this grammar point appears on Student Book page 176. Answer Keys appear on Teacher's Edition page 254.

LESSON 3 Ordering from a Menu

OBJECTIVE
Ordering from a menu

VOCABULARY
appetizers   salads
beverages   sandwiches
desserts   side orders
main dishes soups

WINDOW ON MATH
Computing a Tip

TARGET GRAMMAR
Quantifiers   *page 177*

THINGS TO DO

1 Learn New Words 083

- Have students look at the menu and pictures, and elicit the words they know.
- Have students listen and look at the pictures while you say the words or play the audio.
- Instruct students to circle the words that are new to them.
- Say the words or play the audio a second time. Pause after each word or phrase, and ask the students to repeat and point to the correct picture.
- Put students in pairs and have one say a word or phrase as the partner points to the correct picture. Reverse roles and repeat the activity.
- Read the items on the menu one by one and have students repeat.
- Call on students and ask questions: *What appetizers do you like? Do you eat dessert often?*

LISTENING SCRIPT

Lesson 3, Activity 1: Learn New Words

Look at the menu. Listen to the words. Listen again and repeat. Which words are new to you? Circle them.

1. appetizers — What's your favorite appetizer?
2. soups — What's your favorite soup?
3. salads — What's your favorite salad?
4. main dishes — What's your favorite main dish?
5. sandwiches — What's your favorite sandwich?
6. side orders — What's your favorite side order?
7. desserts — What's your favorite dessert?
8. beverages — What's your favorite beverage?

Pronunciation Note:

- All the new words in this lesson are plurals. Remind students of the three different sounds that plurals can have: *s*, *z*, and *iz*. Review the rules: *s* sound after voiceless consonants, *z* sound after vowels and voiced consonants, and *iz* after *s*, *z*, *sh*, *ch*, *x*, and soft *g*.

EXPANSION ACTIVITY: Favorite Restaurants [Multi-Level]

- Have students bring in menus from their favorite restaurants in your city or town, or bring in menus yourself and have students each choose one.
- Have partners choose several items from their menus and sort them according to their final sounds: *s*, *z*, and *iz*. Call on partners to share items they sorted, and make a list for each sound on the board.

STUDENT BOOK PAGES 78–79   FOOD • 123

Unit 6: Lesson 3

- Put students in small groups to tell about their restaurant. Have them tell their favorite items on the menu, as well as other reasons why they like to go there.
- Have each group decide on one restaurant they could all agree to go to together.
- Call on representatives from each group to tell the class which restaurant they would want to go to and why.

❷ Complete the Chart 084

- Go over the directions, the chart, and the example.
- Play the audio and have students check the answers they hear.
- LOW LEVEL: For lower level students, provide a script of the listening with key words replaced by blanks. Have students fill in the missing words as they listen, then answer the questions.
- Play the audio a second time and have students check their answers.
- Go over the answers as a class. If necessary, replay each item and have students listen again to hear the answer.

LISTENING SCRIPT

Lesson 3, Activity 2: Complete the Chart

Listen to the people ordering at the Casa Alberto Restaurant. Check the types of food they order.

1.
   A: Are you ready to order?
   B: Yes. I'd like a small garden salad and the spaghetti and meatballs.
   A: Do you want something to drink with that?
   B: Yes. I'd like some ginger ale.
   A: Large or small?
   B: Large, please.

2.
   A: Are you ready to order?
   B: Yes. I'll have a large chicken soup and the rice pudding.
   A: Do you want something to drink with that?
   B: Yes. I'll have some tea.
   A: Large or small?
   B: Small, please.

3.
   A: Are you ready to order?
   B: Yes. I'd like to start with a shrimp cocktail and then have the chicken in a basket as my meal.
   A: Do you want something to drink with your meal?
   B: No. Water is fine for me, but I'll have a cup of coffee after my meal.
   A: Large or small?
   B: Large, please.

4.
   A: Would you like to order any dessert today?
   B: Yes. I'll have the cake.
   A: Would you like any ice cream with that?
   B: No. Just the cake is fine. And I'll have some coffee with it.
   A: Large or small?
   B: Small, please.

5.
   A: Are you ready to order?
   B: Yes. I'll have the steak and a small garden salad.
   A: Do you want something to drink with that?
   B: Yes, I'll have some cola.
   A: What size cola?
   B: Large, please.

ANSWER KEY:

Students should check:
1. salad; main dish; beverage
2. soup; dessert; beverage
3. appetizer; main dish; beverage
4. dessert; beverage
5. main dish; salad; beverage

🎯 TARGET GRAMMAR

Quantifiers

The Target Grammar point is used in Activities 2 and 3. Presentation and practice of this grammar point appears on Student Book pages 177–178. Answer Keys appear on Teacher's Edition page 254.

Unit 6: Lesson 3

EXPANSION ACTIVITY: Dinner With an Extraterrestrial [Challenge]

- Put students in small groups.
- Have students imagine they are having dinner with an extraterrestrial creature who is unfamiliar with foods from our planet.
- Have groups write a short scene between the extraterrestrial and themselves in which the extraterrestrial asks about different menu items and the students describe each one. Have them choose foods from Activity 1 and the menu.
- Model an example for students on the board. For example: *Extraterrestrial: What are French fries? Miguel: They are potatoes that are cut and fried in oil. They are hot and delicious! I eat mine with ketchup.*
- Have groups perform their scenes for the class. Lead a discussion about ways that the groups described each item well.

3 Practice the Conversation

- Have students listen and look at the conversation while you read it or play the audio.
- Say the words or play the audio a second time. Pause after each line and ask the students to repeat.
- Check comprehension by asking questions: *Who is having a conversation? What does the customer order?*
- Model the conversation with a student. Have the student read A's lines. Demonstrate how to substitute from the ideas in the boxes below. Cue the student to make the appropriate substitutions.
- Have students work in pairs to practice the conversation, making substitutions from the boxes and using their own ideas.
- Walk around to make sure students understand the activity and provide help if needed.

LISTENING SCRIPT

Lesson 3, Activity 3: Practice the Conversation

Listen to the conversation. Listen again and repeat.

A: Are you ready to order?

B: Yes. I'd like a small onion soup and a chicken sandwich.

A: Do you want something to drink with your sandwich?

B: Yes. I'd like some tea, please.

A: Large or small?

B: Small, please.

EXPANSION ACTIVITY: Role-Play

- Brainstorm ingredients for different items on the menu. For example, ingredients in the fruit salad could include bananas, apples, and grapes.
- Put students in pairs and have them take turns role-playing a customer and a waiter. Have the customer ask the waiter about things on the menu: *What appetizers do you have today? What desserts are on the menu?* and for an explanation of different items: *What is in the fruit salad?* Have the waiter answer the questions.
- Have volunteers perform their role-play for the class.

WINDOW ON MATH

Computing a Tip

A Read the meal receipt and explanation.

- Have students look at the receipt.
- Read the information and ask questions about the information: *How much did the food cost? How much was the tax? How much was the tip?*

Unit 6: Lesson 3

B Complete the chart below.
- Have students complete the chart and then compare answers with a partner.
- Go over the answers with the class.

Culture/Civics Notes:
- Students who are new to the country may not be familiar with American customs regarding tipping. Brainstorm situations in which we normally tip. Point out or elicit that in restaurants we usually tip 20%. Customers often round up to the nearest dollar when tipping, rather than leaving the exact amount.
- Ask students to compute a 20% tip on $10 and $20.
- Brainstorm other situations in which someone might give a tip (in a taxi, in a bar, in a hotel). Discuss how much Americans generally tip in these and other situations.

ANSWER KEY:

B.

Total Food Cost	$16.00	$24.00	$32.00
5% tax	$.80	$1.20	$1.60
20% tip	$3.20	$4.80	$6.40
Total	$20.00	$30.00	$40.00

EXPANSION ACTIVITY: Restaurant Budgeting [Challenge]
- Tell students that each of them has a restaurant budget for the week.
- Give each student an index card and have them write a receipt from a meal on the card. Students should include the name of the restaurant, the items ordered, the amount spent, tax and tip. Each student's receipt should total between $5 and $15. Circulate to make sure that the information on each card is clear.
- You may wish to assign monetary amounts for each receipt before beginning the activity to ensure a wide range of totals is represented. To do so, write a range on the back of each card, such as *$5-7* or *$11-14*. Receipts should be evenly distributed between inexpensive, moderate, and more expensive meals.
- Collect the cards. Put students in groups. Have each student choose a card. For each student in the group, allow $10 in their restaurant budget. For example, a group of three would have a $30 budget and a group of five would have a $50 budget.
- Have each group total up its cards and discover whether they exceeded their weekly restaurant budget. If so, have them look at the receipts and decide which items they would cut (or which restaurants they would not go to again) in order to stay within their budget.
- Have groups share their results with the class.

BIG PICTURE EXPANSION ACTIVITY:
READING—Sam's Family Restaurant
- Make copies of Worksheet 11 (Teacher's Edition page 234) and distribute them to students.
- Have students look at the Big Picture in their books (Student Book pages 76–77).
- Instruct students to complete the activities and then check their answers with a partner.
- Go over the answers with the class.

Unit 6: Lesson 3

ANSWER KEY:

A. Look at the Big Picture. Complete the story with information from the picture.

Sam's Family <u>Restaurant</u> is a fun and friendly place to eat. I went to the restaurant with my daughter and husband. The food was very good. The meatballs are my favorite main dish. The restaurant has great baked desserts, too. Sam's has both tables and <u>booths</u>. You can even sit at the <u>counter</u> and watch the cook work. Sam's has a lot of hostesses and waiters—there were <u>fourteen</u> of them working last night. Susan and <u>Max</u> served our table. They did a great job, but some of the other waiters had problems. One of them tripped and dropped a <u>tray</u> right next to our table. Sam's is usually full of people. Only <u>one</u> table was empty. I saw <u>two</u> other families with children, and one family even brought their dog!

B. Answer the questions.
1. a woman wearing purple clothes and scarf;
2. Some of the waiters had problems;
3. Answers will vary. Students may include the following information: there were many spills and dropped trays; servers cleared the tables; the tables and floors all look clean

BIG PICTURE EXPANSION ACTIVITY:
GRAMMAR—Quantifiers

- Make copies of Worksheet 12 (Teacher's Edition page 235) and distribute them to students.
- Have students look at the Big Picture in their books (Student Book pages 76–77).
- Instruct students to complete the activities and then check their answers with a partner.
- Go over the answers with the class.

ANSWER KEY:

A. Look at the Big Picture. Complete the questions with *How many* or *How much*.
1. How many; 2. How much; 3. How much;
4. How many; 5. How many; 6. How much;
7. How much; 8. How many

B. Answer the questions in complete sentences. Use quantifiers before noncount nouns.
1. There are two bowls on Janet's table.
2. The baby spilled a glass of water.
3. Dot is carrying three plates of food.
4. There are 30 customers and one dog in the restaurant.
5. Four waiters are spilling something.
6. There are at least six bowls of soup.
7. Leo is carrying four glasses of water.
8. Four people are looking at menus.

Grammar Notes:

Some students may not have learned the differences between count and noncount nouns. You may want to review the following points.

- Count nouns can be counted. We can use *a*, *an*, or a number in front of count nouns. They can be singular or plural, and so are followed by different forms of the verb depending on the number.

- Noncount nouns cannot be counted. Nouns that are ideas, are too big or too small, or are category nouns are usually noncount nouns. Noncount nouns are always singular. Unlike count nouns, noncount nouns do not need an article. Liquids are usually noncount, and so require quantity words before we can count them. However, the names of liquids can be count nouns when they refer to a cup or portion of that liquid. For example, a server may ask: *How many coffees do you want?* rather than *How many cups of coffee do you want?*

STUDENT BOOK PAGES 78-79

LESSON 4: Cooking at Home: Thanksgiving

OBJECTIVE
Cooking at home: Thanksgiving

VOCABULARY
bake	fry	mix
boil	heat	peel
cut up	mash	slice

TARGET GRAMMAR
Adjective + noun *page 179*

THINGS TO DO

1 Learn New Words 086

- Have students look at the pictures and elicit the words they know.
- Have students listen and look at the pictures while you say the words or play the audio.
- Instruct students to circle the words that are new to them.
- Say the words or play the audio a second time. Pause after each word or phrase and ask the students to repeat and point to the correct picture.
- Put students in pairs and have one say a word or phrase as the partner points to the correct picture. Reverse roles and repeat the activity.

LISTENING SCRIPT

Lesson 4, Activity 1: Learn New Words

Look at the pictures. Listen to the words. Listen again and repeat. Which words are new to you? Circle them.

1. fry	You can fry an egg.
2. bake	You can bake bread.
3. boil	You can boil water for tea.
4. cut up	You cut up vegetables to cook them.
5. slice	You can slice meat.
6. mix	You mix ingredients.
7. peel	You can peel a potato.
8. mash	You can mash a potato.
9. heat	You heat soup in a pan.

EXPANSION ACTIVITY: Charades

- Write the verbs from this lesson and from previous lessons in this unit on slips of paper (*fry, bake, boil, cut up, slice, mix, peel, mash, heat, set the table, take an order, clear the table, serve food, pour, spill, fall off, trip over*).
- Have volunteers come to the front of the class and act out a word. Elicit the name of the action from the class.
- LITERACY: As students name each word or phrase, write it on the board. When all words have been listed, have students look for similarities and differences in the spelling and pronunciation of words. For example, *bake* and *take (an order)* rhyme, *heat* and *peel* have the same vowel sound but are spelled differently, and so on. Based on the examples students find, go over spelling and pronunciation rules that will help students read more effectively.

2 Preview

- Read the directions and go over the questions with students.
- Have students scan the story and circle the answers.
- Have partners compare their answers.
- Go over the answers with the class. Have volunteers identify the specific part of the story where they found each answer.

ANSWER KEY:
1. B; 2. A; 3. B

Unit 6: Lesson 4

TARGET GRAMMAR

Adjective + Noun

The Target Grammar point is used in Activities 2, 3, and 4. Presentation and practice of this grammar point appears on Student Book page 179. Answer Keys appear on Teacher's Edition page 255.

EXPANSION ACTIVITY: Dates and Numbers [Literacy]

- Have students scan the story and circle any numbers or dates they see, including words that represent numbers (second, fourth, 1621, one, first).
- Review the pronunciation and written forms of dates and ordinal numbers, such as *fourth* and *4th*.
- Have students use a current calendar to determine this year's date for both the Canadian and American Thanksgiving holidays. Have them write a sentence for each, including the number from the story and the date. For example, *The fourth Thursday of November is the 26th*. Help students correctly use dates and ordinal numbers.

3 Check *True* or *False*

- Go over the directions.
- Have students read the story and mark the answer to each question.
- Have students check their answers in pairs.
- Go over the answers with the class. Have students correct each false statement to make it true.

ANSWER KEY:

1. True; 2. True; 3. False; the Pilgrims lived in Europe before they came to the United States; 4. False; today, people usually celebrate Thanksgiving; 5. True

EXPANSION ACTIVITY: Thanksgiving Dinner with All the Trimmings [Low-Level]

- Have students list the dishes from the article that are served for a typical Thanksgiving dinner (turkey, bread stuffing, mashed potatoes, vegetables, cranberry sauce).
- Have students make a poster about each dish using pictures or drawings. Have them label the poster with the name of the dish and, if possible, phrases or simple sentences to describe the dish. For example: *Bread stuffing: It is made with bread. It is stuffed in a turkey*.
- Have students display their posters around the room and read each one to the class.
- For more advanced students, have them find recipes and describe how to make each dish to the class.

4 Write

A. Look at the recipe for mashed potatoes and answer the questions.

- Go over the directions and the questions.
- Have students read the recipe and write the answers.
- Have students check their answers in pairs.
- Go over the answers with the class.

ANSWER KEY:

1. five; 2. five; 3. one-half cup; 4. water, potatoes; 5. potatoes, milk, and butter

B. Write the recipe for a dish you like. Then share it with the class.

- Go over the directions.
- Have students write their recipes and then share them in pairs.
- Have a few students read their recipes to the class.

EXPANSION ACTIVITY: Dictate and Order

- Have students close their books.
- Dictate the five steps in the recipe to students in random order.
- Have students put the sentences in order 1–5.
- After you have checked their work, have volunteers write the sentences on the board.

LESSON 5 Ordering at a Deli

OBJECTIVE
Ordering at a deli

PRONUNCIATION
Intonation Patterns in Sentences and Questions

1 Practice Pronunciation: Intonation Patterns in Sentences and Questions 🎧 087

A. Listen to the sentences. Listen again and repeat.
- Explain that we use rising intonation when asking a yes/no question. We use falling intonation when making statements or asking information questions.
- Have students look at the sentences while you read them or play the audio.
- Say the lines or play the audio a second time, pausing after each line to have students repeat.

LISTENING SCRIPT

Lesson 5, Activity 1: Practice Pronunciation: Intonation Patterns in Sentences and Questions

A. Listen to the sentences. Listen again and repeat.
1. I'd like a small coffee.
2. Would you like something to drink?
3. What size salad?

B. Write the intonation marks over the sentences. Listen to check your answers. 🎧 088
- Go over the directions and the example.
- Have students look at the questions and responses while you read them or play the audio. Have students mark the intonation for each sentence.
- Say the lines or play the audio a second time, pausing after each line to have students repeat.
- Elicit that in conversations 1 and 3 the waiter is asking yes/no questions. In conversations 2 and 4, the waiter is asking for information.

- Put students in pairs to check their answers by repeating the sentences to each other with proper intonation.
- Go over the answers with the class, replaying the audio and demonstrating how to mark intonation using the board as necessary.

LISTENING SCRIPT

Lesson 5, Activity 1: Practice Pronunciation: Intonation Patterns in Sentences and Questions

B Write the intonation marks over the questions and responses. Listen to check your answers.

1. Waiter: Would you like dessert tonight?
   Customer: No, thank you.
2. Waiter: What kind of soup would you like?
   Customer: I'll have the chicken soup.
3. Waiter: Are you ready to order?
   Customer: Yes. I'll have a hamburger.
4. Waiter: What can I get for you?
   Customer: I'll have a salad.

ANSWER KEY:

1. Would you like dessert tonight? ↗
   No, thank you. ↘
2. What kind of soup would you like? ↘
   I'll have the chicken soup. ↘
3. Are you ready to order? ↗
   Yes. I'll have a hamburger. ↘
4. What can I get for you? ↘
   I'll have a salad. ↘

C. Work with a partner. Take turns asking and answering the questions from Activity B.
- Put the students in pairs and have them practice the conversations in random order. Remind the "customers" to respond appropriately, depending on whether the question is asking for information or is a yes/no question.
- Walk around to monitor the activity and provide help as needed.

Unit 6: Lesson 5

> **EXPANSION ACTIVITY: Write Your Own**
> - Have students work individually to write their own *yes/no* questions and questions that ask about options.
> - CHALLENGE: Have more advanced students write conversations that include several questions about the same topic or item. For example, a customer might ask specific questions about a menu item: *Is that baked or fried? Does it come with a side order?*
> - Put students in pairs to practice asking and answering the questions or conversations with correct intonation.

2 Listen and Write 089

- Read the conversation or play the audio.
- Have students put a check next to what each speaker is ordering and write the total cost for each order.
- Read or play the conversation again and have students check their answers.
- Go over the answers with the class.

> **Vocabulary Note:**
> - Point out that *for here* means to eat in the restaurant, and *to go* means to take the food away.

> **LISTENING SCRIPT**
>
> **Lesson 5, Activity 2: Listen and Write**
>
> *Listen to three people ordering at a deli. Check what each person orders. Then write the total you hear for each order.*
>
> 1. A: Can I help you?
>   B: Yes, I'd like a steak sandwich, please.
>   A: Do you want something to drink with that?
>   B: Yes, I'll have a large root beer.
>   A: Okay. That will be $8.00.
> 2. A: What can I get for you?
>   B: I'd like a veggie sandwich.
>   A: Do you want a salad with that?
>   B: No, thank you.
>   A: Would you like something to drink?
>   B: Sure. I'll have a small tea, please.
>   A: That will be $6.25.
> 3. A: Can I help you?
>   B: Yes, I'd like a fruit salad, please.
>   A: Do you want something to drink with that?
>   B: Sure. I'll have a small orange soda.
>   A: For here or to go?
>   B: To go, please.
>   A: That will be $7.50.

> **ANSWER KEY:**
>
> Person 1: -Check: steak sandwich, root beer; Total: $8.00
> Person 2: -Check: veggie sandwich, tea; Total: $6.25
> Person 3: -Check: fruit salad, orange soda; Total: $7.50

> **EXPANSION ACTIVITY: May I Take Your Order? [Multi-Level]**
> - Put students in groups of three. Assign one student to be the customer, one to be the waiter, and one to be an observer.
> - Have students use the chart in Activity 2 to improvise a conversation between the customer and the waiter. Have the waiter take the customer's order, with the customer choosing from items in the chart. Have students model their conversations on the ones they just heard in Activity 2. You may wish to put a written example on the board.
> - Have the observer in each group listen to the conversation and write down the order and the cost of the order, then report it back to the group after the conversation is finished.
> - Have students in the group switch roles so that each student has an opportunity to be the customer, the waiter, and the observer.

Unit 6: Lesson 5

3 Practice the Conversation: Placing a Food Order 🎧 090

- Show students the picture in the book for Activity 3. To set the context, ask questions about the picture: *Who is in the picture? Where are they?*
- Read the conversation or play the audio.
- Read or play the conversation again. Pause after each sentence and ask students to repeat. To confirm understanding, ask comprehension questions about the conversation: *What does B want? What size drink?*
- Point out that there are three pieces of scripted information in the conversation that can be substituted: the order, an item in the order, and the size of that item.
- Model the conversation with a student. Have the student read A's lines. Demonstrate how to substitute *a roast beef sandwich* and *vegetable soup* for the scripted order and item, and *small* for the scripted size. Cue the student to ask about the size of the soup.
- Put students in pairs to practice the conversation, making substitutions from the boxes and using their own ideas.
- Walk around to monitor the activity and provide help as needed.

> **LISTENING SCRIPT**
>
> **Lesson 5, Activity 3: Practice the Conversation: Placing a Food Order**
>
> *Listen to the conversation. Listen again and repeat.*
>
> A: What can I get for you?
> B: I'd like a turkey sandwich.
> A: Would you like something to drink with that?
> B: Sure. I'll have a root beer.
> A: What size root beer?
> B: Large, please.

4 Practice the Conversation: Computing the Cost of a Meal 🎧 091

- Repeat the basic procedure from Activity 3.
- To set the context, ask questions about the menu: *What kind of restaurant is it? What drinks are available?*
- After students have listened to and repeated the conversation line by line, check comprehension by asking more questions: *What does B want? What size? How much is it?*
- Point out that in this conversation students must look at the prices and figure out the total. Give a few examples and elicit the cost of the meal.
- Have students continue practicing the conversation, making substitutions from the boxes and using their own ideas.

> **LISTENING SCRIPT**
>
> **Lesson 5, Activity 4: Practice the Conversation: Computing the Cost of a Meal**
>
> *Listen to the conversation. Listen again and repeat.*
>
> A: Can I help you?
> B: Yes. I'd like a veggie sandwich.
> A: Do you want some chips with that?
> B: No, thank you.
> A: Will that be all for you?
> B: Let's see . . . I'll have a small coffee, too.
> A: That will be $5.50.

LESSON 6: Food Groups

> **OBJECTIVE**
> Food groups

1 Check *True* or *False*

- Have students look at the information about food groups on page 85. Ask questions: *What is this information about? What do the headings tell you?*
- Have students read the information silently, or read aloud line by line and have students repeat.
- Read the first item in Activity 1 and ask if it is true or false. Elicit the correct answer (True) and have students check the box under *True*.
- Have students check *True* or *False* for the other sentences and correct the false statements. Then have them check their answers with a partner.
- Go over the answers with the class.

> **ANSWER KEY:**
> 1. True; 2. False; 3. False; 4. False; 5. True; 6. True; 7. True; 8. False

> **EXPANSION ACTIVITY:** *True* or *False* Teams [Multi-Level]
> - Divide the class into two teams. For larger classes, more teams may be needed.
> - Have each team write true or false statements about the food group information. Each team should write one statement for each student on the team.
> - Have students close their books. Have teams take turns presenting a true or false statement. The answering team earns one point for the correct answer and a bonus point for correcting false statements.
> - You may wish to make sure that both teams have an equal number of false statements so that each team has the opportunity to score an equal number of points.

2 Think About It

- Go over the directions and read the chart aloud.
- Put students in pairs or have them complete the exercise individually.
- Go over the answers with the class. Have students tell why they chose each dinner, and where they found supporting information in the text.

> **ANSWER KEY:**
> 1. a; 2. a; 3. a

> **EXPANSION ACTIVITY: Pass or Fail?**
> - Give each student an index card or a piece of paper.
> - Have students anonymously write down a full day's menu like the ones shown in Activity 2. Students may either write healthy menus that adhere to the guidelines in the food group chart, or they may write menus that include unhealthy choices.
> - Collect the cards. Divide the class into small groups. Have each group draw one card per person.
> - Have groups discuss each menu card they've drawn and assign it a "pass" or "fail" grade based on how healthy it is when compared to the food group chart recommendations.
> - MULTI-LEVEL: Have lower level students point to or name the items on the group's menu that are healthy and unhealthy, giving reasons if possible. Have more advanced students confirm whether they are correct or not, explaining why they think so.
> - Have each group report on one of the menus they examined. Have them tell why they gave it a passing or failing grade.

Unit 6: Lesson 6

3 Your Diet in a Day

- Go over the directions.
- Have students track their diet for one day and then examine the results.
- Put students in pairs to discuss what they discovered.
- Lead a class discussion about diet and where the class needs to improve. Take a poll to find out what common habits students have: do they need to eat more or less of a certain type of food? Have students discuss whether they agree with the information in the food group chart, or whether they believe a different combination of foods is healthier than the one recommended by the USDA. If students disagree with the chart, what is their rationale?

Culture Notes:

- Some students may have strong cultural traditions related to food and eating. You may wish to lead a discussion about this topic in class. Ask students whether it is common or uncommon in their cultures or families to eat the healthy foods recommended by the food group chart.

- Point out that many American families have changed their holiday menus as they have become more health-conscious. Write before and after menu examples on the board, such as this Fourth of July picnic menu: *Before: hot dogs, hamburgers, white bread buns, potato salad, creamy green bean casserole, chocolate cake; After: grilled chicken, turkey burgers, whole wheat buns, grilled vegetables, salad, fruit.*

- Have students tell about traditional dishes their families prepare either for everyday consumption or for special occasions. Are students pressured to eat these foods or to eat more than may be healthy?

- For students who are interested, help them brainstorm strategies for improving their diets, including researching healthier versions of traditional foods.

LESSON 7 — What Do You Know?

1 Listening Review 092

- Go over the directions with the class.
- Read the items or play the audio and have the students mark their answers on the Answer Sheet.
- Walk around to monitor the activity and help students stay on task.
- Have students check their answers with a partner.
- Go over the answers with the class.

LISTENING SCRIPT

Lesson 7, Activity 1: Listening Review

Listen to the conversation. To finish the conversation, listen and choose the correct answer: A, B, or C. Use the Answer Sheet.

1. Did you eat any eggs yesterday?
   A. No, thank you.
   B. Yes, I'd like some eggs.
   C. Yes, I did. I had some for breakfast.

2. Can you bring me a napkin please?
   A. Yes, I'll get one right away.
   B. Yes, you can have one.
   C. Yes, you are.

3. Are you ready to order?
   A. For here, please.
   B. Yes. I'd like a small chicken soup and a salad.
   C. Yes, it is.

4. Do you want something to drink with your sandwich?
   A. Yes, I'd like some french fries please.
   B. Yes, I'd like some ice cream.
   C. No, thank you.

5. What size lemonade?
   A. Large, please.
   B. No, thank you.
   C. Yes, it is.

TESTING FOCUS: Ignoring Distractions

- Tell students that especially during listening exercises, they need to learn to ignore other sounds or things going on in order to focus on what they are hearing.
- Practice this skill by taking students to a busy or noisy part of the building, such as a hallway or cafeteria. Repeat a long list of vocabulary items quickly, or read a paragraph with a great deal of information. Have students focus on your voice and take notes on what you say while ignoring distractions around them. Read the list or paragraph only once. Return to the classroom and discuss the exercise with students. How difficult was it? Were they able to focus better when they consciously made an effort to do so?
- Encourage students to practice this skill outside the classroom, listening to people speak in crowded places such as shopping malls and restaurants.

ANSWER KEY:

1. C; 2. A; 3. B; 4. C; 5. A

2 Listening Dictation 093

- Copy the numbers and lines from the Listening Dictation section on the board.
- Read the first sentence: *Can I help you?* Have a more advanced student write the sentence on the board on the line next to 1. Have students copy the sentence in their books.
- Play the audio and have students write the sentences they hear. Repeat as many times as necessary.
- Put students in pairs to compare answers.
- Have volunteers write the sentences on the board.

Unit 6: Lesson 7

LISTENING SCRIPT

Lesson 7, Activity 2: Listening Dictation

Listen and write the sentences you hear.

1. A: Can I help you?
   B: Yes, I'd like a turkey sandwich and a small coffee.
2. A: Can you bring me a glass of water, please?
   B: Sure. I'll get one for you right away.
3. A: Are you ready to order?
   B: Yes. I'd like the baked fish dinner and an orange juice.
4. A: Do you want something to drink with your green salad?
   B: Sure. I'll have a cup of tea.
5. A: What size soup would you like?
   B: Large, please.

❸ Grammar Review

- Go over the directions.
- Read the first sentence. Elicit the appropriate completion. Have students circle B for item 1.
- Have students answer the rest of the questions.
- Put students in pairs to compare answers.
- Go over the answers with the class.

ANSWER KEY:

1. B; 2. A; 3. A; 4. B; 5. C; 6. B

LEARNING LOG

- Point out the four sections of the Learning Log: *I know these words; I can ask; I can say;* and *I can write*.
- Have students check what they know and what they can do.
- Walk around to note what they don't know or can't do. Use this information to review areas of difficulty.

BIG PICTURE EXPANSION ACTIVITY: WRITING—Describing the Restaurant

- Have students look at the Big Picture in their books (Student Book pages 76–77).
- Ask the class: *What do you see in the restaurant? What are the people eating? What are the waiters doing?* Call on a few students to share their observations with the class.
- Tell the students to write a paragraph about the restaurant. Remind them to look at the Big Picture for ideas. They should use count and noncount nouns and quantifiers if possible.
- Ask students to read their paragraphs to a partner.
- Invite a few volunteers to read their sentences to the class.

Unit 6: Lesson 7

 BIG PICTURE EXPANSION ACTIVITY:
SPEAKING—Assessment: Talking about the Picture

- You can use the Big Picture on Student Book pages 76–77 to place new students in open entry classes, to diagnose difficulties, or to measure progress.

- Work with one student at a time and show them the Big Picture. Ask: *What do you see in the picture? Tell me about the picture*. Tell the student you want him or her to speak for as long as possible. Wait a moment for the student to prepare to answer. If the student has difficulty, you can use prompts: *What do you see in the restaurant? What are the people doing?*

- You can use a rubric like the one below to rate beginning speakers.

4	Exhibits confidence, begins speaking without prompting Uses some complex sentences, although may make mistakes with irregular forms Can use more than one tense
3	Uses sentences, although form may be incorrect Can speak for sustained length of time Responds to prompts, but doesn't need them to begin speaking
2	Can use nouns and verbs Uses phrases Answers informational questions
1	Can name objects Uses single words Can answer *yes/no* questions
0	Cannot say anything independently May be able to point to objects when prompted

TEACHER'S NOTES:

Things that students are doing well:

_____
_____
_____
_____

Things students need additional help with:

_____
_____
_____
_____

Ideas for further practice or for the next class:

_____
_____
_____
_____

UNIT 7 RELATIONSHIPS

UNIT OVERVIEW

LESSON	STUDENT BOOK PAGE	TEACHER'S EDITION PAGE
1. Identifying Relationships	88	139
2. Activities at a Wedding	90	143
3. Communicating in Social Situations	92	147
4. Family Traditions	94	151
5. Disagreeing Politely and Offering Help	96	154
6. Getting Along With Others	98	157
7. What Do You Know?	100	158

Big Picture Expansion Activities

FOCUS	TITLE	SUGGESTED USE
Speaking	What's wrong with it?	Lesson 2
Reading	Sylvia's Story	Lesson 4
Grammar	Word Forms	Lesson 5
Speaking	Assessment: Talking about the Big Picture	Lesson 7
Writing	Comparing Wedding Customs	Lesson 7

Big Picture Expansion Activity Worksheets

FOCUS	TITLE	TEACHER'S EDITION PAGE
13. Reading	Sylvia's Story	236
14. Grammar	Word Forms	237

LESSON 1: Identifying Relationships

OBJECTIVE
Identifying relationships

VOCABULARY

aunt	fiancée	nephew
boss	friend	niece
brother-in-law	grandparents	parents
cousin	landlady	uncle
co-worker	neighbors	

TARGET GRAMMAR

It's, its and *'s*   page 180

THINGS TO DO

1 Learn New Words 094

- Have students look at the family tree diagram and ask what it is and what it shows. Elicit the words they know. Direct their attention to the other pictures and elicit the words they know.
- Have students listen and look at the pictures while you say the words or play the audio.
- Instruct students to circle the words that are new to them.
- Say the words or play the audio a second time. Pause after each word and ask the students to repeat and point to the correct picture.
- Put students in pairs and have one say a word as the partner points to the correct picture. Reverse roles and repeat the activity.
- Call on students and ask questions: *Do you have an aunt? How many nephews do you have? Do you like your neighbors?*

LISTENING SCRIPT

Lesson 1, Activity 1: Learn New Words

Look at the pictures. Listen to the words. Listen again and repeat.

1. grandparents — Manuel and Maria are Juan's grandparents.
2. parents — Tito and Rosa are Juan's parents.
3. aunt — Lupe is Juan's aunt.
4. uncle — Richard is Juan's uncle.
5. cousin — Marco is Juan's cousin.
6. brother-in-law — Paul is Juan's brother-in-law.
7. nephew — Nick is Juan's nephew.
8. niece — Sofia is Juan's niece.
9. fiancée — Lisa is Juan's fiancée.
10. co-worker — Tom is Juan's co-worker.
11. boss — Mr. Li is Juan's boss.
12. friend — Joe is Juan's friend.
13. neighbors — Mr. and Mrs. Nath are Juan's neighbors.
14. landlady — Mrs. Chen is Juan's landlady.

Which words are new to you? Circle them.

TARGET GRAMMAR

It's, its and *'s*

The Target Grammar point is used in Activities and 3. Presentation and practice of this grammar point appears on *Student Book* page 180. Answer Keys appear on Teacher's Edition page 255.

Unit 7: Lesson 1

EXPANSION ACTIVITY: Talking Maps

- Draw a "talking map" on the board to illustrate the people you talk to in the course of the day. It may look something like the one below.
- Point out that a "talking map" can look like a cluster diagram, a real map, a timeline, or any other diagram that will show who the students talk to during the day and the relationships.

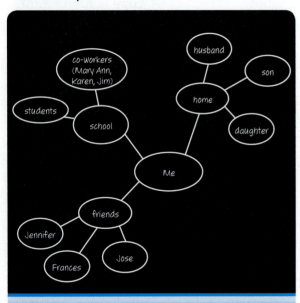

- Distribute paper and have students draw their own "talking maps." Ask them to indicate how much time they spend talking with each person.
- Put students in pairs to share their talking maps.
- Call on students to tell the class about their partners' "talking maps."

2 Listen and Circle *True* or *False* 095

- Go over the directions. Remind students to look at the pictures in the book while they are listening in order to answer each question.
- Play the audio. Pause after each conversation and have students circle *true* or *false*.
- Put students in pairs to compare answers. Play the audio again if necessary to have students confirm their answers.
- MULTI-LEVEL: If you have students at different levels, you may want to pair an advanced student with a less advanced student. The more proficient student can help the less proficient student locate the correct pictures for each question.
- Go over the answers with the class.

LISTENING SCRIPT

Lesson 1, Activity 2: Listen and Circle *True* or *False*

Listen to Juan describe his family relationships. Circle True or False.

My name is Juan. I'm going to tell you about my family.
1. My grandparents' names are Manuel and Maria.
2. One of their children is my Aunt Lupe.
3. Lupe is married to my uncle. His name is Marco.
4. My Aunt Lupe and Uncle Richard have one son. He is my cousin.
5. I have one brother-in-law. His name is Nick.
6. I have a niece, too. Her name is Sofia.

ANSWER KEY:

1. true; 2. true; 3. false; 4. true; 5. false; 6. true

Unit 7: Lesson 1

EXPANSION ACTIVITY: Cloze Spelling [Literacy]

- For students whose native alphabet is not the Roman alphabet, create a worksheet based on the Listening Script in Activity 2 to help them practice writing the correct letters for the sounds they hear. You can use blanks in place of entire words or in place of individual letters. Make your own worksheet or use the sentences below.
- Have students listen to the audio and complete the worksheet.
- Put students in pairs to compare the letters and words they used to complete the worksheet.
- Go over the answers. Pronounce any words for which students have trouble writing the correct letters. Review the sound-letter connection for individual letters, blends, and digraphs as needed.
- Use sentences like these:
  1. My ___arents' name___ are Man___ and ___ia.
  2. One ___ their ___ildren is ___ Aunt ___upe.
  3. Lu___e is marrie___ to my ___ncle. ___ name is ___arco.
  4. My ___ Lupe and Uncle Ri___ard have ___ son. H___ is my ___ousin.
  5. ___ have one ___other-in-l___. His name ___ Nick.
  6. I ha___e a niece, ___. H___ name is ___ofia.

❸ Practice the Conversation 096

- Have students listen and look at the conversation while you read it or play the audio.
- Say the words or play the audio a second time. Pause after each line and ask the students to repeat.
- Check comprehension by asking questions: *Who is having a conversation? What are they talking about?*
- Model the conversation with a student. Have the student read B's lines. Demonstrate how to substitute from the ideas in the boxes below. Cue the student to make the appropriate substitutions.
- Have students work in pairs to practice the conversation, making substitutions from the boxes and using their own ideas.
- Walk around to make sure students understand the activity and provide help if needed.

LISTENING SCRIPT

Lesson 1, Activity 3: Practice the Conversation

Listen to the conversation. Listen again and repeat.

A: Is this your coat?
B: No, it's not mine. It's Maria's.
A: Who is Maria?
B: She's Juan's grandmother.

Unit 7: Lesson 1

EXPANSION ACTIVITY: Whose is it?
[Challenge]

- Divide the class into small groups. For each group, provide them with a set of small cards that are labeled as follows: *Manuel, Maria, Richard, Lupe, Tito, Rosa, Marta.*
- Write the following conversation on the board:

> A: Is this your notebook?
> B: No, it's not mine. It's <u>Lupe's husband's</u>.
> A: Who is <u>Lupe's husband</u>?
> B: <u>He's Richard</u>.

- Have students note the similarities and differences between this conversation and the one in Activity 3.
- To demonstrate the activity, draw cards at random from one of the groups and model the new conversation orally, writing it on the board if needed. For example: Manuel/Rosa: *A: Is this your notebook? B: No, it's not mine. It's Manuel's daughter-in-law's. A: Who is Manuel's daughter-in-law? She's Rosa.* Point out that the new names, relationships, and sometimes pronouns should replace the underlined words in the model conversation.
- One at a time, have each student in each group choose two cards at random and create a new conversation based on the model. Challenge students to reverse the names and repeat the same conversation. For example: Rosa/Manuel: *A: Is this your notebook? B: No, it's not mine. It's Rosa's father-in-law's. A: Who is Rosa's father-in-law? He's Manuel.*

Grammar/Vocabulary Note:

- To complete the Expansion Activity, some students may need to review proper use of apostrophe-*s* for possessives, as well as the titles that signify various family relationships (mother-in-law, sister-in-law, and so on). Be sure to explain that sometimes when using multiple possessives, such as *Lupe's husband's*, we leave out the implied object (*Lupe's husband's notebook*).

Pronunciation Note:

- Point out that the answers to the questions in Activity 3 will involve using contractions (*She's*) and possessive nouns (*Juan's*). Remind students to stress the ending -*s* sounds so that their listeners can hear this important information.

4 Write

- Go over the directions and the examples.
- Distribute paper and have students draw tree diagrams for their families.
- Put students in pairs and have them share the information in their diagrams.

EXPANSION ACTIVITY: Genealogy Stories

- Explain to students that many Americans research their genealogy and identify strongly with their cultural backgrounds and ancestors, keeping alive customs from other countries, cultures, and foregone centuries. Many people make extensive family trees that go back hundreds of years.
- Ask students to share stories about their ancestors. How did they hear these stories? Were they passed down by word of mouth, or are there written documents verifying the stories?
- Try to find out who in the class can tell a story about an ancestor from the furthest back in time. You may wish to share a story of your own or show students genealogical records and documents from your family.

LESSON 2 Activities at a Wedding

OBJECTIVE
Activities at a wedding

VOCABULARY

bride	hug	make a toast
dance	in a bad mood	musicians
gifts	in a good mood	photographer
groom	kiss	shake hands

TARGET GRAMMAR
Possessive pronouns and object pronouns *page 181*

THINGS TO DO

1 Learn New Words 097

- Have students look at the Big Picture in their books (Student Book pages 90–91). Ask students what the picture is of and elicit the words that they know.
- Have students listen and look at the pictures while you say the words or play the audio.
- Instruct students to circle the words that are new to them.
- Say the words or play the audio a second time. Pause after each word or phrase and ask the students to repeat and point to the correct part of the picture.
- Put students in pairs and have one say a word or phrase as the partner points to the correct part of the picture. Reverse roles and repeat the activity.
- Call on students and ask questions, using the new vocabulary: *Is a bride a man or a woman? What does a photographer do? Do you like to dance?*

LISTENING SCRIPT

Lesson 2, Activity 1: Learn New Words

Look at the picture. Listen to the words. Listen again and repeat.

1. bride — Where's the bride?
2. groom — Where's the groom?
3. kiss — Who is kissing Marta?
4. musicians — Where are the musicians?
5. in a bad mood — Who is in a bad mood?
6. make a toast — Who is making a toast?
7. gifts — Where are the gifts?
8. photographer — Where's the photographer?
9. in a good mood — Who is in a good mood?
10. dance — Who is dancing?
11. hug — Who is Joe hugging?
12. shake hands — Who is shaking hands with Ron?

EXPANSION ACTIVITY: What kind of word is it?

- Write the headings *Nouns, Verbs,* and *Adjectives* on the board.
- Put students in pairs and have them write the words from Activity 1 under the appropriate headings. Point out that in the phrases (shake hands) there will be more than one type of word. They should write *shake* under *Verbs* and *hands* under *Nouns.*
- Have students list other words they know in the picture under the appropriate headings.
- When students have finished their lists, elicit the words in each category and write them on the board.

STUDENT BOOK PAGES 90–91

Unit 7: Lesson 2

2 Listen and Circle 098

- Go over the directions. Remind students to look at the pictures in the book while they are listening in order to answer each question.
- Play the audio. Pause after each conversation and have students circle the correct name.
- Put students in pairs to compare answers. Play the audio again if necessary to have students confirm their answers.
- LOW-LEVEL: For students who have trouble with listening comprehension, provide the listening script for them. Have them read the listening script while listening to the audio. Then, pause the audio after each sentence if necessary to allow students to scan the picture to answer the question.
- Go over the answers with the class.

LISTENING SCRIPT

Lesson 2, Activity 2: Listen and Circle

Listen and circle the correct name.

1. He's in a good mood.
2. She's dancing with Tito.
3. She's the bride.
4. He's standing next to the food.
5. He's kissing Marta.
6. He's shaking Ron's hand.
7. He's talking to the photographer.
8. He is making a toast.

ANSWER KEY:

1. Ted; 2. Sylvia; 3. Lisa; 4. Nick; 5. Thomas; 6. Bill; 7. Mr. Li; 8. Richard

EXPANSION ACTIVITY: What's happening? [Low-Level]

- Write the following chart on the board:

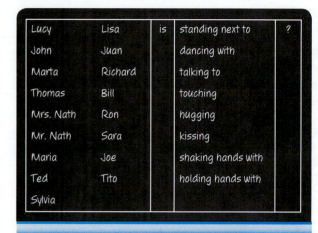

- Have students create at least five sentences based on the picture using the chart. Have them choose a subject, an action, and replace the question mark with an appropriate person or object.
- Model an example or two on the board. For example: *Mrs. Nath is standing next to Mr. Nath* or *Mrs. Nath is standing next to the table*.
- Have students cross out each subject when they use it in a sentence.
- Have partners read their sentences to each other and identify each person in the picture.
- As a further challenge, have students convert their sentences into questions. For example: *Who is standing next to Mr. Nath?* Put students in new pairs to ask and answer questions based on their sentences.

Unit 7: Lesson 2

3 Talk About the Picture

- Have students look at the Big Picture in their books (Student Book pages 90–91).
- To set the context, ask questions about the picture: *How many people do you see? Where are they? What are they doing?* Write any additional vocabulary on the board.
- Ask students to write five sentences about the picture. Remind them to use the words on the board or in Activity 1 if they need help.
- Walk around the room and provide help as needed.
- Put students in pairs. Have them take turns reading their sentences.
- Call on students to read sentences to the class.

EXPANSION ACTIVITY: Compare Traditions [Challenge]

- Put students in small groups of three or four. If possible, group students so that they are with others from similar countries of origin or backgrounds.
- Have students list wedding traditions that are typical of their culture. Have them use the picture and the statements they wrote in Activity 3 for ideas.
- Call on representatives from each group to talk about their traditions.
- As an alternative, after the groups have discussed their traditions, pair each student with someone from a different cultural background. Have them compare and contrast traditions.

BIG PICTURE EXPANSION ACTIVITY: SPEAKING—What's wrong with it?

- Explain that in this activity, students will create incorrect sentences that their partners will correct.
- Model the activity by making an incorrect statement about the picture: *The musicians are dancing* and have students correct you verbally (*The musicians are playing music*).
- Have students write five sentences about the picture that are incorrect.
- Then put students in pairs and have them take turns saying incorrect statements and correcting their partners' statements.
- Call on students to say sentences to the class and elicit the corrections from their classmates.
- As an alternative, divide the class into teams and have each team create incorrect statements. Have members from each team challenge other teams by saying statements and eliciting corrections. A team earns a point when it stumps the other team.

4 Practice the Conversation 099

- Have students listen and look at the conversation while you read it or play the audio.
- Say the words or play the audio a second time. Pause after each line and ask the students to repeat.
- Check comprehension by asking questions: *Who is having a conversation? Who are they talking about?*
- Model the conversation with a student. Have the student read B's lines. Demonstrate how to substitute from the ideas in the boxes below. Cue the student to make the appropriate substitutions.
- Have students work in pairs to practice the conversation, making substitutions from the boxes and using their own ideas.
- Walk around to make sure students understand the activity and provide help if needed.

Unit 7: Lesson 2

LISTENING SCRIPT

Lesson 2, Activity 4: Practice the Conversation

Listen to the conversation. Listen again and repeat.

A: Look at Tito!

B: Who's dancing with him?

A: That's the mother of the bride.

A: Do you know her?

B: Yes, I do. She's very friendly.

 TARGET GRAMMAR

Possessive pronouns and object pronouns

The Target Grammar point is used in Activity 4. Presentation and practice of this grammar point appears on *Student Book* pages 181–182. Answer keys appear on Teacher's Edition page 256.

EXPANSION ACTIVITY: Personal Photos

- Have students bring in photos of graduations, weddings, and other events, or have them draw pictures of typical family events.

- Model the activity with a picture of your own. Walk around and display the photo. Elicit questions from the students: *Who's that sitting next to you? That's my aunt. What's her name? Kathy.*

- Put students in pairs to practice asking and answering questions about their partners' pictures.

LESSON 3: Communicating in Social Situations

OBJECTIVE
Communicating in social situations

VOCABULARY

apologize	criticize	take care of
ask for advice	disagree	talk back
compliment	interrupt	yell at

TARGET GRAMMAR
Indefinite pronouns *page 183*

THINGS TO DO

1 Learn New Words 🎧 100

- Have students look at the pictures and tell what the people are doing. Elicit the vocabulary words they already know.
- Have students listen and look at the pictures while you say the words or play the audio.
- Instruct students to circle the words that are new to them.
- Say the words or play the audio a second time. Pause after each word or phrase and ask the students to repeat and point to the correct picture.
- Put students in pairs and have one say a word or phrase as the partner points to the correct picture. Reverse roles and repeat the activity.
- Call on students and ask questions: *Do you think children should talk back to their parents? Who do you ask for advice?*

LISTENING SCRIPT

Lesson 3, Activity 1: Learn New Words

Look at the pictures. Listen to the words. Listen again and repeat.

1.	ask for advice	He's asking her for advice.
2.	take care of	She's taking care of her grandmother.
3.	compliment	He's complimenting her work.
4.	apologize	He's apologizing.
5.	disagree	They disagree about the food.
6.	yell at	He yelled at the man to slow down.
7.	criticize	He criticized the painter's work.
8.	talk back	The boy talked back to his mother.
9.	interrupt	He interrupted them.

Which words are new to you?
Circle them.

EXPANSION ACTIVITY: When is it appropriate?

- Put students in pairs or small groups to brainstorm situations in which they would do each of the communicative tasks in Activity 1. Note that they may decide that it is never appropriate to engage in some types of communication (for example, talking back).
- Call on representatives from each group to tell the class about their ideas.

STUDENT BOOK PAGES 92-93

Unit 7: Lesson 3

Culture Notes:
- Your students may notice cultural differences in the way that people communicate. For example, people in this country sometimes talk back in situations that would be completely inappropriate in other cultures.
- You may want to point out that disagreement and constructive criticism are generally perceived as healthy in this culture, although yelling at others and talking back are less acceptable.

2 Listen and Write 101

- Go over the directions and the words.
- Play the audio. Pause after each conversation and have students write the number next to the correct word.
- Put students in pairs to compare answers. Play the audio again if necessary to have students confirm their answers.
- Go over the answers with the class.

LISTENING SCRIPT

Lesson 3, Activity 2: Listen and Write

Listen to the conversations. Number the words and phrases from 1–5.

1. A: It's time to go to bed now.
   B: No! I want to stay up and play!
2. A: Wow! You look beautiful in that dress!
   B: Thank you!
3. A: You are so lazy! And you are late every day.
   B: I will try to work harder.
4. A: I'm sorry I forgot to call you yesterday.
   B: That's okay.
5. A: I think this is a great car.
   B: Really? I don't like it!

ANSWER KEY:

- 2 compliment
- 4 apologize
- 5 disagree
- 3 criticize
- 1 talk back

EXPANSION ACTIVITY: Dictation Dialogues [Challenge]

- Play the audio from Activity 2 as a dictation exercise and have students copy down each conversation.
- Put students in pairs to check their work.
- Have volunteers write each conversation on the board and have students peer-correct any errors in spelling or grammar.
- Put students in small groups and assign each group one of the conversations.
- Have the group expand on the conversation by writing additional dialogue that happens either before or after the conversation itself. Students may also add dialogue that happens both before and after the conversation.
- Have groups perform their dialogues for the class.

Unit 7: Lesson 3

3. Practice the Conversation 102

- Have students listen and look at the conversation while you read it or play the audio.
- Say the words or play the audio a second time. Pause after each line and ask the students to repeat.
- Check comprehension by asking questions: *How was B's day? What happened?*
- Model the conversation with a student. Have the student read A's lines. Demonstrate how to substitute from the ideas in the boxes below. Cue the student to make the appropriate substitutions.
- Have students work in pairs to practice the conversation, making substitutions from the boxes.
- Walk around to make sure students understand the activity and provide help if needed.
- Call on volunteers to read one of the variations aloud.

LISTENING SCRIPT

Lesson 3, Activity 3: Practice the Conversation

Listen to the conversation. Listen again and repeat.

A: How was your day?

B: Not so good.

A: What happened?

B: My boss criticized me.

A: That's too bad. What did he say?

B: He said I was careless.

EXPANSION ACTIVITY: Lifestyles of the Rich and Famous [Multi-Level]

- Have students work in groups to rewrite the conversation. Have each group choose three famous people to be person B. Person A should be a friend who is speaking to the famous person.
- Have lower level students suggest the response for how person B is feeling (*great, terrible, fantastic, and so on*), as well as the response person A gives (*that's too bad, great, really?*). Have more advanced students suggest what happened to person B, as well as what the person said to person B.
- Remind students to change the pronouns to *she* as necessary. Encourage students to include extra details in their conversations to make them more interesting.
- Model a conversation on the board. For example:

Person B: Michael Jordan

A: How was your day?

B: Amazing!

A: What happened?

B: I got a letter from one of my fans, a 10-year-old boy.

A: Wow, that's great. What did he say?

B: He said I was the greatest basketball player ever. That really made me feel good.

- Have groups share one or more of their dialogues with the class.

Unit 7: Lesson 3

4 Interview

- Go over the directions and the chart.
- Put students in small groups and have each students in the group interview each other.
- Have groups share any interesting stories that they heard with the class. Students may also wish to tell about ideas on which they completely agreed or disagreed.

> **EXPANSION ACTIVITY: Vote with Your Feet**
>
> - Write *AGREE* on one side of the board and *DISAGREE* on the other.
> - Call a group of students to the front of the class. Tell them that you will read some statements aloud, and they should stand in front of the word that expresses their opinion.
> - Make statements. Create your own or use the ones below. Remind students to move to one side of the board or the other. Call on students to explain their positions.
> - After reading several statements, call a new group of students to the board and repeat the procedure.
> - Possible statements: *It is okay to talk back to your boss if he or she is wrong. You shouldn't disagree with your husband or wife. Parents shouldn't yell at their children. Teachers need to yell at students sometimes. It is okay to ask a friend for advice. It is not okay to ask your children for advice. You shouldn't compliment people too much. If your boss disagrees with you, you should apologize. Children must take care of their parents when they get old.*
> - LOW-LEVEL: For students who may have trouble with listening comprehension, allow them to participate by reading aloud written statements for their classmates instead of reading the statements yourself. After each statement has been read and students have voted, ask the reader a simple question to test his or her comprehension of the question or about how he or she would answer the question.

TARGET GRAMMAR

Indefinite pronouns:
The Target Grammar point is used in Activity 4. Presentation and practice of this grammar point appears on *Student Book* page 183. Answer Keys appear on Teacher's Edition page 256.

LESSON 4 — Family Traditions

OBJECTIVE
Family traditions

TARGET GRAMMAR
Can, could, would, and *may* for requests and offers   page 184

WINDOW ON MATH
Calculating Time Changes

THINGS TO DO

1 Predict
- Have students look at the title and the pictures. Remind them that we can often guess what a reading will be about by looking at it before we read it.
- Have the students read the sentences in Activity 1, or read each sentence aloud and have students repeat.
- Have students check *I think so* or *I don't think so* after each sentence.
- Have students read the interview, or read the interview aloud as they read along. Have students check their answers as you read.
- Go over the answers with the class. Have students show where in the reading they found the information for each answer.

EXPANSION ACTIVITY: Creative Descriptions
- Have students look at the picture of The Four Brothers on page 95.
- Have students write sentences or paragraphs using their imaginations to describe the people in the photo. Tell students that they can invent any details they wish, such as favorite activities, places the group has traveled, and so on. Students may describe the group as a whole or individuals from the group.

- **LOW-LEVEL:** Have students in pairs make a list of things they see in the picture using words they already know or a bilingual dictionary. If possible, have them write simple sentences about the picture, such as: *There are five men; One man is wearing a hat;* and so on.
- Have students present their ideas to the class. Lead a discussion about how students imagined the people's lives differently.

2 Read and Take Notes
- Have students read the interview again and complete the sentences.
- Have students check their answers with a partner.
- Go over the answers with the class.

ANSWER KEY:
1. questions.
2. eleven.
3. Australia.
4. Conti.
5. Italian.
6. custom.

TARGET GRAMMAR
Can, could, would, and *may* for requests and offers

The Target Grammar point is used in Activity 2. Presentation and practice of this grammar point appears on *Student Book* pages 184–185. Answer Keys appear on Teacher's Edition page 256.

Unit 7: Lesson 4

Pronunciation Note:

- You may notice that students have trouble reading long sentences aloud. Point out that native speakers don't read or say long sentences very quickly. Instead, we say groups of words quickly. These groups of words usually represent a thought group (prepositional phrases, short sentences, long verb phrases, or long noun phrases). As students complete the Reading Practice expansion for Activity 2, encourage them to say phrases fluently and quickly, pausing when natural for breathing and for cueing the listener that information is beginning or ending.

EXPANSION ACTIVITY: Reading Practice [Low-Level]

- Read the interview aloud line by line. Have students make a slash whenever they hear you pause to take a breath. Read naturally, but pause long enough for them to notice the pause.
- Go over where they should have marked the text. Point out that you paused at periods and commas. Point out that in long sentences, you paused to make the text more understandable. For example, you could pause before *Like borrowing things without asking or taking too long in the bathroom*, and so on.
- Put students in pairs and have them read the interview aloud, pausing briefly at the slash marks to practice natural phrasing. Then have them switch roles.

BIG PICTURE EXPANSION ACTIVITY: Reading—Sylvia's Story

- Make copies of Worksheet 13 (Teacher's Edition page 236) and distribute them to students.
- Have students look at the Big Picture in their books (Student Book pages 90–91)
- Instruct students to complete the activities and then check their answers with a partner.
- Go over the answers with the class.

ANSWER KEY:

A. 1. False; 2. True; 3. True; 4. True; 5. False; 6. True

❸ Write

- Go over the directions and the questions.
- Have students write two more questions.
- Put students in pairs and have them take turns asking and answering the questions. Remind them to write down their partners' answers.
- Have students copy the questions and answers on a separate piece of paper in an interview format. Remind them to use the interview on page 95 as a model.
- When students have written up their interview, have them exchange their interviews with their partners to check that the write-ups are correct.
- Have volunteers reenact their interviews for the class.

Unit 7: Lesson 4

EXPANSION ACTIVITY: Guess Who?
[Multi-Level]

- Collect the interviews that students wrote in Activity 3.
- Have two volunteers come to the front of the class and read one of the interviews aloud, with one student playing the role of the interviewer and the other playing the student answering the questions. Make sure the readers do not tell which students they are playing.
- Have the class guess who each pair of volunteers is portraying. After students have guessed, have the original students from the interview stand up to reveal the answer.

EXPANSION ACTIVITY: Pin the Clock on the Map

- Draw a small clock and cut it out.
- Display a large map on a bulletin board.
- Have students take turns pinning the clock on the map using a push pin. Blindfold each student first or have the students close their eyes so they cannot see where they are pinning the clock.
- Have students look at the country where they pinned the clock and tell what time it is there compared to where you live. Students may need to consult a time zone chart to do this if your map is not divided into time zones.

WINDOW ON MATH
Calculating Time Changes

- Go over the information and the example in the box.
- Have students calculate the times and write their answers.
- Put students in pairs to check their answers.
- Go over the answers with the class.

ANSWER KEY:

1. 11 A.M.; 2. 10 P.M.; 3. 1 P.M.

LESSON 5  Disagreeing Politely and Offering Help

OBJECTIVE
Disagreeing politely and offering help

PRONUNCIATION
Suffixes and Syllable Stress

1 Practice Pronunciation: Suffixes and Syllable Stress 🎧 103

A. Listen to the words and underline the syllable that receives the most stress. Listen again and repeat.

- Go over the directions and the information in the box.
- Have students look at the words while you say them or play the audio.
- Say the words or play the audio a second time, pausing after each word to have students repeat.
- Read the words or play the audio a third time, and have students underline the stressed syllable.
- Go over the answers with the class.

LISTENING SCRIPT

Lesson 5, Activity 1: Practice Pronunciation: Suffixes and Syllable Stress

A. Listen to the words and underline the syllable that receives the most stress. Listen again and repeat.

Base word	+ suffix
1. problem	problematic
2. tradition	traditional
3. apology	apologize
4. critic	criticize
5. invite	invitation
6. marry	marital
7. music	musician
8. photograph	photographic

ANSWER KEY:

A.
1. <u>prob</u> lem   prob le <u>mat</u> ic
2. tra <u>di</u> tion   tra <u>di</u> tion al
3. a <u>pol</u> o gy   a <u>pol</u> o gize
4. <u>crit</u> ic   <u>crit</u> i cize
5. in <u>vite</u>   in vi <u>ta</u> tion
6. <u>mar</u> ry   <u>mar</u> i tal
7. <u>mu</u> sic   mu <u>si</u> cian
8. <u>pho</u> to graph   pho to <u>graph</u> ic

B. Write the words in the correct place in the chart.

- Have students work individually to write the words in the chart.
- Have students compare their charts with a partner.
- Go over the answers with the class.

ANSWER KEY:

B.

-ic suffix	-ize suffix	-al suffix	-ion / -ian suffix
problematic	apologize criticize	marital traditional	identification invitation musician

Which suffixes change the syllable stress?
<u>-ic, -ion, and -ian</u>

Unit 7: Lesson 5

BIG PICTURE EXPANSION ACTIVITY:
Grammar—Word Forms

- Make copies of Worksheet 14 (Teacher's Editon page 237) and distribute them to students.
- Have students look at the Big Picture in their books (Student Book pages 90–91).
- Instruct students to complete the activities and then check their answers with a partner.
- Go over the answers with the class.
- Have students read the sentences aloud. Remind them to focus on their pronunciation. Correct if necessary.

ANSWER KEY:

1. customs; 2. customary; 3. photograph;
4. religious; 5. respect; 6. musical; 7. invited;
8. employer; 9. apologized; 10. problematic

❷ Practice the Conversation: Disagreeing Politely 🎧 104

- Show students the picture in the book for Activity 2. To set the context, ask questions about the picture: *Who is in the picture? Where are they?*
- Read the conversation or play the audio.
- Read or play the conversation again. Pause after each sentence and ask students to repeat.
- To confirm understanding, ask comprehension questions about the conversation: *Who likes the movie? What does B think?*
- Point out that there are four pieces of scripted information in the conversation that can be substituted: two statements about A's opinion, one about B's opinion, and a suggestion.
- Model the conversation with a student. You read A's part and have the student read B's lines. Demonstrate how to substitute *terrific pizza* and *think it's delicious* from the first box below. Cue the student to suggest *too salty*, then respond by suggesting *order from the other restaurant*.
- Put students in pairs to practice the conversation, making substitutions from the boxes and using their own ideas.
- Walk around to monitor the activity and provide help as needed.

LISTENING SCRIPT

Lesson 5, Activity 2: Practice the Conversation: Disagreeing Politely

Listen to the conversation. Listen again and repeat.

A: This is a great movie.

B: Do you really think so?

A: Yes, I love it. Don't you?

B: No, not really. I think it's kind of boring.

A: Okay. Let's watch the other movie.

B: Okay!

EXPANSION ACTIVITY: Mingle [Multi-Level]

- Have students think of their favorite movie, book, song, teacher, subject, or sport.
- Have students write down a statement of their opinion and then memorize it.
- Model the activity. State an opinion: *Joe's Burgers is a great restaurant*. Call on a student and cue him or her to continue the conversation as in Activity 1. Elicit an opposing opinion: (*I think the food is too fattening*). For less advanced students, appropriate responses may be shorter statements (*I disagree*) or restatements of the speaker's opinion (*You think Joe's Burgers is a great restaurant*.)
- Have students stand and walk around the room, taking turns stating their opinions and expressing disagreement. Encourage them to interact with as many people as they can in the time allowed.

Unit 7: Lesson 5

❸ Practice the Conversation: Offering to Help 🎧 105

- Repeat the basic procedure from Activity 2.
- To set the context, ask questions about the picture: *Who do you see? What are they talking about?*
- After students have listened to and repeated the conversation line by line, check comprehension by asking: *What did A offer to do?*
- Have students continue practicing the conversation, making substitutions from the boxes and using their own ideas.
- CHALLENGE: For students at a more advanced level, have them continue the conversation by improvising new dialogue. Tell them to imagine that the people talking are going to do a new activity now. Have person B suggest the new action and person A either accept or decline.

> **LISTENING SCRIPT**
>
> **Lesson 5, Activity 3: Practice the Conversation: Offering to Help**
>
> *Listen to the conversation. Listen again and repeat.*
>
> A: Can I help you with the dishes?
>
> B: Thanks for offering, but I'm all set.
>
> A: Is there something else I can do?
>
> B: Well, you could clear the kitchen table.
>
> A: Sure. I'd be happy to clear it!

❹ Practice the Conversation: Asking for Clarification 🎧 106

- Repeat the basic procedure from Activity 2.
- To set the context, ask questions about the picture: *Who do you see? What are they doing?*
- After students have listened to and repeated the conversation line by line, check comprehension by asking: *What does A ask B to do? How does B respond?*
- Have students continue practicing the conversation, making substitutions from the boxes and using their own ideas.

> **LISTENING SCRIPT**
>
> **Lesson 5, Activity 4: Practice the Conversation: Asking for Clarification**
>
> *Listen to the conversation. Listen again and repeat.*
>
> A: Could you mail this invitation for me?
>
> B: Sure. No problem.
>
> A: It needs to get there by tomorrow.
>
> B: So should I send it by Express Mail?
>
> A: Yes, that would be great.
>
> B: Okay. I'll go to the post office now to send it.

LESSON 6: Getting Along with Others

OBJECTIVE
Getting along with others

1 Preview and Check *True* or *False*

- Read the directions and go over the statements with students.
- Have students scan the title and the photograph on page 99 and check *True* or *False*.
- Have partners compare their answers.
- Go over the answers with the class. Have volunteers tell why they chose the answers they did.

ANSWER KEY:
1. True; 2. False; 3. False; 4. True;

2 Read and Match

- Go over the directions.
- Have students read the article and complete the matching exercise.
- Have students check their answers with a partner.
- Go over the answers with the class.

ANSWER KEY:
1. d; 2. a; 3. f; 4. b; 5. e; 6. h; 7. c; 8. g

EXPANSION ACTIVITY: That Depends [Challenge]

- Introduce students to the phrase *that depends*. Explain that we use it when our response to something might change based on what happens.
- Write a model question and answer on the board. For example:
  - Q. Do you agree that you shouldn't take things personally?
  - A. That depends. It's true that sometimes co-workers are just in a bad mood. But sometimes co-workers say things to hurt your feelings on purpose.
- Put students in groups to discuss the suggestions from the article. Have them tell whether they disagree with any of the ideas, using the phrase *that depends*.
- Have groups report to the class about any interesting scenarios they discussed.

3 Interview

- Go over the directions and the chart.
- Put students in pairs and have them ask and answer questions to complete the chart about their partners.
- Have volunteers tell the class about their partners.

EXPANSION ACTIVITY: Setting Goals

- Have students look at their results from the chart in Activity 3. Ask them if there are any areas where they could improve their performance at work.
- Have students write sentences or a paragraph telling how their performance could be better. Then, have them write two or three specific strategies to improve their performance.
- LOW-LEVEL: Help students complete sentence frames such as the following to tell about their work performance and goals: *I can <verb> better if I <action>. I shouldn't <verb> at work because <reason>. I will improve <problem> by <solution>.*
- Students may share their ideas with a partner or in groups if desired.

LESSON 7: What Do You Know?

1 Listening Review 107

- Go over the directions with the class.
- Read the items or play the audio and have the students mark their answers on the Answer Sheet.
- Walk around to monitor the activity and help students stay on task.
- Have students check their answers with a partner.
- Go over the answers with the class.

LISTENING SCRIPT

Lesson 7, Activity 1: Listening Review

Look at the pictures and listen. Choose the correct answer: A, B, or C. Use the Answer Sheet.

1. A: This is Mrs. Sanchez. She's my landlady.
   B: Nice to meet you, Mrs. Sanchez.
2. A: Where do your grandparents live?
   B: In California.
3. A: Look at Barbara!
   B: Who's that dancing with her?
   A: That's one of her friends.
4. A: Where's the photographer?
   B: She's over there by the gifts.
5. A: How was your day?
   B: Not so good.
   A: What happened?
   B: My daughter talked back to me.

TESTING FOCUS: Using Visuals to Aid Comprehension

- Have students look at the pictures. Elicit the words for family relationships that they know.
- Tell them that pictures and other visuals can help them to understand the context of something they are listening to. Explain that they will comprehend more if they use their background knowledge before they listen to or read something.
- Ask them to predict what the listening will be about using the picture.

ANSWER KEY:

1. C; 2. A; 3. C; 4. A; 5. B

2 Listening Dictation 108

- Copy the numbers and lines from the Listening Dictation section on the board.
- Read the first sentence: *How many cousins do you have?* Have a more advanced student write the sentence on the board on the line next to 1. Have students copy the sentence in their books.
- Play the audio and have students write the sentences they hear. Repeat as many times as necessary.
- Put students in pairs to compare answers.
- Have volunteers write the sentences on the board.

158 • UNIT 7   STUDENT BOOK PAGES 100–101

Unit 7: Lesson 7

LISTENING SCRIPT

Lesson 7, Activity 2: Listening Dictation

Listen and write the sentences you hear.

1. A: How many cousins do you have?
   B: Twelve.
2. A: Who's shaking Bill's hand?
   B: That's Ron.
3. A: Do you know him?
   B: Yes, I do. He's a nice guy.
4. A: How was your day?
   B: Not so good. My boss criticized me.
5. A: Can I help you clean the house?
   B: Thanks for offering, but I'm all set.

❸ Grammar Review

- Go over the directions.
- Read the first sentence. Elicit the appropriate completion. Have students circle C for item 1.
- Have students answer the rest of the questions.
- Put students in pairs to compare answers.
- Go over the answers with the class.

> **ANSWER KEY:**
>
> 1. C; 2. B; 3. B; 4. B; 5. A; 6. B

LEARNING LOG

- Point out the four sections of the Learning Log: *I know these words; I can ask; I can say;* and *I can write.*
- Have students check what they know and what they can do.
- Walk around to note what they don't know or can't do. Use this information to review areas of difficulty.

BIG PICTURE EXPANSION Activity: SPEAKING— Assessment: Talking about the Picture

- You can use the Big Picture on Student Book pages 90–91 to place new students in open entry classes, to diagnose difficulties, or to measure progress.
- Work with one student at a time and show them the Big Picture. Ask: *What do you see in the picture? Tell me about the picture.* Tell the student you want him or her to speak for as long as possible. Wait a moment for the student to prepare to answer. If the student has difficulty, you can use prompts: *What do you see in the picture? Who do you see in the picture? What are the people doing?*
- You can use a rubric like the one below to rate beginning speakers.

4	Exhibits confidence, begins speaking without prompting Uses some complex sentences, although may make mistakes with irregular forms Can use more than one tense
3	Uses sentences, although form may be incorrect Can speak for sustained length of time Responds to prompts, but doesn't need them to begin speaking
2	Can use nouns and verbs Uses phrases Answers informational questions
1	Can name objects Uses single words Can answer *yes/no* questions
0	Cannot say anything independently May be able to point to objects when prompted

Unit 7: Lesson 7

 BIG PICTURE EXPANSION ACTIVITY:
Writing—Comparing Wedding Customs

- Have students look at the Big Picture in their books (Student Book pages 90–91).
- Ask the class questions: *What do you see at this wedding? Do you have any of these customs? Did you go to a wedding? What was it like?*
- Model the activity for the students. Tell about a wedding you went to. Write comparative sentences on the board: *I went to my sister's wedding. Her wedding was bigger than Juan's wedding. My sister wore a longer dress than I did.*
- Write headings on the board: *Juan and Lisa's wedding*, and _____ *wedding*. Tell students to copy the headings on a piece of paper and write in the name of the people whose wedding they attended.
- Have students brainstorm ideas and write them under the headings.
- Have students write a paragraph comparing the two weddings.
- Put students in pairs to take turns reading their paragraphs to their partners.

TEACHER'S NOTES:

Things that students are doing well:
_____
_____
_____
_____
_____
_____

Things students need additional help with:
_____
_____
_____
_____
_____
_____

Ideas for further practice or for the next class:
_____
_____
_____
_____
_____
_____
_____
_____

UNIT 8: HEALTH

UNIT OVERVIEW

LESSON	STUDENT BOOK PAGE	TEACHER'S EDITION PAGE
1. Identifying Body Parts	102	162
2. Describing Illnesses and Injuries	104	165
3. Activities in an Emergency Room	106	168
4. Reading Medicine Labels	108	172
5. Talking to Health Professionals	110	176
6. Reading a Medical Advertisement	112	179
7. What Do You Know?	114	180

Big Picture Expansion Activities

FOCUS	TITLE	SUGGESTED USE
Grammar	*Should* and *Shouldn't*	Lesson 2
Speaking	Patient and Doctor	Lesson 3
Reading	Doctor's Orders	Lesson 4
Speaking	Assessment: Talking about the Big Picture	Lesson 7
Writing	What happened at the ER?	Lesson 7

Big Picture Expansion Activity Worksheets

FOCUS	TITLE	TEACHER'S EDITION PAGE
15. Grammar	*Should* and *Shouldn't*	238
16. Reading	Doctor's Orders	239

LESSON 1: Identifying Body Parts

OBJECTIVE
Identifying body parts

VOCABULARY

back	hip	skin
bone	joint	tooth
brain	lungs	waist
heart	muscle	wrist

TARGET GRAMMAR

Can and *could* for ability *page 186*

THINGS TO DO

1 Learn New Words 109

- Have students look at the diagram of the body and elicit the words they know. Make sure they can name ankle, arm, chest, ear, elbow, eye, finger, foot, hand, head, knee, leg, mouth, nose, shoulder, stomach, toe, throat, and wrist. Point out that the review vocabulary is labeled on the illustration.
- Have students listen and look at the pictures while you say the words or play the audio.
- Have students circle words that are new to them.
- Say the words or play the audio a second time. Pause after each word and ask the students to repeat the word and point to the correct picture.
- Put students in pairs and have one say a word as the partner points to the correct picture. Reverse roles and repeat the activity.
- Call on students and ask questions: *Where do you have a bone? Where is your brain? Where is your heart? Is your shoulder a joint?*

LISTENING SCRIPT

Lesson 1, Activity 1: Learn New Words

Look at the pictures. Listen to the words. Listen again and repeat.

1. brain	It's a brain.
2. lungs	They're lungs.
3. heart	It's a heart.
4. wrist	It's a wrist.
5. skin	It's skin.
6. back	It's a back.
7. tooth	It's a tooth.
8. muscle	It's a muscle.
9. waist	It's a waist.
10. hip	It's a hip.
11. joint	It's a joint.
12. bone	It's a bone.

Which words are new to you? Circle them.

EXPANSION ACTIVITY: Draw it! [Low-Level]

- Divide the class into teams.
- Explain to students that they will draw as their classmates identify the body part.
- Model the activity. Draw an elbow on the board and elicit the name of the body part.
- Call a member from each team to the front of the room. Whisper the name of a body part to each "artist" and tell the student to begin drawing. Note that you should include the new words from Activity 1 as well as the review vocabulary labeled on the illustration. Their teammates should try to name the body part.
- The first team to correctly name the body part (no matter who draws it best) earns a point.

2 Write

- Have students look at the chart. Go over the directions.
- Read the first column and example: *I have muscles in my arm*. Point out that arm is written next to number 1. Read the sentence stem again and elicit another way to complete it (*I have muscles in my leg*).

Unit 8: Lesson 1

- Have students list more parts of the body in each column, and then compare lists with a partner.
- Call on students to tell the class what they listed in each column.

> **ANSWER KEY:**
>
> - I have muscles in my: *Possible answers include* heart, hip, waist, back, *and other body parts* except *bone, blood, tooth, skin, and ear.*
> - I have bones in my: *Possible answers include* hip, back, head, chest, arm, shoulder, elbow, wrist, finger, *etc., but do not include* muscle, blood, heart, stomach, brain, lungs, skin, tooth, *or* eye.
> - My _____ is a joint: *Possible answers include* shoulder, elbow, wrist, hip, knee, *and* ankle.

EXPANSION ACTIVITY: Category Sort

- Copy all the words from Activity 1 (including the review vocabulary labeled on the illustration) on slips of paper (one word per slip).
- Give each student a slip.
- Tell the students that when you call out a category, they should move and stand with other students whose words fit that category. For example, if you say *joints* and *no joints*, students with joints on their slips of paper (elbow, shoulder, ankle, hip, knee, wrist) should group together while the other students should stand in a separate group.
- Call on a few students in each category to name their body part.
- Call out categories. Use your own ideas or these: *joints/no joints, muscles/no muscles, bones/no bones, above the waist/below the waist, two or more/only one, bigger than your head/equal to or smaller than your head.*

❸ Check *True, False,* or *I Don't Know*

- Have students look at the activity. Go over the directions.
- Read the first statement and ask students if it is true, false, or if they don't know. Elicit the correct answer (*True*) and have them check *True*.
- Explain that the *I don't know* column can help students identify things they might want to learn. Point out that it is often a good idea to identify information we don't know because this can help us set learning goals.
- Have students read the statements and check their statements.
- Have students check their answers in pairs.
- Go over the answers with the class. Have students correct each false statement orally to make it true.

> **ANSWER KEY:**
>
> 1. True; 2. True; 3. True; 4. False; teeth do not have hair; 5. False; your heart moves your blood around, or your muscles move your body around; 6. True; 7. True; 8. True

🎯 TARGET GRAMMAR

Can and *could* for ability

The Target Grammar point is used in Activity 3. Presentation and practice of this grammar point appears on *Student Book* pages 186–187. Answer Keys appear on Teacher's Edition page 257.

Unit 8: Lesson 1

EXPANSION ACTIVITY: *True/False* Scramble
[Multi-Level]

- Divide the class into small groups. Have each group write the vocabulary words from Activity 1 on slips of paper and put them into a paper bag.
- Have students in each group take turns drawing two body parts from the bag. Have the student make a statement about the two body parts and tell it to the group. For example, for the words *hip* and *heart*, the student might say: *The heart moves blood to the hip* (true).
- Have the group tell whether it is true or false. Have more advanced students correct false statements to make them true.

4 Work Together

- Review left and right.
- Read the directions. Go over the examples.
- Put students in pairs to have them take turns giving and following instructions.

EXPANSION ACTIVITY: Simon Says

- Tell students that you are going to play a game called *Simon Says*. Students should follow the instruction if the person says *Simon says* before the instruction. They should not follow the instruction if the person does not say *Simon says* before the instruction.
- Model the activity. Start with: *Simon says, "Stand up,"* so that all students are standing. Give an instruction such as: *Simon says, "Point to your left ear."* Gesture for students to point to their left ears. Then say: *Point to your right ear*. If students begin to point, shake your head no. Give a few more instructions with and without saying *Simon says* and make sure students understand the game. If students make a mistake, they are out of the game and should sit down.
- Have a volunteer come to the front of the class to give instructions while the rest of the class follows. Continue with various volunteers.
- CHALLENGE: To increase the difficulty of the activity, call out one instruction while acting out another. For example, say *Simon says, "Point to your left elbow,"* then point to your right knee. Remind students to do what you say, not what you do. Invite advanced students to continue the game by leading the class.

LESSON 2: Describing Illnesses and Injuries

OBJECTIVE
Describing illnesses and injuries

VOCABULARY

bleed	cut	fracture
blister	feel dizzy	infection
bruise	feel nauseous	rash
burn	fever	shock
cold	flu	sprain

TARGET GRAMMAR
Should and shouldn't for advice *page 188*

THINGS TO DO

1 Learn New Words 110

- Have students look at the pictures and elicit the words they know.
- Have students listen and look at the pictures while you say the words or play the audio.
- Instruct students to circle the words that are new to them.
- Say the words or play the audio a second time. Pause after each word or phrase and ask the students to repeat the word and point to the correct picture.
- Put students in pairs and have one say a word or phrase as the partner points to the correct picture. Reverse roles and repeat the activity.
- Call on students and ask questions: *Do you have a cut? When do you get a fever? What is the flu?*

LISTENING SCRIPT

Lesson 2, Activity 1: Learn New Words

Look at the pictures. Listen to the words. Listen again and repeat. Which words are new to you? Circle them.

1. burn — It's a bad burn.
2. cut — It's a deep cut.
3. fracture — It's a bad fracture.
4. sprain — It's a sprain.
5. bruise — It's a bruise.
6. shock — He got a shock from the electric cord.
7. rash — She has a rash on her leg.
8. fever — She has a fever.
9. cold — Bill has a cold.
10. flu — Sara has the flu.
11. infection — She has an infection on her finger.
12. feel dizzy — Tom feels dizzy.
13. blister — Jacob has a blister on his hand.
14. feel nauseous — Lisa feels nauseous.
15. bleed — The cut on his arm is bleeding.

EXPANSION ACTIVITY: Bingo Board

- Tell students you are going to read a story. If they hear a word, they should put a check mark on the correct picture on pages 104 and 105. When they have checked all the boxes, they should call "Bingo."
- Create a story or read the one below. Read at a normal pace.

> Lisa is a nurse at the school. The children at the school come to the nurse's office when something is wrong. Today, she sees a lot of children. Three of them have cuts, one has a rash and two feel nauseous. Five children have bruises from the playground, and one feels dizzy from the swings. One child has a fever because of an infection, and four have colds. One has the flu. She sends one little girl to the emergency room because Lisa thinks the girl has a fracture, but it is just a sprain. A little boy hurts his nose, and it begins to bleed. Lisa gets a blister on her foot because she is wearing new shoes and she has to run around so much. At the end of the day the maintenance man comes in to see her. He got a shock from the electrical cord. It leaves a burn on his hand.

STUDENT BOOK PAGES 104–105

Unit 8: Lesson 2

- When you finish telling or reading the story, ask students how many pictures they put a check mark next to. Read the story again if necessary.

❷ Listen and Write 111

- Go over the directions and remind students to use the pictures to answer each question.
- Play the audio. Pause after each conversation and have students write the correct name in each blank.
- Put students in pairs to compare answers. Play the audio again if necessary to have students confirm their answers.
- Go over the answers with the class.
- LOW LEVEL: For students who have trouble with listening comprehension, provide a copy of the listening script as a cloze. Replace several words of the script with blank lines. Have students listen to the conversations and fill in the missing words. Then have them answer the questions.

LISTENING SCRIPT

Lesson 2, Activity 2: Listen and Write

Listen and look at the pictures. Write the name of the person that has the illness or injury.

1. A: Is your cold getting any better?
   B: I don't think so.
   A: Maybe you should go home and rest.
   B: Maybe you're right.
2. A: Are you okay?
   B: No. I'm feeling dizzy.
   A: Maybe you should sit down.
   B: Maybe you're right.
3. A: Your cut is still bleeding.
   B: I know.
   A: Maybe you should put more pressure on it.
   B: Maybe you're right.
4. A: Are you okay?
   B: No. I'm feeling nauseous.

   A: Maybe you should drink some ginger ale.
   B: Maybe you're right.
5. A: Is your flu getting any better?
   B: I don't think so.
   A: Maybe you should see a doctor.
   B: Maybe you're right.
6. A: Is your fever getting any better?
   B: I don't think so.
   A: Maybe you should take some medicine.
   B: I already did.

ANSWER KEY:

1. Bill; 2. Tom; 3. Mark; 4. Lisa; 5. Sara; 6. Abby

EXPANSION ACTIVITY: More Advice [Multi-Level]

- Divide the class into three groups. Assign each group one of the following pictures: 1 (burn), 5 (bruise), 7 (rash).
- Have each group write a conversation based on the ones they heard in Activity 2. Provide the listening script as a model if needed for students at lower levels. Encourage advanced students to help their peers with spelling and correct sentence formation.
- Have two students from each group perform the conversation for the class.

◯ TARGET GRAMMAR

Should and *shouldn't* for advice
The Target Grammar point is used in Activities 2 and 3. Presentation and practice of this grammar point appears on Student Book page 188. Answer Keys appear on Teacher's Edition page 257.

❸ Practice the Conversation 112

- Have students listen and look at the conversation while you read it or play the audio.
- Say the lines or play the audio a second time. Pause after each line and ask the students to repeat.

Unit 8: Lesson 2

- Check comprehension by asking questions: *What's wrong with B? What did A suggest?*
- Model the conversation with a student. Have the student read B's lines. Demonstrate how to substitute from the ideas in the boxes below.
- Have students work in pairs to practice the conversation, making substitutions from the boxes and using their own ideas.
- Walk around to make sure students understand the activity and provide help if needed.
- Call on volunteers to read one of the variations aloud.

> **LISTENING SCRIPT**
>
> **Lesson 2, Activity 3: Practice the Conversation**
>
> *Listen to the conversation. Listen again and repeat.*
>
> A: Is your fever getting any better?
>
> B: No, I don't think so. Do you think I should see a doctor?
>
> A: Yes. And I think you should drink more liquids.
>
> B: Maybe you're right.

> **EXPANSION ACTIVITY: Comparing Remedies [Challenge]**
>
> - Put students in small groups of three or four. Have them discuss what they would do for the following problems: a rash, a fever, a cold, the flu, feeling nauseous, a burn.
> - Call on representatives from each group to share their ideas with the class.

❹ Find Someone Who

- Go over the directions.
- Have students move around the room to talk to classmates and fill out the chart. If some students prefer not to discuss their personal medical history, have them participate by telling about a time when someone they know had an illness or injury. As an alternative, assign each student a secret fictional illness and then begin the mingle activity.
- Call on students to tell what they found out. Have volunteers tell about their injuries and illnesses if they wish.

> **EXPANSION ACTIVITY: At the Movies**
>
> - Have students brainstorm movies or television shows they've seen in which characters suffer from the illnesses and injuries they've learned about today. Have students tell how the ailments fit into the plot of the story, and what was done to help each person.
> - You may wish to show a video clip from a medical drama or film. Have students listen for words they learned in this lesson. Then, ask them to retell the gist of what was happening in the video.

> **BIG PICTURE EXPANSION ACTIVITY: GRAMMAR—*Should* and *Shouldn't***
>
> - Make copies of Worksheet 15 (Teacher's Edition page 238) and distribute them to students.
> - Have students look at the Big Picture in their books (Student Book pages 106–107).
> - Instruct students to complete the activities and then check their answers with a partner. Have partners discuss their answers to Part C.
> - Go over the answers with the class.
> - Have volunteers tell what they wrote in Part C. Lead a discussion about the students' ideas.
>
> **ANSWER KEY:**
>
> A. 1. c; 2. e; 3. a; 4. b; 5. d
> B. 1. Fred, shouldn't; 2. Nina, shouldn't; 3. Bill, should; 4. Tommy, shouldn't; 5. Mia, should; 6. Lupe, should
> C. Answers will vary.

LESSON 3: Activities in an Emergency Room

OBJECTIVE
Activities in an emergency room

VOCABULARY

admissions desk	radiology
bandage	sling
cast	splint
crutches	stitches
emergency room	waiting area
examining room	wheelchair
ice pack	x-ray

 TARGET GRAMMAR

Adverbs of degree *page 189*

THINGS TO DO

1 Learn New Words 113

- Have students look at the Big Picture in their books (Student Book pages 106–107).
- Ask the students what they see in the picture, and elicit the words that they know.
- Have students listen and look at the pictures while you say the words or play the audio.
- Instruct students to circle the words that are new to them.
- Say the words or play the audio a second time. Pause after each word or phrase and ask the students to repeat the word and point to the correct part of the picture. Put students in pairs and have one say a word or phrase as the partner points to the correct picture. Reverse roles and repeat the activity.
- Call on students and ask questions: *What do you use for a fracture? A sprain? If you can't walk?*

LISTENING SCRIPT

Lesson 3, Activity 1: Learn New Words

Look at the picture. Listen to the words. Listen again and repeat.

1.	emergency room	Where's the emergency room?
2.	examining room	Where's the examining room?
3.	x-ray	He got an X-ray.
4.	radiology	Where's the radiology department?
5.	stitches	She got stitches.
6.	sling	He has a sling.
7.	ice pack	He has an ice pack.
8.	admissions desk	Where's the admissions desk?
9.	splint	He has a splint.
10.	wheelchair	He's in a wheelchair.
11.	waiting area	Where's the waiting area?
12.	crutches	She has crutches.
13.	cast	She has a cast.
14.	bandage	She has a bandage.

Which words are new to you? Circle them.

EXPANSION ACTIVITY: The Doctor Is In [Challenge]

- Put students in pairs and give each student eight index cards.
- One person should write or draw words for illnesses and injuries (*blister, infection, cut, burn, fracture, sprain, bruise, rash*). The other person should write or draw words for treatments (*bandage, medicine, cast, sling, splint, ice pack, x-ray, stitches*).
- Have students mix each set of cards and draw one ailment and one treatment. Have them discuss whether the ailment can be helped or cured by the treatment. If not, have them suggest what treatment would be more effective.
- Have volunteers explain one of their pairings to the class, telling how they would treat each illness.

Unit 8: Lesson 3

Culture Note:

- Lead a discussion about "folk" medicine. Ask students if there are any traditional healing methods used in their cultures or countries of origin. For example, point out that many people use the aloe vera plant to soothe burns. Have students tell about traditional remedies that have worked (or not worked) for them. You may wish to have more advanced students research why certain remedies might be effective based on scientific observations.

❷ Listen and Circle *True* or *False* 🎧 114

- Go over the directions. Remind students to use the pictures in the book while they are listening to answer each question.
- Play the audio. Pause after each conversation and have students circle *True* or *False*.
- Put students in pairs to compare answers. Play the audio again if necessary to have students confirm their answers.
- MULTI-LEVEL: If you have students at different levels, you may want to pair an advanced student with a less advanced student. The more proficient student can help the less proficient student locate the correct pictures for each question.
- Go over the answers with the class.

LISTENING SCRIPT

Lesson 3, Activity 2: Listen and Circle *True* or *False*

Listen to the sentences and look at the picture. Circle True or False.

1. The emergency room is very empty.
2. Alice is in the waiting room.
3. Alex is in the examining room.
4. Nina's ankle looks pretty painful.
5. Ben is in a wheelchair. He has a splint on his leg.
6. Fred is in the waiting room. He is probably waiting to get stitches.

ANSWER KEY:

1. False; 2. True; 3. False; 4. True; 5. True; 6. False

EXPANSION ACTIVITY: Around-the-World *True* or *False*

- Assign each student a person or location from the Big picture. Have them write one *true* and *one* false statement about their person or place on a note card. Circulate as students write to check that sentences make sense.
- Have students leave their books on their desks open to the Big Picture and the note cards next to the book. Have students number each statement with numbers you give them. Explain that each desk will be a "station" on an around-the-world tour. Students will stop at each station to decide whether the statements are true or false.
- Have students number a piece of paper with the number of statements that were written. Students begin by writing *true* or *false* for the statements on their desk, making sure they write the answers next to the correct numbers on their paper.
- After a set time limit (30 seconds, for example), have students move to the next station to write *true* or *false* for the next set of statements. Be sure to establish beforehand in which direction students will move.
- Have students continue through the stations until they have responded to all of the statements. Then ask students to review the answers as a class.

Unit 8: Lesson 3

 TARGET GRAMMAR

Adverbs of degree

The Target Grammar point is used in Activities 2 and 4. Presentation and practice of this grammar point appears on *Student Book* page 189. Answer Keys appear on Teacher's Edition page 257.

3 Talk About the Picture

- Have students look at the Big Picture in their books (Student Book pages 106–107).
- To set the context, ask questions about the picture: *How many people do you see? Where are they? What are they doing?*
- Write any additional vocabulary on the board.
- Ask students to write five questions about the picture. Remind them to use the words on the board or from Activity 1 if they need help.
- Walk around the room and provide help as needed.
- Put students in pairs. Have them take turns asking and answering questions.
- Call on students to ask questions of their classmates.

EXPANSION ACTIVITY: How do you say it?
[Low-Level]

- Put lower level students in pairs and have them look at the Big Picture in their books (Student Book pages 106–107). If possible, have students work with a partner who speaks the same native language.
- On the board, write the sentences: *How do you say _____ in English?* and *_____ in English is _____.* Go over the sentences with students and model an example with a word they already know. For example: *How do you say* adios *in English?* Adios *in English is* goodbye.
- Have partners identify objects in the picture they do not know. Have them use bilingual dictionaries to look up each word in English. Have them use the word in their native language and in English to complete the sentences from the board orally.
- For partners who do not speak the same native language, modify the sentences as follows: *How do you say this in English? In English, you say _____.* The student should point to the unknown object when saying *this* in the first sentence.

 BIG PICTURE EXPANSION ACTIVITY: SPEAKING—Patient and Doctor

- Put students in pairs. Walk around the room and assign each pair a patient in the picture.
- Have students create conversations between the patient and a doctor or nurse. Tell them that each speaker should have at least three lines. They should discuss the problem, how it happened or how long they have had it, and a possible treatment.
- Walk around the room to monitor the activity and provide help as needed.
- Have pairs perform their conversations in front of the class. Ask the class to point to the patient in the Big Picture.

Unit 8: Lesson 3

④ Practice the Conversation 115

- Have students listen and look at the conversation while you read it or play the audio.
- Say the lines or play the audio a second time. Pause after each line and ask the students to repeat.
- Check comprehension by asking questions: *Who is having a conversation? What is wrong with B? What did they do at the emergency room?*
- Model the conversation with a student. Have the student read A's lines. Demonstrate how to substitute from the ideas in the boxes below. Cue the student to make the appropriate substitutions.
- Have students work in pairs to practice the conversation, making substitutions from the boxes.
- Walk around to make sure students understand the activity and provide help if needed.

LISTENING SCRIPT

Lesson 3, Activity 4, Practice the Conversation

Listen to the conversation. Listen again and repeat.

A: What happened to your leg? It looks very painful.

B: I sprained my knee. I had to go to the emergency room.

A: Did they take an X-ray?

B: Yes, and then they put this splint on my knee.

EXPANSION ACTIVITY: Unscramble It

- Write phrases from the conversation on index cards or slips of paper.

   What happened
   to your leg?
   It looks
   very painful
   I sprained
   my knee.
   I had to go
   to the emergency room.
   Did they
   take an x-ray?
   Yes, and then
   they put this splint
   on my knee.

- Call students to the front of the room and give each a phrase. Have students memorize the phrases. Collect the slips.
- Have students repeat their phrases and put themselves in the correct order to re-create the conversation.
- When they are organized, have each student recite his or her part of the conversation. Have the class listen and confirm whether the order is correct.

LESSON 4: Reading Medicine Labels

OBJECTIVE
Reading medicine labels

VOCABULARY
capsule
cream
over the counter
prescription
tablet
teaspoon

TARGET GRAMMAR
Adverbs of frequency page 190

WINDOW ON MATH
Ounces, Tablespoons, and Teaspoons

THINGS TO DO

1 Learn New Words 116

- Have students look at the pictures and elicit the words they know.
- Have students listen and look at the pictures and make sure they listen while you say the words or play the audio. Make sure students understand the difference between an over-the-counter (OTC) medication and a prescription medication.
- Say the words or play the audio a second time. Pause after each word and ask the students to repeat the word and point to the correct picture.
- Put students in pairs and have one say a word as the partner points to the correct picture. Reverse roles and repeat the activity.
- Call on students and ask questions: *Do you take tablets? Do you have any prescription medicines? Where do you get OTC medicines?*

LISTENING SCRIPT

Lesson 4, Activity 1: Learn New Words

Look at the medicine labels. Listen to the words. Listen again and repeat.

1.	tablet	Take two tablets.
2.	teaspoon	Take two teaspoons.
3.	cream	Use the cream two times a day.
4.	prescription	You need to see the doctor to get a prescription.
5.	OTC	The medicine is OTC.
6.	capsule	Take two capsules.

EXPANSION ACTIVITY: What about you?

- Write the following questions on the board: *Which medicines do you have at home? What forms do the medicines come in (tablets, capsules, etc.)? How often do you usually take medicine? What do you usually take medicine for?*
- Put students in pairs and have them take turns asking and answering the questions.
- LOW LEVEL: Bring several kinds of OTC medicines to the classroom. Have lower level students look at each bottle and identify what form it is. Provide a model sentence, such as *Aspirin is a tablet*. Have students use the model to write new sentences, substituting the name of a medicine and its form.
- Call on students to tell the class something about what their partner said.

TARGET GRAMMAR

Adverbs of frequency
The Target Grammar point is used in Activities 1, 2, and 3. Presentation and practice of this grammar point appears on *Student Book* pages 190–191. Answer Keys appear on Teacher's Edition page 258.

172 • UNIT 8   STUDENT BOOK PAGES 108-109

Unit 8: Lesson 4

> **Pronunciation Note:**
> - Students may have difficulty pronouncing the names of medications. Write each word on the board and help students identify the individual syllables, drawing slash marks between each syllable, as in *hy/dro/cor/ti/sone*. Help students practice pronouncing the first syllable, then the first and second syllable together, and so on, adding a syllable each time.

❷ Read and Take Notes

- Have students look at the chart and elicit the types of information they need to know.
- Have students read the labels and complete the chart.
- Have students check their answers with a partner.
- Go over the answers with the class.

ANSWER KEY:

Name of Medicine	Form	How much?	How often?
A. Acetaminophen	tablet	2	every 4–6 hours
B. Ampicillin	liquid	1 teaspoon	3 times/day
C. Hydrocortisone	cream	—	3–4 times/day
D. Max-Relief	capsule	1	every 12 hours

EXPANSION ACTIVITY: Game [Challenge]

- Write the following in large letters on pieces of paper to show the students, or just read them aloud: *Which medicine is a _____ ? Which medicine is for _____ ? Which medicine do you take _____ ? Which medicine has _____ ?*
- Write headings on the board: *What form? What problem? How often? How many?* Under each heading write point values of 100, 200, 300, and 400. Each answer will be the name of a medicine.
- Divide the class into teams. Have teams take turns selecting a category and point value. The category and point values can be called in any order.
- Ask a question based on the corresponding square in the table below, and have the team that selected the square answer the question: *Which medicine has 12 in the package?*
- If the team that selects a question gives an incorrect answer, the other team has a chance to answer.
- Each correct answer earns the indicated point value.
- Once a question has been answered correctly, mark off the point value for that column so that it cannot be called again.
- Play until all questions have been asked and all point values have been marked off.

Point	Which medicine is a _____ ?	Which medicine is for _____ ?	Which medicine do you take _____ ?	Which medicine has ___ ?
100	capsule	a rash	3–4 times/day	12 in a package
200	liquid	sneezing	every 12 hours	150 mg per dose
300	cream	an ear infection	every 4–6 hours	325 mg per tablet
400	tablet	muscle aches	3 times/day	100 in a container

ANSWER KEY:

Point	What form?	What problem?	How often?	What size?
100	Max-Relief	hydrocortisone	hydrocortisone	Max-Relief
200	ampicillin	Max-Relief	Max-Relief	ampicillin
300	hydrocortisone	ampicillin	acetaminophen	acetaminophen
400	acetaminophen	acetaminophen	ampicillin	acetaminophen

❸ Check *True* or *False*

- Go over the directions. Have students check *True* or *False* for each statement.
- Have students compare answers with a partner and correct the false statements.
- Go over the answers with the class.

Unit 8: Lesson 4

ANSWER KEY:

1. False. It's for adults and children over 12;
2. True; 3. False. Only Max-Relief is OTC;
4. True; 5. False. They usually take ampicillin when they have an ear infection, or They usually use hydrocortisone cream when they have a rash; 6. True.

EXPANSION ACTIVITY: Practicing *Yes/No Questions* [Multi-Level]

- Have students rewrite the sentences from Activity 3 as *yes/no* questions. Have more advanced students help lower level students write questions correctly.
- Put students in pairs to practice asking and answering the questions.

ANSWER KEY:

1. Can children older than six take acetaminophen? No. It's for adults and children over 12.
2. Should you swallow hydrocortisone cream? No, you shouldn't.
3. Are ampicillin and Max-Relief OTC? No, they aren't. Only Max-Relief is OTC.
4. Do people sometimes take acetaminophen for a toothache? Yes, they do.
5. Do people usually take ampicillin when they have a rash? No, they usually take hydrocortisone when the have a rash, or No, they usually take ampicillin when they have an ear infection.
6. Can you use the ampicillin after 2013? No, you can't.

④ Write

- Go over the directions and the example in the chart. Explain to students that they can complete the chart the way it is or they can make a chart using different medicines.
- Have students complete their chart, and then share their answers with a partner.
- Have volunteers tell what they wrote in their chart. For students who completed the chart in the book, go over the answers.

ANSWER KEY:

Acetaminophen: headache, backache, muscle aches, toothache, a cold
Max-Relief: fever, headache, body aches, runny nose, sneezing
Hydrocortisone: pain, swelling, and itching due to rashes

EXPANSION ACTIVITY: Dialogues

- Have partners write short dialogues using the chart from Activity 4. In the dialogue, one person should complain of a symptom and the other should respond with a recommended medicine. For example:
A: *I have a runny nose.* B: *You should take Max-Relief.*
- Have volunteers perform their dialogues for the class.

Vocabulary Note:

- Students may be confused about use of capital and lowercase letters for medicines. Explain that on a label or package (as in label A on page 109) a capital letter is always used.

BIG PICTURE EXPANSION ACTIVITY: READING—Doctor's Orders

- Make copies of Worksheet 16 (Teacher's Edition page 239) and distribute them to students.
- Have students look at the Big Picture in their books (Student Book pages 106–107).
- Instruct students to complete the activities and then check their answers with a partner.
- Go over the answers with the class.

ANSWER KEY:

1. Alice, a burn; 2. Ann, a leg fracture;
3. Mia, a cut; 4. Tommy, a wrist sprain

Unit 8: Lesson 4

WINDOW ON MATH

Ounces, Tablespoons, and Teaspoons

- Go over the information in the box.
- Have students look at the first item. Elicit the answer (*6*) and have them write it on the line.
- Have students complete the sentences and check their answers with a partner.
- Go over the answers with the class.

ANSWER KEY:

1. 6; 2. 1/2; 3. 1; 4. 1/2; 5. 3

EXPANSION ACTIVITY: Metric Measurements

- Have students look up equivalent measurements for ounces, tablespoons, and teaspoons in the metric system (milliliters, grams).
- Write a list of measurements on the board, such as *2 tablespoons of sugar, 4 ounces of milk,* and so on. Have partners work together to convert each measurement into milliliters or grams. Note: 1 ounce (U.S. measurement) = 29.57 milliliters; 1 tablespoon (U.S.) = 14.79 grams; 1 teaspoon (U.S.) = 4.93 grams.
- Go over the answers with the class.

LESSON 5: Talking to Health Professionals

OBJECTIVE
Talking to health professionals

PRONUNCIATION
Can and can't

1 Practice Pronunciation: *can* and *can't* 🎧 117

A. Listen to the sentences. Listen again and repeat.

- Have students look at the words while you say them or play the audio.
- Say the sentences or play the audio a second time, pausing after each sentence to have students repeat.
- Make sure students can distinguish between the unstressed vowel sound in *can* and the greater stress in *can't*.

LISTENING SCRIPT

Lesson 5, Activity 1: Practice Pronunciation: Can and Can't

A. Listen to the sentences. Listen again and repeat.

1. Children can take some medicines.
2. Children can't take aspirin.
3. You can fill this prescription at the drugstore.
4. You can't take the medicine after the expiration date.
5. Can I play soccer?
6. Can't I play soccer?

B. Listen to the sentences. Underline the word you hear. 🎧 118

- Have students look at the sentences while you say them or play the audio.
- Say the sentences or play the audio a second time. Have the students underline the word they hear.
- Have students check their answers with a partner.
- Go over the answers with the class.

LISTENING SCRIPT

Lesson 5, Activity 1: Practice Pronunciation: Can and Can't

B. Listen to the sentences. Underline the word you hear.

1. He can't come to school today.
2. She can go back to work.
3. Bob can play soccer today.
4. She can't walk without crutches.
5. I can exercise today.
6. Tara can't take off her bandage.

ANSWER KEY:
1. can't; 2. can; 3. can; 4. can't; 5. can; 6. can't

C. Work with a partner. Take turns reading the sentences in Activity B. Respond with *Oh, good* or *That's too bad*.

- Put the students in pairs.
- Read the directions. Go over the example.
- Have them take turns reading sentences from Activity B. Remind them to choose only one of the options in each sentence: *He can come to school today*, and to use correct pronunciation. Partners should respond appropriately depending on the sentence, with *Oh, good*, or *That's too bad*.
- Walk around to monitor the activity and provide help as needed.
- Call on students to say a sentence, and elicit the appropriate response from another student.

Pronunciation Note:
- You may want to point out to students that native speakers often distinguish between *can* and *can't* by the fact that *can* is usually unstressed and *can't* is usually stressed, rather than by the final *t* sound. Many speakers swallow the final *t* sound in *can't*.

Unit 8: Lesson 5

> **EXPANSION ACTIVITY: Listening Practice**
> - Have each student write the word *can* on one side of an index card and the word *can't* on the other side.
> - Make statements using *can* and *can't*. Have students hold up the word they hear.
> - You may wish to have volunteers make statements for their classmates.

❷ Practice the Conversation: Describing an Illness 119

- Have students look at the picture in the book for Activity 2. To set the context, ask questions about the picture: *Who is in the picture? Where are they?*
- Read the conversation or play the audio.
- Read or play the conversation again. Pause after each sentence and ask students to repeat.
- To confirm understanding, ask comprehension questions about the conversation: *What is A's problem? When can she go in?*
- Point out that there are three pieces of scripted information in the conversation that can be substituted: A's problem, B's question, and when there is an opening.
- Model the conversation with a student. Have the student read A's lines. Cue the student to say *an ear infection*. Demonstrate how to substitute *you have a fever* and *later today* from the boxes below.
- Put students in pairs to practice the conversation, making substitutions from the boxes and using their own ideas.
- Walk around to monitor the activity and provide help as needed.

> **LISTENING SCRIPT**
>
> **Lesson 5, Activity 2: Practice the Conversation: Describing an Illness**
>
> *Listen to the conversation. Listen again and repeat.*
>
> A: I'd like to make an appointment as soon as possible.
> B: What's the problem?
> A: I have a high fever.
> B: Do your joints hurt?
> A: Yes. Can the doctor see me today?
> B: I have an opening this afternoon.
> A: Great. I'll take it.

> **Grammar/Vocabulary Notes:**
> - Point out that *I'll* is a contraction for *I will*. We often use it to volunteer to do something, or in response to an offer.
> - Make sure that students understand that *an opening* is an open appointment time.

❸ Practice the Conversation: Following Instructions 120

- Repeat the basic procedure from Activity 2.
- To set the context, ask questions about the picture: *Who do you see? What are they doing?*
- After students have listened to and repeated the conversation line by line, check comprehension by asking: *What does A tell B to do? What does B ask?*
- Have students continue practicing the conversation, making substitutions from the boxes and using their own ideas.

> **LISTENING SCRIPT**
>
> **Lesson 5, Activity 3: Practice the Conversation: Following Instructions**
>
> *Listen to the conversation. Listen again and repeat.*
>
> A: What happened?
> B: I fell down in a soccer game and hurt my elbow.
> A: It looks like you have a sprain. Use this sling until the next appointment.
> B: Okay.
> A: Also, here's a prescription for some pain medication.
> B: How often do I take it?
> A: Take one tablet two times a day. Don't take more than that.
> B: Can I play soccer?
> A: No. Not until I see you again.

STUDENT BOOK PAGES 110-111

Unit 8: Lesson 5

> **EXPANSION ACTIVITY: Beanbag Toss**
> **[Low-Level]**
> - Tell students that when you say a medical problem, they should respond with a treatment.
> - Toss a ball or beanbag and call a student's name. Then say a medical problem: *a sprain of the wrist*. Elicit one treatment: *a sling*.
> - Have the student toss the beanbag to another student as he or she says a medical problem. Continue until all the students have participated.

4 Listen and Write 121

- Go over the directions and the appointment cards.
- Play the audio. Pause after each conversation and have students fill out the appointment cards.
- Put students in pairs to compare answers. Play the audio again if necessary to have students confirm their answers.
- Go over the answers with the class.
- CHALLENGE: Have advanced students work in pairs to write down as much of the conversations as they can remember. Have them perform their reconstructed dialogues for the class, then play back the audio so they can check their work.

> **LISTENING SCRIPT**
>
> **Lesson 5, Activity 4: Listen and Write**
>
> *Listen to two people making doctor's appointments. Fill out the appointment cards.*
>
> 1.
>
> A: I'd like to make an appointment with Dr. Thomas.
>
> B: What kind of appointment do you need?
>
> A: A routine checkup, please.
>
> B: Let's see. It looks like I have an opening on the 15th at 9 A.M.
>
> A: Great. I'll take it!
>
> B: And your name please?
>
> A: It's Andy Chen. C-H-E-N.
>
> B: Okay, Andy, that's 9 A.M. on November 15th with Dr. Thomas. See you then!
>
> A: Thank you!
>
> 2
>
> A: Does Dr. Levine want to see you again?
>
> B: Yes. She said to come back in two weeks.
>
> A: Is it for a follow-up appointment or a routine check up?
>
> B: A follow-up appointment.
>
> A: Okay. Let's see. It looks like I have an opening on the 23rd at 2 P.M
>
> B: That's perfect.
>
> A: And your name please?
>
> B: It's Lily Smith. S-M-I-T-H.
>
> A: Okay Lily, that's 2 P.M. on April 23rd with Dr. Levine. See you then!
>
> B: Thank you!

> **ANSWER KEY:**
>
> 1. Name: Andy Chen; Date: November 15; Time: 9 A.M.; Doctor: Dr. Thomas
> 2. Name: Lily Smith; Date: April 23; Time: 2 P.M.; Doctor: Dr. Levine

LESSON 6 — Reading a Medical Advertisement

OBJECTIVE
Reading a medical advertisement

1 Read and Check *True* or *False*

- Read the directions and go over the statements with students.
- Have students scan the flyer on page 113 and check *True* or *False*. Point out the asterisk at the top of the flyer and its explanation at the bottom.
- Have partners compare their answers.
- Go over the answers with the class. Have volunteers tell why they chose the answer they did.
- LOW LEVEL: Have lower level students scan the article and underline five vocabulary words they do not know. Help students pronounce each word. Have them read the sentence containing each word and guess at its meaning. Then have students look the words up in a bilingual dictionary.

ANSWER KEY:
1. True; 2. False; 3. False; 4. False; 5. True; 6. False

2 Read and Take Notes

- Have students read the flyer again and complete the chart.
- Have students check their answers with a partner.
- Go over the answers with the class.

ANSWER KEY:
1. Newton Recreation Center; 2. Oct. 5, (9:00 to 11:30 A.M.) and Oct. 23, (4:00 to 6:00 P.M.); 3. to protect yourself from the flu; 4. everyone, but especially children, pregnant women, people with heart and lung disease, and people 65 and older; 5. $30.00, or free for seniors 65 years and older; 6. death, allergic reactions such as breathing problems, rash, muscle weakness, or feeling dizzy

3 Interview

- Go over the directions and the questions.
- Put students in pairs and have them ask and answer questions with their partner.
- Have volunteers tell the class about their partners.

EXPANSION ACTIVITY: Researching Vaccines [Challenge]

- Have students research the history of specific vaccines or new vaccines that have become available in recent years. Have them find out when each vaccine was developed and what benefits it provides. In addition, have them find out whether a vaccine is controversial at all, and if so, why.
- Have students write a short paragraph about the vaccine they chose.
- Have students share what they found out with the class. Lead a discussion about the information. You may wish to invite a medical professional to speak to your class. If so, have the students prepare questions in advance to ask the speaker.

LESSON 7: What Do You Know?

❶ Listening Review 122

- Read the directions with the class. Read the items or play the audio and have the students mark their answers on the Answer Sheet.
- Walk around to monitor the activity and help students stay on task.
- Have students check their answers with a partner.
- Go over the answers with the class.

LISTENING SCRIPT

Lesson 7, Activity 1: Listening Review

Look at the pictures and listen. Choose the correct answer: A, B, or C. Use the Answer Sheet.

1. Your brain is in your head.
2. A: Is your burn getting any better?
   B: No, I don't think so.
3. A: What happened to your leg?
   B: I sprained my ankle.
   A: You should use an ice pack.
4. A: How often do I take it?
   B: Take one capsule three times a day.
5. A: I'd like to make an appointment as soon as possible.
   B: What's the problem?
   A: I have a rash.

ANSWER KEY:

1. B; 2. C; 3. A; 4. B; 5. C

❷ Listening Dictation 123

- Copy the numbers and lines from the Listening Dictation section on the board.
- Read the first sentence: *Is your flu getting any better?* Have a more advanced student write the sentence on the board on the line next to 1. Have students copy the sentence in their books.
- Play the audio and have students write the sentences they hear. Repeat as many times as necessary.
- Put students in pairs to compare answers.
- Have volunteers write the sentences on the board.

LISTENING SCRIPT

Lesson 7, Activity 2: Listening Dictation

Listen and write the words you hear.

1. A: Is your flu getting any better?
   B: No, I don't think so.
2. A: What happened to your hand?
   B: I burned it.
3. A: Did they put an ice pack on it?
   B: Yes, and then they gave me these crutches.
4. A: What happened?
   B: I fell down and hurt my hip.
5. A: How often do I take it?
   B: Take one tablet four times a day.

❸ Grammar Review

- Go over the directions.
- Read the first sentence. Elicit the appropriate completion. Have students circle *A* for item 1.
- Have students answer the rest of the questions.
- Put students in pairs to compare answers.
- Go over the answers with the class.

ANSWER KEY:

1. A; 2. B; 3. B; 4. A; 5. C; 6. C

TESTING FOCUS: Predicting

- Have students cover the answers for question 1 in Activity 3. Have them read the statement.
- Ask students to predict what word would best complete the sentence. Write their suggestions on the board. Have students agree on one or two answers that they think are best or most likely.
- Have students uncover the answers for question 1 and check whether their predicted answer(s) are included. Have them mark the answer they think is correct.
- Go over the answer with the class. Have them tell whether predicting was helpful, and if so, why.

Unit 8: Lesson 7

LEARNING LOG

- Point out the four sections of the Learning Log: *I know these words; I can ask; I can say;* and *I can write.*
- Have students check what they know and what they can do.
- Walk around to note what they don't know or can't do. Use this information to review areas of difficulty.

BIG PICTURE EXPANSION ACTIVITY:
SPEAKING— Assessment: Talking about the Picture

- You can use the Big Picture on Student Book pages 106–107 to place new students in open entry classes, to diagnose difficulties, or to measure progress.
- Work with one student at a time and show them the Big Picture. Ask: *What do you see in the picture? Tell me about the picture.* Tell the student you want him or her to speak for as long as possible. Wait a moment for the student to prepare to answer. If the student has difficulty, you can use prompts: *What do you see in the emergency room? Who do you see in the emergency room? What are the people doing?*
- You can use a rubric like the one below to rate beginning speakers.

4	Exhibits confidence, begins speaking without prompting
	Uses some complex sentences, although may make mistakes with irregular forms
	Can use several tenses
3	Uses sentences, although form may be incorrect
	Uses more than one tense
	Can speak for sustained length of time
	Responds to prompts, but doesn't need them to begin speaking
2	Can use nouns and verbs
	Uses phrases
	Answers informational questions
1	Can name objects
	Uses single words
	Can answer yes/no questions
0	Cannot say anything independently
	May be able to point to objects when prompted

Unit 8: Lesson 7

 BIG PICTURE EXPANSION ACTIVITY:
Writing—What happened at the ER?

- Have students look at the Big Picture in their books (Student Book pages 106–107).
- Ask the class: *What problems do you see? What do you think happened next?*
- Model the activity for the students. Tell about the trip to the emergency room from one patient's point of view. For example: *I am a dancer. During class one day, I slipped on the floor and hurt my leg. My friend and teacher took me to the emergency room. I waited in the waiting room for a while. Then I went to radiology and they took an x-ray. It was just a sprain, so they put a bandage on it and gave me crutches.* Have students name the person you are describing (Nina).
- Give the students five minutes to choose a character in the picture and brainstorm ideas.
- Have students write a story. Remind them to tell what happened, what the problem is, and what the people did in the emergency room.
- Put students in pairs to take turns reading their paragraphs to their partners.

TEACHER'S NOTES:

Things that students are doing well:
_____
_____
_____
_____

Things students need additional help with:
_____
_____
_____
_____

Ideas for further practice or for the next class:
_____
_____
_____
_____

UNIT 9: HOME AND SAFETY

UNIT OVERVIEW

LESSON	STUDENT BOOK PAGE	TEACHER'S EDITION PAGE
1. Identifying Actions	116	184
2. Identifying Problems at Home	118	187
3. A Fire Emergency	120	190
4. Safety Tips	122	193
5. Talking About Emergencies	124	196
6. Home Emergency Plans	126	199
7. What Do You Know?	128	200

Big Picture Expansion Activities

FOCUS	TITLE	SUGGESTED USE
Grammar	What happened?	Lesson 3
Speaking	Question Challenge	Lesson 3
Reading	How to Escape From a Fire	Lesson 4
Speaking	Assessment: Talking About the Big Picture	Lesson 7
Writing	Order of Events	Lesson 7

Big Picture Expansion Activity Worksheets

FOCUS	TITLE	TEACHER'S EDITION PAGE
17. Grammar	What happened?	240
18. Reading	How to Escape From a Fire	241

LESSON 1 Identifying Actions

OBJECTIVE
Identifying actions

VOCABULARY

lock	put back	turn off
pick up	shut off	turn on
plug in	take out	unlock
put away	turn down	unplug

 TARGET GRAMMAR

Simple past review *page 192*

THINGS TO DO

1 Learn New Words 124

- Have students look at the pictures. Elicit the words they know.
- Have students listen and look at the pictures while you say the words or play the audio.
- Instruct students to circle the words that are new to them.
- Say the words or play the audio a second time. Pause after each word or phrase and ask the students to repeat and point to the correct picture.
- Put students in pairs and have one say a word or phrase as the partner points to the correct picture. Reverse roles and repeat the activity.
- Call on students and ask questions: *What do you shut off? Do you lock a coffeepot? What can you do to a fan?*

LISTENING SCRIPT

Lesson 1, Activity 1: Learn New Words

Look at the pictures. Listen to the words. Listen again and repeat.

1. shut off — Shut off the alarm clock.
2. plug in — Plug in the coffeepot.
3. pick up — Pick up the newspaper.
4. put away — Put away the dishes.
5. take out — Take out the milk.
6. turn on — Turn on the radio.
7. turn off — Turn off the radio.
8. put back — Put back the milk.
9. turn down — Turn down the heat.
10. lock — Lock the door.
11. unlock — Unlock the door.
12. unplug — Unplug the coffeepot.

EXPANSION ACTIVITY: Pronoun Practice

- Explain to students that you will make requests and they will respond with a question about the request, using the pronoun *it*. For example, if you say: *Luis, will you please shut off the TV?* Luis might ask: *How do I shut it off?*
- Brainstorm sample questions and write them on the board.
- Call on students and make a request, eliciting a question in response.
- Continue the activity until all the students have had a chance to participate.
- Alternatively, have students continue the activity by making requests of each other.

Grammar Note:

- Point out that many of the new words are two-word verbs, that is, they are formed by a verb and a particle. Remind students that if they use a pronoun, the pronoun goes between the verb and the particle (*plug it in*). You may want to point out that prefixes usually change the meaning of the word that they precede (*un-* means the opposite). Ask students to identify the opposite of *lock* and *plug in* (*unlock, unplug*).

Unit 9: Lesson 1

2 Write

- Have students look at the chart. Have them copy the chart on paper.
- Put students in pairs to brainstorm a list of items that are in each room in the pictures. Have them list the objects on the chart.
- Call on students to share their ideas with the class.
- Explain that students will tell about the man's actions this morning. Go over the example.
- Have students take turns telling their partners about what the man did.
- Call on students to share their ideas with the class.

ANSWER KEY:

Answers will vary. Charts may include the following:

Bedroom	Kitchen	Living Room
a lamp	a window	a stereo
a clock	curtains	a radio
a bed	a coffeepot/	a lamp
a glass of	coffeemaker	a thermostat
water	a coffee cup	a TV
a pillow	cabinets	pictures
a window	a refrigerator	
curtains	a heater	
	milk	
	a spoon	

EXPANSION ACTIVITY: Sequencing [Multi-Level]

- Have students close their books. Dictate sentences about the pictures (without providing the following numbers). For lower level students, you may wish to provide a cloze exercise of the sentences you read, having them fill in missing words instead of writing the whole sentence. Create your own sentences or use the ones below.

    The man locked the door. (5)
    He plugged in the coffeepot. (2)
    He took out the milk. (3)
    The man turned off the alarm clock. (1)
    He turned down the heat. (4)

- Have students compare sentences with a partner.
- Tell students to put the sentences in order, writing *1* next to the first action and so on.
- Have volunteers write the sentences in the correct sequence on the board.

3 Listen and Write 125

- Go over the directions and remind students to use the pictures to answer each question.
- Play the audio. Pause after each conversation and have students write the correct picture number in each blank.
- Put students in pairs to compare answers. Play the audio again if necessary to have students confirm their answers.
- Go over the answers with the class.

LISTENING SCRIPT

Lesson 1, Activity 3: Listen and Write

Listen to the instructions. Write the number of the picture.

Thanks, Katia, for checking on the house while I am gone. I'm going to go over some instructions.

First, use this key to unlock the door.

Second, turn on one or two lights. You can leave them on at night.

Third, take out the trash on Tuesday night. Wednesday is trash day.

Fourth, when you leave, make sure you turn down the heat. The thermostat is in the hall.

After that, unplug the coffeepot if you used it.

Finally, the most important thing—remember to lock all the doors.

Call me with any questions. I'll see you on the 19th.

ANSWER KEY:

First, 11; Second, 6; Third, 5; Fourth, 9; After that, 12; Finally, 10

Unit 9: Lesson 1

EXPANSION ACTIVITY: Closing Time
[Multi-Level]

- Have students brainstorm various job titles and list them on the board. Encourage students to include a wide variety of professionals such as zookeeper, bus driver, florist, athlete, and so on.
- Put students in small groups of mixed levels. Have each group choose one of the jobs listed, making sure no jobs are repeated.
- Have groups imagine what tasks their professional would have to do at the end of a day of work. For example, a bus driver might have to file incident reports, log miles, refill the bus with gas, and so on. Lower level students might draw pictures or use a bilingual dictionary to make suggestions. Have more advanced students help put their ideas into words.
- Have groups list a sequence of steps that the professional would take each day at the end of work, using words such as *first, next,* and *finally*.
- Have groups share their lists with the class.

4 Practice the Conversation 126

- Have students listen and look at the conversation while you read it or play the audio.
- Say the words or play the audio a second time. Pause after each line and ask the students to repeat.
- Check comprehension by asking questions: *What are they talking about? What did B do?*
- Model the conversation with a student. Have the student read B's lines. Demonstrate how to substitute from the ideas in the boxes below. Cue the student to make the appropriate substitutions.
- Have students work in pairs to practice the conversation, making substitutions from the boxes and using their own ideas.
- Walk around to make sure students understand the activity and provide help if needed.

LISTENING SCRIPT

Lesson 1, Activity 4: Practice the Conversation

Listen to the conversation. Listen again and repeat.

A: Oh, no. We'd better hurry, or we'll be late.
B: Did you unplug the coffeepot?
A: Yes, and I put away the milk.
B: Good. I turned off the TV.
A: Thanks. Let's go!

TARGET GRAMMAR

Simple past review
The Target Grammar point is used in Activity 4. Presentation and practice of this grammar point appears on *Student Book* pages 192–193. Answer Keys appear on Teacher's Edition page 258.

EXPANSION ACTIVITY: Write It Out

- Tell students to pretend that they are going away on a trip. Have them write two to-do lists: one for themselves, to remember what they must do before they leave (Turn down the heat) and one for someone who will check on the house/apartment (Take the trash out on Wednesday).
- Put students in pairs to compare lists.
- Call on students to tell the class about something on their lists.
- CHALLENGE: Have advanced students write sentences about the items on their lists, telling the consequences that could happen if each item is not completed.

LESSON 2

Identifying Problems at Home

OBJECTIVE
Identifying problems at home

VOCABULARY

bathtub	key	space heater
clog	leak	stick
clothes dryer	overheat	toaster oven
drain	pipe	toilet
drawer	roof	valve
faucet	sink	window
hair dryer	sliding door	

THINGS TO DO

1 Learn New Words 127

- Have students look at the pictures. Elicit the words they know.
- Have students listen and look at the pictures while you say the words or play the audio.
- Instruct students to circle the words that are new to them.
- Say the words or play the audio a second time. Pause after each word or phrase and ask the students to repeat the word and point to the correct picture.
- Put students in pairs and have one say a word or phrase as the partner points to the correct picture. Reverse roles and repeat the activity.
- Call on students and ask questions: *What do you have in a bathroom? What can stick? What can overheat?*

LISTENING SCRIPT

Lesson 2, Activity 1: Learn New Words

Look at the pictures. Listen to the words. Listen again and repeat.

Things that leak
1. valve — A valve can leak.
2. faucet — The faucet is leaking.
3. pipe — The pipe is leaking.
4. roof — The roof is leaking.

Things that overheat
5. toaster oven — A toaster oven can overheat.
6. space heater — The space heater is overheating.
7. clothes dryer — The clothes dryer is overheating.
8. hair dryer — The hair dryer is overheating.

Things that clog
9. drain — A drain can clog.
10. sink — The sink is clogged.
11. toilet — The toilet is clogged.
12. bathtub — The bathtub is clogged.

Things that stick
13. window — A window can stick.
14. key — The key is stuck.
15. drawer — The drawer is stuck.
16. sliding door — The sliding door is stuck.

EXPANSION ACTIVITY: Descriptions

- Have students draw a box around the pictures of items 2–4, 6–8, and 10–12. Point out that they now have a 3 x 3 grid.
- Tell students that you will give descriptions of some of the words on the grid. As they hear a word described, they should write the number of the description on the picture.
- Create your own description or use the ones below.
  1. *You brush your teeth here. You can wash your hands here too.* (sink)
  2. *This is something that covers your house. It stops the rain from coming in your living room.* (roof)
  3. *This is in your bathroom. You can sit on it.* (toilet)
  4. *You can use this after you take a shower. It can make you look beautiful.* (hair dryer)

Unit 9: Lesson 2

5. *Some people don't take a shower. Instead they use this to wash their bodies.* (bathtub)
6. *This takes water from one place to another.* (pipe)
7. *Water comes out of this. You can turn on hot water or cold water.* (faucet)
8. *This is something you can use to get warm. You plug it into the wall.* (space heater)
9. *When your shirts and pants are wet, you can put them in here.* (clothes dryer)

- Have students compare their answers with a classmate. Go over the answers with the class. Ask students how many they got right.
- CHALLENGE: Have advanced students write their own descriptions. Remind them that they cannot use words in the description that are in the name. For example, when describing *hair dryer*, they can't use *hair* or *dry*. Have volunteers read their descriptions to the class. It doesn't matter if the words are repeated.

❷ Practice the Conversation 128

- Have students listen and look at the conversation while you read it or play the audio.
- Say the lines or play the audio a second time. Pause after each line and ask the students to repeat.
- Check comprehension by asking questions: *What is A calling about? What's the problem this time?*
- Model the conversation with a student. Have the student read B's lines. Demonstrate how to substitute from the ideas in the boxes below. Cue the student to make the appropriate substitutions.
- Have students work in pairs to practice the conversation, making substitutions from the boxes and using their own ideas.
- Walk around to make sure students understand the activity and provide help if needed.

LISTENING SCRIPT

Lesson 2, Activity 2: Practice the Conversation

Listen to the conversation. Listen again and repeat.

A: Hi. This is your tenant in apartment 101.
B: Hi. What can I do for you?
A: Could you please take a look at my refrigerator?
B: Is the door stuck again?
A: No. This time it's leaking.
B: Okay. I'll be over as soon as I can.

Vocabulary Note:
- Students may be unfamiliar with some of the vocabulary in this conversation: *tenant, take a look, be over.* Encourage them to guess the meanings of these words and phrases.

EXPANSION ACTIVITY: Beanbag Toss [Low-Level]

- Tell students that you will say a room and they will answer with a problem with something in the room. For example, if you say: *bathroom*, a student might answer *The sink is leaking, The toilet is clogged,* and so on. Tell students that they cannot say the same problem twice.
- Call on a student and toss a beanbag or ball as you say a room. Elicit a problem with something in the room. Classmates should listen to the problem and correct it if necessary.
- The student should toss the beanbag to a classmate, saying another room and eliciting a different problem.
- Continue the activity until all students have had a chance to participate.

188 • UNIT 9   STUDENT BOOK PAGES 118-119

Unit 9: Lesson 2

3 Listen and Write 129

- Go over the directions and the chart
- Play the audio. Pause after each conversation and have students write the problem in the chart.
- Put students in pairs to compare answers. Play the audio again if necessary to have students confirm their answers.
- Go over the answers with the class.

LISTENING SCRIPT

Lesson 2, Activity 3: Listen and Write

Listen to the telephone messages. Write the problem.

You have four messages. To listen to your messages, press 1.

First message: Hi. This is the tenant in Apartment 103. We've got a problem. The roof is leaking. Can you come over right away?

Second message: This is John Burke in 210. The clothes dryer is overheating. Could you check it out, please?

Third message: Sorry to bother you, but this is Lisa in Apartment 507. The kitchen sink is clogged again. It's really making a mess.

Fourth message: Hey. I'm the tenant in Apartment 401. My key is stuck in the front door. Would you get it out for me?

ANSWER KEY:

1. The roof is leaking; 2. The clothes dryer is overheating; 3. The kitchen sink is clogged; 4. The key is stuck in the front door.

EXPANSION ACTIVITY: Excuses, Excuses [Challenge]

- Have more advanced students work in pairs to expand one of the conversations they heard in Activity 3. Tell them that the building manager can't come or doesn't want to fix the problem. Have them write why he can't or won't come, as well as how the tenant responds.
- Have partners perform their conversations for the class.

4 Write

- Go over the directions.
- Have students complete the maintenance request form for a problem in Activity 3.
- Put students in pairs and have them tell about the problem.

EXPANSION ACTIVITY: Role-Play

- Have students copy the maintenance request form.
- Put students in pairs and have them role-play the conversation between a tenant and the building manager as in Activity 3. Have the building manager complete the form.

LESSON 3 — A Fire Emergency

OBJECTIVE
A fire emergency

VOCABULARY

ambulance	evacuate	hydrant
attach	fire escape	ladder
climb	fire truck	rescue
cover	firefighter	spray
crawl	hose	smoke

TARGET GRAMMAR
Series of commands *page 194*

THINGS TO DO

1 Learn New Words 130

- Have students look at the Big Picture in their books. Ask students what the picture is about and elicit the words they know.
- Have students listen and look at the picture while you say the words or play the audio.
- Instruct students to circle the words that are new to them.
- Say the words or play the audio a second time. Pause after each word or phrase and ask the students to repeat and point to the correct part of the picture.
- Put students in pairs and have one say a word as the partner points to the correct part of the picture. Reverse roles and repeat the activity.
- Call on students and ask questions: *What does a firefighter do? Where are there fire escapes?*

LISTENING SCRIPT

Lesson 3, Activity 1: Learn New Words

Look at the picture. Listen to the words. Listen again and repeat.

1. smoke	There's a lot of smoke.
2. spray	They spray water on the fire.
3. fire escape	They are going down the fire escape.
4. rescue	He is rescuing the man.
5. climb	The man is climbing down.
6. evacuate	The residents need to evacuate the building.
7. ladder	He is on the ladder.
8. ambulance	The ambulance is in front of the building.
9. cover	The woman covers her mouth.
10. firefighter	The firefighter is spraying water.
11. hose	The hose brings water to the fire.
12. crawl	The man crawls under the smoke.
13. hydrant	The firefighter attaches the hose to the hydrant.
14. attach	The firefighter needs to attach the hose.
15. fire truck	The fire truck is next to the building.

EXPANSION ACTIVITY: Spelling Rule Review [Literacy]

- For students who need practice with the rules of spelling and pronunciation, go over words from the vocabulary list. Use examples like these:
    1. vowel + consonant + e = long vowel sound (smoke, escape, evacuate, hose, firefighter)
    2. silent b (climb)
    3. silent gh (firefighter)
- Help students brainstorm other words that follow the same spelling rules.

Unit 9: Lesson 3

 BIG PICTURE EXPANSION ACTIVITY:
GRAMMAR—What Happened?

- Make copies of Worksheet 17 (Teacher's Edition page 240) and distribute them to students.
- Have students look at the Big Picture for Unit 9, Lesson 3 in their books (Student Book pages 120–121). Instruct students to complete the activities and then check their answers with a partner.
- Go over the answers with the class.

ANSWER KEY:

A. 1. flew; 2. stood; 3. fought; 4. put; 5. took; 6. held; 7. came, heard; 8. got; 9. had
B. Answers will vary. Possible answers include: 1. She drove the ambulance; 2. She went down the fire escape; 3. He told people about the fire; 4. He saw a woman who needed help.

❷ Talk About the Picture

- Have students look at the Big Picture in their books.
- To set the context, ask questions about the picture: *How many people do you see? Where are they? What are they doing?*. Write any additional vocabulary on the board.
- Ask students to write five sentences about the picture. Remind them to use the words on the board or in Activity 1 if they need help.
- Walk around the room and provide help as needed.
- Put students in pairs. Have them take turns reading their sentences.
- Call on students to read sentences to the class.

EXPANSION ACTIVITY: Vocabulary Builder

- Have lower level students look at the picture and identify five objects for which they do not know the names in English.
- Have students look up each object in a bilingual dictionary or ask a more advanced classmate the name of the object. Have them write a list of the five words and their translations.
- Put students in pairs and have them share their lists. Have partners choose three words and write one sentence using each word.
- CHALLENGE: Have more advanced students look up technical words or words with narrow definitions shown in the picture, such as *nozzle, puddle, hover,* and so on.

 BIG PICTURE EXPANSION ACTIVITY:
SPEAKING—Question Challenge

- Divide the class into teams. Have each team member create a question about the picture. Have them memorize their questions.
- Give students three minutes to memorize as much as they can about the picture. Have students close their books.
- Have teams take turns asking questions of an opposing team member. Each correct answer earns the team a point. Continue the activity until all students have asked and answered a question.

❸ Put in Order

- Have the students read the sentences or read the sentences aloud and have students repeat.
- Go over the directions. Point out that the first event in the story is indicated by a number 1.
- Have students put the story in order and then check their answers with a classmate.
- Go over the answers with the class.

Unit 9: Lesson 3

ANSWER KEY:

1. Sam turned on the space heater.
2. He went to bed.
3. The heater overheated.
4. The smoke alarm went off.
5. He woke up.
6. He smelled smoke.
7. He called 911.
8. The fire trucks arrived.

EXPANSION ACTIVITY: Strip Story [Challenge]

- Write another story on strips of paper, one sentence per strip. Make enough copies so each student will have a strip, but make sure that all strips form part of a complete story. Create your own story or use the one below.

    *Mary woke up.
    She turned off her alarm clock.
    She turned on the space heater in her bedroom.
    She went downstairs to make breakfast.
    Mary smelled smoke.
    She thought the smoke was from her breakfast, but it was the space heater upstairs.
    She called 911.
    She went outside.
    The firefighters came and saw Mary outside.*

- Give each student a strip and have them memorize the sentence.
- Have students stand and walk around the room, reciting their sentences to classmates. Have them stand in a group with classmates, so that each student in the group has a different sentence. Together the group's sentences should form one complete version of the story. Then have them stand in order and recite the sentences.

❹ Practice the Conversation 131

- Have students listen and look at the conversation while you read it or play the audio.
- Say the lines or play the audio a second time. Pause after each line and ask the students to repeat.
- Check comprehension by asking questions: *What should the people not do? What should they do?*

- Model the conversation with a student. Have the student read B's lines. Demonstrate how to substitute from the ideas in the boxes below. Cue the student to make the appropriate substitutions.
- Have students work in pairs to practice the conversation, making substitutions from the boxes and using their own ideas.
- Walk around to make sure students understand the activity and provide help if needed.

LISTENING SCRIPT

Lesson 3, Activity 4: Practice the Conversation

Listen to the conversation. Listen again and repeat.

A: What should we do if there is a fire?

B: Call 911. Don't take the elevator.

A: Should we go down the stairs?

B: Yes, if possible. Or go down the fire escape.

A: Okay.

⭕ TARGET GRAMMAR

Series of commands

The Target Grammar point is used in Activity 4. Presentation and practice of this grammar point appears on Student Book page 194. Answer Keys appear on Teacher's Edition page 259.

EXPANSION ACTIVITY: More Disasters!

- Brainstorm other emergencies or disasters that could happen, such as tornadoes or car crashes.
- Put students in groups. Assign each group one emergency. Have the group rewrite the conversation from Activity 4 using their disaster.
- Have group members role-play their new conversation for the class. Lead a discussion after each one, asking whether each suggestion is a good idea.

LESSON 4 — Safety Tips

OBJECTIVE
Safety tips

VOCABULARY

Celsius	overheat
Fahrenheit	overload
overflow	temperature

TARGET GRAMMAR
Adverbs of point in time *page 195*

WINDOW ON MATH
Converting Temperatures

THINGS TO DO

1 Learn New Words 🎧 132

- Have students look at the illustration in their books. Ask students what the picture is about and elicit the words they know.
- Have students listen and look at the picture while you say the words or play the audio.
- Say the words or play the audio a second time. Pause after each word or phrase and ask the students to repeat and point to the correct part of the picture as possible. For words not illustrated specifically in the picture (*Celsius, Fahrenheit*), provide other examples.
- Put students in pairs and have one say a word as the partner points to the correct part of the picture. Reverse roles and repeat the activity.
- Call on students and ask questions: *What is overheated? Which things have a high temperature?*

LISTENING SCRIPT

Lesson 4, Activity 1: Learn New Words

Listen to the words. Listen again and repeat.

1. overload — Don't overload the outlet.
2. overheat — The space heater can overheat.
3. overflow — The sink overflowed.
4. temperature — The temperature is too high.
5. Celsius — They use the Celsius temperature scale in most countries.
6. Fahrenheit — We use the Fahrenheit temperature scale in the United States.

EXPANSION ACTIVITY: Name that Temperature

- Choose several locations around the world. Before class, find out the current temperature in each location. Be sure to choose a variety of climates.
- Write one location on the board. Have students guess what the temperature is there today. Write their guesses on the board, using either Celsius or Fahrenheit (but not both).
- After students have guessed, tell the correct temperature. Have students convert the temperature into the alternative measurement (Celsius or Fahrenheit). Have students use the information from Window on Math to make their calculations.
- Continue until you have reviewed and converted the temperature for each location chosen.
- LOW LEVEL: Have lower level students write sentences about the temperature in each place. Provide a sentence frame such as *The temperature in _____ is _____.*

STUDENT BOOK PAGES 122-123

Unit 9: Lesson 4

2 Think About the Topic

- Have students silently look at the picture and think about the problems it shows for a few minutes.
- Have partners discuss what problems they saw in the picture.
- Have volunteers share their ideas with the class.

ANSWER KEY:

Possible answers include: candle burning near curtain; towel on hot stove; cooking food unattended; electrical cord under rug; heater too close to curtain; overloaded electrical outlet; flammable material (canister) near heater

---

EXPANSION ACTIVITY: Creative Writing [Challenge]

- Put students in small groups.
- Have students look at the picture and imagine a story that is happening. For example, students may imagine that the man is dreaming, that someone who is not in the picture is cooking dinner, or that the smoke detector is about to go off.
- Have groups write a short story telling what they imagined, using as many words they've learned in the unit as possible.
- Have groups share their stories with the class.

---

3 Read and Take Notes

- Have students look at the chart so they know what information to look for when they read. Have them copy the chart on another sheet of paper so they have enough room to include all the information.
- Have students read the article silently, or read each it in a round robin style, with each student reading part of it aloud.
- Have students work individually to complete the chart and then compare charts with a partner.
- Call on students and have them tell what they wrote under *Do* and *Don't*.

ANSWER KEY:

Do: keep materials away from stove; lock up matches and lighters; keep space heaters three feet from flammable materials; unplug appliances that smoke or smell odd; store flammable materials away from heated appliances; keep flammable things away from heat sources; throw out oily rags or store them in sealed containers; keep kids three feet from a hot stove

Don't: leave food on/in the stove/oven/microwave unattended; run electrical cords under rugs; overload electrical sockets with plugs; fold electric blankets while they're plugged in; leave a lit candle unattended; smoke in bed;

BIG PICTURE EXPANSION ACTIVITY: READING—How to Escape from a Fire

- Make copies of Worksheet 18 (Teacher's Edition page 241) and distribute them to students.
- Have students look at the Big Picture for Unit 9, Lesson 3 in their books (Student Book pages 120–121).
- Instruct students to complete the activities and then check their answers with a partner.
- Go over the answers with the class.

ANSWER KEY:

A. 1. False; 2. True; 3. False; 4. I don't know.; 5. True; 6. False

B. 1. Answers will vary. Possible answers: People are using the fire escape./ No one went to the roof./ Some people went to the window./ One man is crawling under the smoke; 2. Answers will vary.

Unit 9: Lesson 4

EXPANSION ACTIVITY: Phrasal Verbs and Prepositions [Literacy]

- Have students scan the article they read for Activity 3 and circle the phrasal verbs and prepositions they see (verbs: *lock up, plugged in, throw out;* prepositions: *away from*).
- Explain that when students read, they should look for phrases as well as try to identify individual words. Point out that if they do not look for phrases, they could become confused about meaning. For example, have students tell the difference between *throw* and *throw out* and how it affects the meaning of the sentence in the chart.
- Have students list other phrasal verbs and prepositions they know. Discuss examples as a class, telling the meaning and how each phrase is used.

4 Write

- Go over the directions.
- Read the example aloud. Point out the expressions of time. Brainstorm other expressions that tell the order of events (*A few years ago, last month, then, after that*).
- Put students in pairs to tell about an emergency that they or someone they know experienced.
- Have students write the story.
- Call on students to read their stories to the class.

EXPANSION ACTIVITY: Sequence Strips

- Have students write or rewrite their stories from Activity 4 on strips of paper or index cards, one sentence per strip.
- Have students shuffle the strips and then exchange stories with a classmate.
- Have students put their partners' strips in order.

TARGET GRAMMAR

Adverbs of point in time

The Target Grammar point is used in Activity 4. Presentation and practice of this grammar point appears on Student Book pages 195–196. Answer Keys appear on Teacher's Edition page 259.

WINDOW ON MATH

Converting Temperatures

A Read the information below.

- Have students read the information silently or read it aloud to them.
- Ask questions: *Do we use Fahrenheit or Celsius to report temperatures here? What is the temperature today? What temperature is that in Celsius? How do we convert Fahrenheit to Celsius?*
- Go over the examples.

B Convert these temperatures.

- Work through the first problem with the class.
- Have students convert the temperatures, and then check their answers with a partner.
- Go over the answers with the class.

ANSWER KEY:

1. 0; 2. 30; 3. 104; 4. 59

LESSON 5 Talking About Emergencies

OBJECTIVE
Talking about emergencies

PRONUNCIATION
L versus R Sounds

1 Practice Pronunciation: L versus R Sounds 🎧 133

A. Listen to the pairs of words. Listen again and repeat.

- Have students look at the list of words. Point out that there are six pairs of words in the list. Each pair sounds almost the same, except one word has an L sound, and the other has an R sound.
- Have students look at the words while you say them or play the audio.
- Say the words or play the audio a second time, pausing after each word to have students repeat.

LISTENING SCRIPT

Lesson 5, Activity 1: Practice Pronunciation: L versus R Sounds

A. Listen to the pairs of words. Listen again and repeat.

1. file	fire	4. lamp	ramp
2. while	wire	5. list	wrist
3. call	car	6. light	right

B. Listen to the pairs of sentences. Listen again and repeat. 🎧 134

- Have students look at the sentences while you say them or play the audio.
- Say the sentences or play the audio a second time, pausing after each word to have students repeat.

LISTENING SCRIPT

Lesson 5, Activity 1: Practice Pronunciation: L versus R Sounds

B. Listen to the pairs of sentences. Listen again and repeat.

1. It will be a while.	It will be a wire.
2. There's a file in the supply closet.	There's a fire in the supply closet.
3. Take a light.	Take a right.

C. Work with a partner. Take turns reading each sentence and choosing a response.

- Model the activity. Read the first sentence with *while: It will be a while.* Ask students which response is appropriate (*How long?*)
- Put students in pairs. Have students take turns reading a sentence with one of the word choices, and responding appropriately.

EXPANSION ACTIVITY: Words We Know

- Put students in small groups to brainstorm other words with the *l* or *r* sounds that they find difficult.
- Call on students to share their ideas. Write the words on the board. The list might include: *rain/lane, play/pray, fly/fry, long/wrong, rink/link.*
- Have individuals use the words in sentences. Tell students to raise their right hand if the word has an *r* sound and their left hand if the word has an *l* sound.
- **LOW LEVEL** Have lower level students make illustrated flash cards for several of the word pairs, with a word on one side and a picture on the other. Have partners take turns holding up a picture and having each other say the word it represents. You may wish to have a more advanced student listen to them and model pronunciation as needed.

Unit 9: Lesson 5

❷ Practice the Conversation: Reporting Emergencies 🎧 135

- Show students the picture in the book for Activity 2. To set the context, ask questions about the picture: *Who is in the picture? Where are they?*
- Read the conversation or play the audio.
- Read or play the conversation again. Pause after each sentence and ask students to repeat.
- To confirm understanding, ask comprehension questions about the conversation: *What is the man calling about? Where is the fire?*
- Point out that there are three pieces of scripted information in the conversation that can be substituted: A tells about an emergency and gives a location, and B tells what help is coming.
- Model the conversation with a student. You read A's part and have the student read B's lines. Demonstrate how to substitute *someone is breaking into a house* and *315 Market Street* from the first box below. Cue the student to say *A police car is on the way.*
- Put students in pairs to practice the conversation, making substitutions from the boxes and using their own ideas.
- Walk around to monitor the activity and provide help as needed.

LISTENING SCRIPT

Lesson 5, Activity 2: Practice the Conversation: Reporting Emergencies

Listen to the conversation. Listen again and repeat.

A: Is this 911?

B: Yes. What's your emergency?

A: I'm calling to report a fire.

B: What is the location?

A: 1524 South Main Street.

B: A fire truck is on the way.

❸ Practice the Conversation: Talking About Safety Problems 🎧 136

- Repeat the basic procedure from Activity 2.
- To set the context, ask questions about the picture: *Who do you see? What are they looking at?*
- After students have listened to and repeated the conversation line by line, check comprehension by asking: *What is the problem? What does B suggest doing?*
- Have students continue practicing the conversation, making substitutions from the boxes and using their own ideas.

LISTENING SCRIPT

Lesson 5, Activity 3: Practice the Conversation: Talking About Safety Problems

Listen to the conversation. Listen again and repeat.

A: Oh, no. We've got a problem.

B: What's the matter?

A: The dryer overheated and the wires melted.

B: We'd better call an electrician right away.

A: Good idea. I'm worried about a fire.

❹ Listen and Write 137

- To set the context, ask questions about the picture: *Who do you see? What is the woman doing?*
- Have students read the news report.
- Read the conversation or play the audio. Have students write the missing words.
- Read or play the conversation again as students check their answers.
- Put students in pairs to compare their answers.
- Go over the answers with the class.

Unit 9: Lesson 5

LISTENING SCRIPT

Lesson 5, Activity 4: Listen and Write

Listen to the news report. Write the missing words. Listen again and check your answers.

This is Channel 5 news at 9:00 A.M. We have breaking news of a major fire in the 2000 block of Main Street, at the Landview Apartments. We don't have many details yet, but we do know that 45 families had to leave their homes at 5:30 this morning. Firefighters and other emergency personnel are on the scene. We'll bring you more news as the story develops. Drivers should take North Street instead.

ANSWER KEY:

This is Channel 5 news at <u>9:00 A.M</u>. We have breaking news of a major <u>fire</u> in the 2000 block of <u>Main Street</u>, at the Landview Apartments. We don't have many details yet, but we do know that <u>45</u> families had to leave their homes at <u>5:30</u> this morning. <u>Firefighters</u> and other emergency personnel are on the scene. We'll bring you more news as the story develops. Drivers should take <u>North</u> Street instead.

EXPANSION ACTIVITY: Breaking News
[Challenge]

- Have students work in groups to write a news report, using the one from Activity 4 as a model. Brainstorm ideas with students as necessary, making a list of the kinds of stories that they might hear on the news.

- Have one member from each group deliver the news report to the class. Have students retell the details they heard in each report.

LESSON 6: Home Emergency Plans

OBJECTIVE
Home emergency plans

1 Talk About It
- Go over the directions.
- Have partners work together to list emergencies.
- Call on students to share their ideas with the class.

EXPANSION ACTIVITY: Emergencies Around Town
- Brainstorm ideas with students about emergencies that they might witness during the course of a normal day. For example, they might see an accident while driving to work, someone might choke on food at a restaurant, and so on.
- Discuss with students what they would do in each situation.
- LOW-LEVEL: Help students write a list of the emergencies discussed. Have them use a bilingual dictionary if necessary to be sure they understand the meaning of important words. Help students write sentences that they could use for each emergency, such as *Call an ambulance.*

Culture/Civics Note:
- Tell students about Good Samaritan laws in the United States and the protection they offer to people who help someone in an emergency situation. You may also wish to explain the origin of the phrase (the tale of the Good Samaritan) and ask students if they have similar tales in their cultures or countries of origin.

2 Read and Match
- Go over the directions.
- Have students read the article and answer the questions.
- Put students in pairs to check their answers.
- Go over the answers with the class.

ANSWER KEY:
1. b; 2. d; 3. a; 4. c; 5. f; 6. e

3 Make a Plan
- Have students read the article and check the activities they've completed in the past year. Then have them write three activities they intend to do in the next year.
- Have volunteers share their ideas with the class. Discuss any new ideas, having students give their opinions.

EXPANSION ACTIVITY: What's the Procedure? [Challenge]
- Have students go online to find out the emergency procedures for their neighborhood or your school or area. You may wish to have a media specialist or an information technology specialist in your school help students find relevant websites or other resources that would tell this information.
- Have students report the information to the class.

LESSON 7 What Do You Know?

1 Listening Review 138

- Go over the directions with the class.
- Read the items or play the audio and have the students mark their answers on the Answer Sheet.
- Walk around to monitor the activity and help students stay on task.
- Have students check their answers with a partner.
- Go over the answers with the class.

> **LISTENING SCRIPT**
>
> **Lesson 7, Activity 1: Listening Review**
>
> *You will hear part of a conversation. To finish the conversation, listen and choose the correct answer: A, B, or C. Use the Answer Sheet.*
>
> 1. A: Oh, no. We've got a problem.
>   A. What's the matter?
>   B. I don't know.
>   C. Yes, I can.
> 2. A: What's your location?
>   A. There's a fire.
>   B. 564 9th Street.
>   C. Thank you.
> 3. A: Could you please take a look at my kitchen sink?
>   B: Is it leaking again?
>   A. In an hour.
>   B. Apartment 13A.
>   C. No. This time it's clogged.
> 4. A: What is the emergency?
>   A. Someone had a car accident.
>   B. At the corner of Main and Pine Streets.
>   C. I don't think so.
> 5. A: Hi. This is the tenant in Apartment 19B. The sliding door is stuck.
>   A. Is it the window again?
>   B. Okay. I'll be right over.
>   C. Thank you.

> **ANSWER KEY:**
>
> 1. A; 2. B; 3. C; 4. A; 5. B

2 Listening Dictation 139

- Copy the numbers and lines from the Listening Dictation section on the board.
- Read the first sentence: *Please turn off the lights.* Have a more advanced student write the sentence on the board on the line next to 1. Have students copy the sentence in their books.
- Play the audio and have students write the sentences they hear. Repeat as many times as necessary.
- Put students in pairs to compare answers.
- Have volunteers write the sentences on the board.

> **TESTING FOCUS: Listening Effectively**
>
> - Remind students that when they listen for dictation, every word is important. However, students need to remember to continue listening actively even when their mind is stuck on a particular word. Encourage students to stop thinking about words they don't know or don't hear properly the first time, but instead to keep listening to the rest of the conversation so they don't miss other important information.
> - Remind students that if they miss words during the first listening, they can leave blank spaces and go back to fill them in during subsequent listenings.

> **LISTENING SCRIPT**
>
> **Lesson 7, Activity 2: Listening Dictation**
>
> *Listen. Write the sentences you hear.*
>
> 1. Please turn off the lights.
> 2. The hair dryer is overheating.
> 3. The fire truck is next to the hydrant.
> 4. Don't use the elevator.
> 5. You can use the fire escape.

Unit 9: Lesson 7

❸ Grammar Review
- Go over the directions.
- Read the first sentence. Elicit the appropriate completion. Have students circle C for item 1.
- Have students answer the rest of the questions.
- Put students in pairs to compare answers.
- Go over the answers with the class.

ANSWER KEY:

1. C; 2. A; 3. C; 4. A; 5. A; 6. B

LEARNING LOG
- Point out the four sections of the Learning Log: *I know these words; I can ask; I can say;* and *I can write.*
- Have students check what they know and what they can do.
- Walk around to note what they don't know or can't do. Use this information to review areas of difficulty.

BIG PICTURE EXPANSION ACTIVITY:
SPEAKING—Assessment: Talking about the Picture

- You can use the Big Picture on student Book pages 120–121 to place new students in open entry classes, to diagnose difficulties, or to measure progress.
- Work with one student at a time and show them the Big Picture. Ask: *What do you see in the picture? Tell me about the picture.* Tell the student you want him or her to speak for as long as possible. Wait a moment for the student to prepare to answer. If the student has difficulty, you can use prompts: *What do you see in the picture? Who do you see in the picture? What are they doing?*
- You can use a rubric like the one below to rate beginning speakers.

4	Exhibits confidence; begins speaking without prompting Uses some complex sentences, although may make mistakes with irregular forms Can use more than one tense
3	Uses sentences, although form may be incorrect Can speak for a sustained length of time Responds to prompts, but doesn't need them to begin speaking
2	Can use nouns and verbs Uses phrases Answers informational questions
1	Can name objects Uses single words Can answer *yes/no* questions
0	Cannot say anything independently May be able to point to objects when prompted

Unit 9: Lesson 7

BIG PICTURE EXPANSION ACTIVITY:
WRITING—Order of Events

- Have students look at the Big Picture (Student Book pages 120–121).
- Ask the class questions: *What do you think caused the fire? What happened next? What happened after that? How do you think the mother on the third floor feels?*
- Have students write a paragraph describing the fire from the point of view of one of the people in the picture. Remind them to use the simple past to describe the actions that have already happened.
- Put students in pairs to take turns reading their paragraphs to their partners.

TEACHER'S NOTES:

Things that students are doing well:
_____
_____
_____
_____

Things students need additional help with:
_____
_____
_____
_____

Ideas for further practice or for the next class:
_____
_____
_____
_____

UNIT 10 WORK

UNIT OVERVIEW

LESSON	STUDENT BOOK PAGE	TEACHER'S EDITION PAGE
1. Identifying Jobs	130	204
2. Evaluating Job Skills	132	207
3. At a Career Center	134	210
4. Job Tips	136	213
5. Communicating with an Employer	138	216
6. Understanding Job Ads and Applications	140	219
7. What Do You Know?	142	221

Big Picture Expansion Activities

FOCUS	TITLE	SUGGESTED USE
Grammar	What do we have to do?	Lesson 1
Speaking	Describe and Identify	Lesson 3
Reading	My New Job	Lesson 4
Speaking	Assessment: Talking about the Big Picture	Lesson 7
Writing	Describing Activities at a Career Center	Lesson 7

Big Picture Expansion Activity Worksheets

FOCUS	TITLE	TEACHER'S EDITION PAGE
19. Grammar	What do we have to do?	242
20. Reading	My New Job	243

LESSON 1 Identifying Jobs

OBJECTIVE
Identifying jobs

VOCABULARY

accountant	electrician	nursing assistant
administrative assistant	home health aide	painter restaurant manager
assembler	hotel desk clerk	welder
bricklayer	machine operator	X-ray technician
chef		
computer programmer		

 TARGET GRAMMAR

Have to, don't have to, and *must* page 197

THINGS TO DO

1 Learn New Words 140

- Have students look at the pictures and elicit the words they know.
- Have students listen and look at the pictures while you say the words or play the audio.
- Instruct students to circle the words that are new to them.
- Say the words or play the audio a second time. Pause after each word or phrase and ask the students to repeat and point to the correct picture.
- Put students in pairs and have one say a word as the partner points to the correct picture. Reverse roles and repeat the activity.
- Call on students and ask questions: *Do you know an accountant? Which people build or make things?*

LISTENING SCRIPT

Lesson 1, Activity 1: Learn New Words

Look at the pictures. Listen to the words. Listen again and repeat. Which words are new to you? Circle them.

1. computer programmer — He is a computer programmer.
2. accountant — She is an accountant.
3. administrative assistant — She is an administrative assistant.
4. home health aide — She is a home health aide.
5. X-ray technician — She's an X-ray technician.
6. nursing assistant — He is a nursing assistant.
7. assembler — She is an assembler.
8. machine operator — He is a machine operator.
9. painter — He is a painter.
10. electrician — He is an electrician.
11. bricklayer — She is a bricklayer.
12. welder — He is a welder.
13. chef — She is a chef.
14. restaurant manager — He is a restaurant manager.
15. hotel desk clerk — She is a hotel desk clerk.

EXPANSION ACTIVITY: Draw It [Low-Level]

- Divide the class into teams.
- Explain to students that one member from each team will draw as their classmates identify the job.
- Model the activity. Draw a job and have the students name it.
- Call a member from each team to the front of the room. Whisper the same job title to each "artist" and tell them to begin. Their teammates should try to name the job.
- The first team to correctly name the job (no matter who draws it best) earns a point.

2 Talk About the Pictures

- Have students look at the pictures in their books.
- Go over the directions and the questions. Point out that students should write their own idea for question 5.
- Have partners discuss the jobs together, answering the questions.
- Walk around the room and provide help as needed.
- Go over the answers with the class. Have volunteers tell their original ideas for question 5.

Unit 10: Lesson 1

ANSWER KEY:

Answers will vary.
1. accountant, restaurant manager, hotel desk clerk; possibly computer programmer and administrative assistant; 2. home health aide, X-ray technician, nursing assistant; 3. chef, restaurant manager; 4. electrician; 5. Answers will vary.

EXPANSION ACTIVITY: Twenty Questions

- Divide the class into teams. Tell students they will ask *yes/no* questions to find out what job a person has.
- Brainstorm other jobs (mechanic, office manager, plumber, stylist, mover, construction worker, truck driver, landscaper, child care worker, teacher, dentist, sales clerk, bus driver, machinist, pharmacist, doctor, police officer, nurse, cashier).
- Brainstorm appropriate questions and write them on the board: *Do you work in _____? Do you work with _____? Do you work with other people?*
- Model the activity. Tell students you are thinking of a job title. Tell them to ask you *yes/no* questions in order to find out what job you are thinking of. Remind them to look at the board for ideas for questions.
- When students feel they have enough clues, they can guess what the job is. Each time they guess incorrectly, their team is penalized with one strike. In the end, the team with the fewest strikes wins. Continue until one team guesses the job.
- Have volunteers come to the front of the room. Whisper a job, either one from Activity 1 or from the brainstormed list of jobs.
- Have the other students ask *yes/no* questions. Remind them if they guess too early (*Are you an electrician?*) and are incorrect, they will receive strikes.

3 Listen and Circle 141

- Go over the directions and the questions.
- Play the audio. Pause after each conversation and have students circle the correct answer.
- Put students in pairs to compare answers. Play the audio again to have students confirm their answers.
- LOW LEVEL: Help lower level students prepare for listening by having them predict the answer for each question. For example, for question 1, ask them whether salespeople usually talk a lot.
- Go over the answers with the class.

LISTENING SCRIPT

Lesson 1, Activity 3: Listen and Circle

Listen to the conversation. Circle the correct words.

A: What kind of job do you think you want? Something in sales?
B: No, I don't want to be a salesperson. A salesperson has to work with people. I like to work alone.
A: How about something in construction?
B: Well, I'm not very strong.
A: Hmm. A bricklayer must be strong, but what about a welder?
B: But I'm not a man.
A: A welder doesn't have to be a man. A lot of welders are women.
B: I don't think I want to wear a lot of safety equipment. What about an accountant?
A: Sure. An accountant doesn't have to wear safety equipment. But an accountant has to have a special certificate.

ANSWER KEY:

1. has to; 2. has to; 3. doesn't have to; 4. doesn't have to; 5. has to

◉ TARGET GRAMMAR

Have to, don't have to, and *must*
The Target Grammar point is used in Activity 3. Presentation and practice of this grammar point appears on Student Book pages 197–198. Answer Keys appear on Teacher's Edition page 260.

Unit 10: Lesson 1

EXPANSION ACTIVITY: Requirements for Work

- Divide the class into two groups. Give each group at least 10 small pieces of paper.
- Tell students that they will write down job titles and personal characteristics. Assign one group the task of writing job titles and the other group the task of writing personal characteristics. Students may use ideas from the vocabulary list and previous activities in this lesson, or create their own ideas.
- Collect the job titles and put them in a paper bag. Put the personal characteristics in a separate bag.
- Have volunteers draw one piece of paper from each bag and discuss whether the job title requires the personal characteristic. For example, if students drew *welder* and *outgoing*, they might say that a welder doesn't have to be outgoing since he or she works alone much of the time. This activity may be done as a class or with groups drawing their own pieces of paper.

Culture Note:

- You may wish to lead a discussion about which jobs are appropriate for men and women. Have students cite examples of people who do jobs traditionally done by the opposite sex. For example, point out that there are many more male nurses today than there were in previous decades. Have students talk about their own cultures or countries of origin and tell whether it is acceptable for people to cross gender lines for work.

4 Find Someone Who

- Go over the directions and the example.
- Have students look at the list and elicit the questions they should ask. If necessary, write them on the board.
- Have students stand and walk around the room, asking questions. Remind them to write the person's name down if he or she can answer *yes* to the question.

- Call on students to tell about someone he or she talked to (*Ivan likes to work with numbers*).

EXPANSION ACTIVITY: Job Descriptions [Challenge]

- Write a job on the board (a nursing assistant). Brainstorm ideas of what a person in that job has to do and doesn't have to do. Write the ideas on the board.
- Put students in pairs and assign them a job. Have the pairs write a job description for that job using *has to/doesn't have to*. Tell them not to write the name of the job on the description.
- Put two pairs of students together and have them exchange job descriptions. Have them guess what job is being described.

BIG PICTURE EXPANSION ACTIVITY: GRAMMAR—What do we have to do?

- Make copies of Worksheet 19 (Teacher's Edition page 242) and distribute them to students.
- Have students look at the Big Picture in their books (Student Book pages 134–135).
- Instruct students to complete the activities and then check their answers with a partner.
- Go over the answers with the class.

ANSWER KEY:

A. 1. has to; 2. doesn't have to; 3. has to; 4. doesn't have to; 5. don't have to; 6. has to; 7. don't have to; 8. have to

B. If you want to get a job at this company, you <u>have to</u> dress neatly, but you <u>don't have to</u> wear a suit. You <u>have to</u> come on time. Before the interview, you <u>have to</u> fill out an application. You can bring a résumé, but you <u>don't have to</u> bring photos or evaluations. These aren't necessary. You <u>don't have to</u> be a certain age or gender. We employ men and women of all ages. For our machine operator positions, you <u>have to</u> work from 3 to 7 P.M.

LESSON 2  Evaluating Job Skills

OBJECTIVE
Evaluating job skills

VOCABULARY

communicate ideas effectively	manage time efficiently
follow directions	organize information
have computer skills	resolve conflicts
help other people	work independently
	work well with others

TARGET GRAMMAR
Adverbs of manner *page 199*

THINGS TO DO

1 Learn New Words 142

- Have students look at the pictures and elicit the words they know.
- Have students listen and look at the pictures while you say the phrases or play the audio.
- Say the words or play the audio a second time. Pause after each phrase and ask the students to repeat and point to the correct picture.
- Put students in pairs and have one say a phrase as the partner points to the correct picture. Reverse roles and repeat the activity.
- Call on students and ask questions: *Do you have computer skills? Why is it important to work well with others?*

LISTENING SCRIPT

Lesson 2, Activity 1: Learn New Words

Look at the pictures. Listen to the words. Listen again and repeat.

1. communicate ideas effectively — Are you able to communicate ideas effectively?
2. resolve conflicts — Can you resolve conflicts?
3. organize information — Do you organize information well?
4. have computer skills — Do you have computer skills?
5. work well with others — Do you work well with others?
6. help other people — Do you like to help other people?
7. work independently — Can you work independently?
8. manage time efficiently — Do you manage time efficiently?
9. follow directions — Do you follow directions well?

TARGET GRAMMAR

Adverbs of manner
The Target Grammar point is used in Activities 1, 2, and 3. Presentation and practice of this grammar point appears on Student Book pages 199–200. Answer Keys appear on Teacher's Edition page 260.

EXPANSION ACTIVITY: Continuum
[Multi-Level]

- Have the students stand at the front of the room.
- Tell students that they will place themselves along a continuum, rating their own job skills.
- Say a job skill (*have computer skills*). Indicate one side of the room is for those with excellent computer skills; the other side is for students with no computer skills. For students who have a moderate amount of computer skills, have them self-assess their skills as *very good, okay,* and *not very good*. Have students stand along the continuum where appropriate. Have students take note of where their classmates are standing.
- Continue with the other skills.
- Note: You can use this type of exercise to help pair students for other activities, matching a student of a high skill level with a student of a low skill level. For example, if you plan to have students do an online search, pair students from one end of the computer skills continuum with students from the other end.

Unit 10: Lesson 2

❷ Listen and Check 143

- Go over the directions.
- Read the conversation or play the audio. Have students check their answers.
- Put students in pairs to compare their answers.
- Go over the answers with the class.

LISTENING SCRIPT

Lesson 2, Activity 2: Listen and Check

Listen to the conversation. Check the skills the person has.

A: I'm interested in the position of administrative assistant.

B: Okay. Do you have any experience?

A: Yes, I do. I was an administrative assistant for five years.

B: What skills do you have for this position?

A: I'm very good at organizing information and managing my time.

B: Do you work well with people?

A: Yes, I do. I like to help people. I'm also good at resolving conflicts.

B: What are some areas you need to improve?

A: Well, I want to improve my computer skills. They could be stronger.

B: Okay. We'll call you with our decision next week.

ANSWER KEY:

Students should check: resolve conflicts, organize information, work well with others, help other people, manage time.

Grammar Note:

- You may wish to review the gerunds used in this exercise, showing how each one can be used as a subject although it is formed from a verb. Write an example on the board that shows various usage of a verb and its gerund, such as *I like to help people; I like helping people; helping people is nice.*

EXPANSION ACTIVITY: Dictation

- Have students in groups write down as much of the dialogue as they can remember, using the cues from Activity 2.
- Play the audio from Activity 2 two times, stopping after each listening to have groups revise the dialogue they wrote. Have them try to write the dialogue word-for-word if possible.
- LOW LEVEL: Have lower level students work in groups. Provide them with sentence strips from the dialogue, one line per strip. For each line of dialogue, delete one or two words. Have students listen the first time to order the strips. Have them listen the second time to fill in the missing words.
- Have volunteers write each line of the dialogue on the board and have students peer-correct any errors in spelling or grammar.
- Have students look at the listening script and identify any mistakes they made. Review the most common mistakes that the students made as a whole.

❸ Practice the Conversation 144

- Have students listen and look at the conversation while you read it or play the audio.
- Say the words or play the audio a second time. Pause after each line and ask the students to repeat.
- Check comprehension by asking questions: *What job does A want? What skill is needed?*
- Model the conversation with a student. Have the student read A's lines. Demonstrate how to substitute from the ideas in the boxes below. Cue the student to make the appropriate substitutions.
- Have students work in pairs to practice the conversation, making substitutions from the boxes.
- Walk around to make sure students understand the activity and provide help if needed.
- Call on volunteers to read one of the variations aloud.

Unit 10: Lesson 2

LISTENING SCRIPT

Lesson 2, Activity 3: Practice the Conversation

Listen to the conversation. Listen again and repeat.

B: I'm interested in the bricklayer position.

A: Do you follow directions well?

B: Yes, I do.

A: Excellent. That's what we need.

EXPANSION ACTIVITY: Your Family [Multi-Level]

- Have students write sentences telling what their family members are good or not good at doing. Write examples on the board, such as: *My sister is good at managing time effectively.* Alternately, provide a sentence frame, such as *(Person) is (not) good at (skill).* You may wish to have lower level students work together.
- Next, have students rewrite each sentence using an adverb of manner. For example: *My sister manages time well.*
- Put students in pairs or groups to share their sentences. Have more advanced students help lower level students correct their sentences for grammar, spelling, and punctuation.
- Have volunteers read sentences to the class. Find out whose family members have skills in common, if desired.

4 How About You?

- Have students look at the self-survey. Ask about the first item: *Who is excellent at organizing information? Who needs to improve their organization skills?* Have students check the appropriate box to describe their skills.
- Have students rate their skills on their own.
- Put students in pairs to share their evaluations, following the example as a model.
- Call on students to tell the class about their skills.

EXPANSION ACTIVITY: Interview/Write

- Have students write questions about the skills in Activity 3 (*How are your computer skills?*).
- Put students in pairs and have them interview their partners.
- Have students write about their partners.
- Call on students to tell the class about their partners' skills (*Yuliya has average computer skills. She needs to improve her time management.*).

LESSON 3  At a Career Center

OBJECTIVE
At a career center

VOCABULARY

application	day shift	job applicant
appointment	evening shift	night shift
career center	full time	part time
career counselor	interview	résumé

TARGET GRAMMAR
Compound sentences with *and*, *but*, and *or*   page 201

THINGS TO DO

1 Learn New Words 145

- Have students look at the Big Picture in their books (Student Book pages 134–135). Elicit the words they know.
- Have students listen and look at the pictures while you say the words or play the audio.
- Say the words or play the audio a second time. Pause after each word or phrase and ask the students to repeat and point to the correct part of the picture.
- Put students in pairs and have one say a word as the partner points to the correct part of the picture. Reverse roles and repeat the activity.

LISTENING SCRIPT
Lesson 3, Activity 1: Learn New Words

Look at the picture. Listen to the words. Listen again and repeat.

1. career center — Where is the career center?
2. career counselor — Who is the career counselor?
3. application — Do you have your application?
4. resume — Did you bring a résumé?
5. interview — When is your interview?
6. job applicant — Are you a job applicant?
7. full-time — Are you looking for a full-time job?
8. part-time — Are you looking for a part-time job?
9. day shift — When does the day shift start?
10. evening shift — When does the evening shift start?
11. night shift — When does the night shift start?
12. appointment — Did you make an appointment?

EXPANSION ACTIVITY: Want Ads [Literacy]

- Bring in want ads from the newspaper or have students bring in ads. Put students in pairs, and give each pair several ads.
- Have students decide whether the ads are part-time or full-time and if the ads mention a shift. Point out that some ads may use abbreviations for these terms.
- Elicit any abbreviations they might find for the new vocabulary words. Write the abbreviations on the board (eves, p/t, f/t). You may wish to review other common abbreviations that may appear (EOE, Ltd., yrs.)
- Call on students to tell the class about the ads they looked at.

Unit 10: Lesson 3

2 Talk About the Picture

- Have students look at the Big Picture in their books (Student Book pages 134–135). Ask questions: *Who do you see? Who do you think wants a new job? What ads do you see?*
- Have students write five ideas or sentences about the picture.
- Put students in pairs to read their sentences.
- Call on students to share their ideas with the class.

> **EXPANSION ACTIVITY: Creative Writing [Challenge]**
>
> - Have more advanced students work with a partner to choose a character from the Big Picture.
> - Have students write a telephone conversation between the character and someone the character knows who is not pictured (a spouse, friend, or other person). The conversation should take place before or after the Big Picture and should describe what the character plans to do at the career center or what happened to the character while he or she was there.
> - Have partners perform their conversations for the class.

> **BIG PICTURE EXPANSION ACTIVITY: SPEAKING—Describe and Identify**
>
> - Put students in groups of five or six.
> - Walk around the room and quietly assign each student a character in the picture.
> - Have the students work individually to list qualities of the person they were assigned.
> - Have students take turns describing their characters to the other members of the group who will try to identify the person.
> - Call on volunteers to describe a person in the picture to the class. Have the class identify the person being described.

3 Practice the Conversation 146

- Have students listen and look at the conversation while you read it or play the audio.
- Say the words or play the audio a second time. Pause after each line and ask the students to repeat.
- Check comprehension by asking questions: *What job did B have before? What shift would B like to work?*
- Model the conversation with a student. Have the student read B's lines. Demonstrate how to substitute from the ideas in the boxes below. Cue the student to make the appropriate substitutions.
- Have students work in pairs to practice the conversation, making substitutions from the boxes.
- Walk around to make sure students understand the activity and provide help if needed.
- Call on volunteers to read one of the variations aloud.

STUDENT BOOK PAGES 134-135

WORK • 211

Unit 10: Lesson 3

LISTENING SCRIPT

Lesson 3, Activity 3: Practice the Conversation

Listen to the conversation. Listen again and repeat.

A: Do you have any experience as an electrician?

B: Yes, I do. I worked as one in my country.

A: Are you good at working on a team?

B: Yes, I am. I had to work on a team in my last job.

A: Would you like to work the day shift or the night shift?

B: I'd like the day shift, but I can work either one.

 TARGET GRAMMAR

Compound sentences with *and*, *but*, and *or*

The Target Grammar point is used in Activity 3. Presentation and practice of this grammar point appears on Student Book page 201. Answer Keys appear on Teacher's Edition page 261.

EXPANSION ACTIVITY: Role-Play

- Put students in pairs to role-play an interview.
- Have students choose a job based on their own interests.
- Have them take turns asking and answering the questions in a mock interview. Point out that they may use the conversations in Activity 3 as a model, as well as inventing new questions.
- Walk around the room to monitor the activity and provide help as needed.
- LOW LEVEL: For lower level students, have them role-play one of the conversations from Activity 3. You may wish to have them write out the conversation first and then have them read it aloud.
- Call on volunteers to perform the role-play in front of the class.

LESSON 4: Job Tips

OBJECTIVE
Job tips

TARGET GRAMMAR
Negative compound sentences *page 202*

WINDOW ON MATH
Overtime Pay

THINGS TO DO

1 Preview

- Have students look at the pictures. Elicit the words they know. Ask questions: *What is he doing? Who are the people? Where is the woman?*
- Have students read the title of the article and look at the pictures to guess what the article is about. Have them check one box.
- Call on students to share their ideas with the class.

Academic Notes:

- Your students have practiced previewing a reading before, and so probably realize the importance of using visuals and titles to predict content. Remind them that predicting what a reading will be about helps them to activate background knowledge. They will understand more of the content if they recall what they already know about the subject first.
- This article has a title and subheadings. Point out that special formatting such as bold-faced type helps identify subheadings. Subheadings often help organize information and highlight key points.

EXPANSION ACTIVITY: Unscramble
[Multi-Level]

- Write the following on the board:

> kas ssutinoeq
> on lsonprae sclal
> og no emit
> ypa nnittatoe
> sders paatlipreyopr

- Tell the students that these scrambled words are key words from the subheadings. Have them work in pairs to unscramble the words and write the phrases. Have lower level students work on the shorter words and more advanced students work on the longer words.
- Call on volunteers to write the phrases on the board.

ANSWER KEY:

Ask questions, no personal calls, go on time, pay attention, dress appropriately.

2 Read and Take Notes

- Have students look at the chart.
- Go over the directions.
- Have students read the article and take notes on the chart.
- Put students in pairs to compare their charts.
- Write an example negative compound sentence on the board using ideas from the reading. For example: *You shouldn't take too long for lunch, and you shouldn't make personal calls.*
- Call on students to share their ideas with the class. Have students write negative compound sentences using two of the ideas from the chart.

STUDENT BOOK PAGES 136–137

Unit 10: Lesson 4

ANSWER KEY:

Things You Should Do	Things You Shouldn't Do
• dress appropriately • get to work on time • pay attention to introductions • ask plenty of questions	• take too long for lunch • make personal telephone calls

 TARGET GRAMMAR

Negative compound sentences
The Target Grammar point is used in Activity 2. Presentation and practice of this grammar point appears on Student Book page 202. The grammar practice may help students with Activity 3. Answer Keys appear on Teacher's Edition page 261.

EXPANSION ACTIVITY: Illustrate a Tip
[Low-Level]

- Distribute paper and drawing supplies. Have students choose one of the tips to illustrate.
- Tell them they can show someone doing the correct thing or someone doing the incorrect thing. For example, for the first point, a student might draw someone dressed neatly and cleanly, while another student might draw a person who is unkempt.
- When students are finished, have volunteers show their illustrations to the class and elicit from the rest of the class what the artists are trying to convey.
- Alternatively, stage a gallery crawl. Display student illustrations on the walls of the classroom. Number the illustrations. Have students walk around the classroom writing the number and the tip they think is being illustrated. Go over the answers with the class.

 BIG PICTURE EXPANSION ACTIVITY:
READING—My New Job

- Make copies of Worksheet 20 (Teacher's Edition, page 243) and distribute them to students.
- Have students look at the Big Picture in their books (Student Book pages 134–135).
- Instruct students to complete the activities and then check their answers with a partner.
- Go over the answers with the class.

ANSWER KEY:

A. 1. gray; 2. She has black hair; She is wearing a gray dress; 3. He wore casual clothes; 4. He went to work early; 5. excited and embarrassed
B. 1. 40 hours; 2. Yes, you'll get overtime if you work more than 40 hours; 3. from 11 P.M. to 7 A.M.

❸ Write

- Go over the directions and the example.
- Have students work independently or in pairs to write their stories.
- Have volunteers read their stories to the class. Have the class tell what the person did right and wrong, discussing each action.

Unit 10: Lesson 4

EXPANSION ACTIVITY: A Different Point of View

- After students have completed Activity 3, have them reread their stories and then write a new one from another person's point of view, such as the character's supervisor or coworker. Have the new narrator notice things that the character did right or wrong.
- MULTI-LEVEL: Have lower level students work with more advanced students who share the same native language. Have students discuss their ideas in both English and their native language. Have the more advanced students help the lower level students translate their ideas correctly into English. You may want to allow students to use bilingual dictionaries as needed.
- Have volunteers share their original story and then their new follow-up story. Have the class discuss how the two together tell more of the whole story than just one person's viewpoint alone.

WINDOW ON MATH

A Read the information below.
- Have students look at the information. Have them read silently as you read aloud.
- Ask comprehension questions: *How many hours do you have to work before you get overtime? How much is overtime pay? What does "time and a half" mean?*
- Go over the example.

B Answer the word problems.
- Have students answer the problems.
- Walk around the room to monitor the activity and provide help as needed.
- Put students in pairs to check their answers.
- Go over the answers with the class.

ANSWER KEY:
1. $588.00; 2. $1100.00

EXPANSION ACTIVITY: More Practice

- Put students in pairs to create two new problems.
- Have them exchange problems with another pair and solve them.
- Ask volunteers to show how they solved the problems on the board.

LESSON 5: Communicating with an Employer

OBJECTIVE
Communicating with an employer

PRONUNCIATION
Intonation in *Yes/No* and *Wh-* Questions

1 Practice Pronunciation: Intonation in *Yes/No* and *Wh-* Questions 🎧 147

A. Listen to the questions. Listen again and repeat.

- Explain to students that we often let the listener know we are asking a question by using rising intonation. In *yes/no* questions, our intonation is even until the last word, and then it goes up. In *wh-* questions, our intonation drops, then rises on the most important word before dropping again.
- Have students look at the questions while you say them or play the audio.
- Say the questions or play the audio a second time, pausing after each line to have students repeat.

LISTENING SCRIPT

Lesson 5, Activity 1: Practice Pronunciation: Intonation in *Yes/No* and *Wh-* Questions

A. Listen to the questions. Listen again and repeat.

Intonation in *Yes/No* Questions

Are you applying for this position?
Did you work before?
Did you travel?
Did you supervise others?
Do you have any questions?

Intonation in *Wh-* Questions

Why are you applying for this position?
Where did you work before?
What did you do?
How many people did you supervise?
What questions do you have?

B. Write three more questions of each type that an employer might ask in an interview.

- Have students create three more *yes/no* questions and three more *Wh-* questions that might be asked in an interview.
- Walk around to monitor the activity and provide help as needed.

C. Work with a partner. Role-play a job interview. Ask and answer the questions.

- Put students in pairs to take turns asking and answering the interview questions.
- Call on students to ask other students the questions in front of the class.

EXPANSION ACTIVITY: Lights, Camera, Action [Multi-Level]

- Videotaping can help your students improve their intonation. If possible in your class setting, arrange for a video camera.
- Record your students as they role-play single questions or an entire interview. Have lower level students write answers to each question first, then read the written questions and answers while videotaping. Have more advanced students improvise answers to each other's written questions.
- Point out that there are many things to notice in the videotape, but for this exercise, they should only focus on intonation. Otherwise, they may become overwhelmed.
- Have students listen to the videotape and draw lines and arrows over their questions to show what their intonation was like. Have them discuss with a partner how to improve intonation.

Unit 10: Lesson 5

② Practice the Conversation: Describing Skills and Experience 🎧 148

- Show students the picture in the book for Activity 2. To set the context, ask questions about the picture: *Who is in the picture? Where are they?*
- Read the conversation or play the audio.
- Read or play the conversation again. Pause after each sentence and ask students to repeat.
- To confirm understanding, ask comprehension questions about the conversation: *What does B enjoy? What did B do before?*
- Point out that there are five pieces of scripted information in the conversation that can be substituted.
- Model the conversation with a student. Have the student read A's lines. Demonstrate how to make substitutions.
- Put students in pairs to practice the conversation, making substitutions from the boxes and using their own ideas.
- Walk around to monitor the activity and provide help as needed.

LISTENING SCRIPT

Lesson 5, Activity 2: Practice the Conversation: Describing Skills and Experience

Listen to the conversation. Listen again and repeat.

A: Why are you applying for this position?
B: I enjoy working with people.
A: Are you willing to travel?
B: Yes, I am. In my last job, I had to travel.
A: I see. Tell me about your experience with office work.
B: I worked as an administrative assistant for three years.

③ Practice the Conversation: Phoning in an Excuse 🎧 149

- Repeat the basic procedure from Activity 2.
- To set the context, ask questions about the picture: *Who do you see? What are they doing?*
- After students have listened to and repeated the conversation line by line, check comprehension by asking: *Why is Magda calling?*
- Play the rest of the audio track. Point out to students that they will use these phrases to practice conversation.
- Have students continue practicing the conversation, making substitutions from the boxes and using their own ideas.

LISTENING SCRIPT

Lesson 5, Activity 3: Practice the Conversation: Phoning in an Excuse

Listen to the conversation. Listen again and repeat.

A: Hello. Is this Mr. Roberts?
B: Yes, it is.
A: This is Magda Perkins. I'm sorry, but I can't come in today. I'm really sick.
B: I hope you feel better.
A: Thank you.

Listen to these expressions. Listen again and repeat.

Oh, I'm sorry. I hope we'll see you later.

That's terrible. I hope she's okay.

That's too bad. Take it easy.

Okay. We'll see you when you get here.

Unit 10: Lesson 5

> **EXPANSION ACTIVITY: Phoning in Instructions**
>
> - Put students in groups.
> - Have groups write a continuation of one of the conversations from Activity 3. In the conversation, have the person who is phoning in leave instructions for someone in the office. For example, they may ask the receptionist to forward calls, or they may ask a co-worker to fill in at a meeting.
> - LOW LEVEL: Have lower level students write a conversation from the viewpoint of the person receiving the call. Using the information from the existing conversation, have students write a short conversation in which the call recipient tells someone what happened. For example, in the first example from Activity 3, Mr. Roberts might tell a co-worker what happened to Magda. Write an example on the board as needed, such as this:
>
>   Mr. Roberts: Magda can't come in today.
>
>   Co-worker: Why not?
>
>   Mr. Roberts: She is really sick.
>
> - Point out to students the language that is reused from the original example.
> - Have groups role-play their new conversations for the class.

> **Culture Note:**
>
> - Make sure students are aware of when employees may be expected to call in: when they are going to be absent (for sickness or emergency) and when they are going to be late.

❹ Practice the Conversation: Talking About Work Schedules 🎧 150

- Repeat the basic procedure from Activities 2 and 3.
- To set the context, ask questions about the picture: *Who do you see? Where are they?*
- After students have listened to and repeated the conversation line by line, check comprehension by asking: *What does the man want?*
- Play the rest of the audio track. Point out to students that they will use these phrases to practice conversation.
- Have students continue practicing the conversation, making substitutions from the boxes and using their own ideas.

LISTENING SCRIPT

Lesson 5, Activity 4: Practice the Conversation: Talking About Work Schedules

Listen to the conversation. Listen again and repeat.

A: Ms. Garcia, can I talk to you for a minute?

B: Sure. What is it?

A: I usually have Mondays off, but can I have Tuesday off this week?

B: Is it important?

A: Yes, I have a doctor's appointment.

B: OK. I'll see what I can do.

A: Thank you. I appreciate it.

Listen to these expressions. Listen again and repeat.

I'll try.

I'll work something out.

I think I can arrange that.

We'll figure something out.

LESSON 6: Understanding Job Ads and Applications

OBJECTIVE
Understanding job ads and applications

1 Read and Identify

- Have students look at the job ads. Ask questions: *What are these? Where can you see ads like these? What jobs are they for?*
- Have students look at the items in Activity 1. Point out that it is helpful to know what information is required before you read.
- Have students read the ads and check their answers.
- Have students check their answers with a partner.
- Go over the answers with the class.

ANSWER KEY:

1. Jobs A and E; 2. Jobs B, C, and E; 3. Jobs A and C; 4. Job E; 5. Jobs A and E; some students may also say Job D for servers and managers; 6. Job B; 7. Job B; 8. Job D

Language Note:

- Point out to students that in Job C, experience with computers is "a plus." Explain that this means that it may help the applicant's chances at being hired, but it is not a requirement.

EXPANSION ACTIVITY: I wouldn't like it! [Challenge]

- Put students in pairs to ask about the jobs in the ads. Tell students that they are going to practice using negative compound sentences.
- Model the activity with a student. Ask: *Would you like to be a nursing assistant?* Cue the student to respond with *I'd like it because _____ and _____*, giving two reasons they would like the job, or *I would not like it because _____ and ___(not)___* giving two reasons they wouldn't like the job. Write an example on the board if needed, such as: *I wouldn't like to be a restaurant manager because it is stressful and you can't go home early*.
- Have students take turns asking and answering questions.
- Have volunteers share their thoughts with the class, using negative compound sentences.

2 Check *True* or *False*

- Have students look at the application on page 141. Ask questions: *What is this? What information is on the application? Who is applying for a job?*
- Have students read the sentences and check *True* or *False*. Then have them correct the false statements.
- Have students compare answers with a classmate.
- Go over the answers with the class.
- Ask students which job in Activity 1 Oscar should apply for and why.

ANSWER KEY:

1. True; 2. False. He studied electronic technology; 3. False. He went to college for 1.5 years; 4. True; 5. False. He would rather work the 1st shift; 6. False. His starting salary was $12/hour; 7. False. He supervises five people; 8. True; 9. True

Unit 10: Lesson 6

EXPANSION ACTIVITY: What About You?

- Have students copy the chart under EDUCATION from the application on page 141 on a piece of paper. Then have them fill out the chart for themselves. Remind them to include your English class in the chart.
- LOW-LEVEL: Help students understand what is required from the employment application. For example, point out that some of the phrases are shortened, such as: *Reason for leaving: What was your reason for leaving?* Other instructions use imperatives, such as *State Job Title and Describe Your Work.* Go over any other questions students may have.
- Walk around the room and provide help as needed.
- Have students talk about their education with a partner.
- As a variation, bring in applications, or have students search online for application forms. Have students complete the application for themselves.
- Point out that the information is often the same across different applications, but that it is sometimes in different places.
- Suggest that students keep a draft of an application on hand so that they have something to refer to when they are filling out applications for a real job.

LESSON 7: What Do You Know?

1 Listening Review 151

- Go over the directions with the class.
- Read the items or play the audio and have the students mark their answers in the Answer Sheet box.
- Walk around to monitor the activity and help students stay on task.
- Have students check their answers with a partner.
- Go over the answers with the class.

LISTENING SCRIPT

Lesson 7, Activity 1: Listening Review

You will hear a question. Listen to the conversation. You will hear the question again. Then choose the correct answer: A, B, or C. Use the Answer Sheet.

1. What is Mark's job?
   - A: Hey, Mark. Are you still working in construction?
   - B: No, I'm an accountant now.
   What is Mark's job?
   - A. He's a bricklayer.
   - B. He's a construction worker.
   - C. He's an accountant.
2. Where does Tina work?
   - A: Hi, Tina. What do you do now?
   - B: I'm a chef.
   Where does Tina work?
   - A. at a hospital
   - B. at a restaurant
   - C. at a school
3. What is Lidia good at?
   - A: So, Lidia, I see you work in an office. Are you good at following directions?
   - B: Yes, I think so. I follow directions very well.
   What is Lidia good at?
   - A. She is good at helping people.
   - B. She is good at organizing information.
   - C. She is good at following directions.
4. How long did the speaker work there?
   - A: I worked there for three years.
   - B: What did you do?
   - A: I was an assembler.
   How long did the speaker work there?
   - A. an assembler
   - B. two years
   - C. three years
5. What's the problem?
   - A: I'm so sorry. I can't come to work today.
   - B: What's the matter?
   - A: I'm really sick.
   What's the problem?
   - A. The caller is sick.
   - B. The caller is late.
   - C. The caller's car broke down.

ANSWER KEY:

1. C; 2. B; 3. C; 4. C; 5. A

2 Listening Dictation 152

- Copy the numbers and lines from the Listening Dictation section on the board.
- Read the first sentence: *A welder doesn't have to be a man.* Have a more advanced student write the sentence on the board on the line next to 1. Have students copy the sentence in their books.
- Play the audio and have students write the sentences they hear. Repeat as many times as necessary.
- Put students in pairs to compare answers.
- Have volunteers write the sentences on the board.

LISTENING SCRIPT

Lesson 7, Activity 2: Listening Dictation

Listen and write the sentences you hear.

1. A welder doesn't have to be a man.
2. I'm good at helping people.
3. Are you willing to travel?
4. I want to work the day shift.
5. I'm sorry. I can't come to work today.

Unit 10: Lesson 7

③ Grammar Review

- Go over the directions.
- Read the first sentence. Elicit the appropriate completion. Have students circle A for item 1.
- Have students answer the rest of the questions.
- Put students in pairs to compare answers.
- Go over the answers with the class.

TESTING FOCUS: Process of Elimination

- Tell students that when filling in missing verbs, it can be helpful to examine the question carefully before reading the answers. For example, students might look at the subject of the question and decide whether it is plural or singular. From this information, they can figure out that the verb needed is also singular or plural.
- After students have determined whether the subject is singular or plural, have them eliminate any answers that do not qualify. This makes choosing the correct answer easier.

ANSWER KEY:

1. A; 2. A; 3. B; 4. A; 5. C; 6. C

LEARNING LOG

- Point out the four sections of the Learning Log: *I know these words; I can ask; I can say;* and *I can write.*
- Have students check what they know and what they can do.
- Walk around to note what they don't know or can't do. Use this information to review areas of difficulty.

BIG PICTURE EXPANSION ACTIVITY:
SPEAKING—Assessment: Talking about the Picture

- You can use the Big Picture on Student Book Pages 134–135 to place new students in open entry classes, to diagnose difficulties, or to measure progress.
- Work with one student at a time and show them the Big Picture. Ask: *What do you see in the picture? Tell me about the picture.* Tell the student you want him or her to speak for as long as possible. Wait a moment for the student to prepare to answer. If the student has difficulty, you can use prompts: *What do you see in the career center? Who do you see in the waiting room? What are the people doing?*
- You can use a rubric like the one below to rate beginning speakers.

4	Exhibits confidence, begins speaking without prompting Uses some complex sentences, although may make mistakes with irregular forms Can use more than one tense
3	Uses sentences, although form may be incorrect Can speak for sustained length of time Responds to prompts, but doesn't need them to begin speaking
2	Can use nouns and verbs Uses phrases Answers informational questions
1	Can name objects Uses single words Can answer *yes/no* questions
0	Cannot say anything independently May be able to point to objects when prompted

Unit 10: Lesson 7

 BIG PICTURE EXPANSION ACTIVITY:
Writing—Describing Activities at a Career Center

- Have students look at the Big Picture in their books (Student Book pages 134–135).
- Ask the class: *What do job applicants do when they get to the office? What do the employees do in the office?*
- Have students brainstorm ideas to prepare to write.
- Have students write a paragraph about what people do in a personnel office.
- Put students in pairs to take turns reading their paragraphs to their partners.

TEACHER'S NOTES:

Things that students are doing well:
_____
_____
_____
_____

Things students need additional help with:
_____
_____
_____
_____

Ideas for further practice or for the next class:
_____
_____
_____
_____

Unit 1: Lesson 4 Big Picture Expansion Activity

WORKSHEET #1

Name: _____   Date: _____

Reading: Greg Works Hard

A. Look at the Big Picture on Student Book pages 8–9. Read the story. Then find Greg in the picture. Check *True* or *False*.

   Greg works hard. He is a student. He has a part-time job. Every day he goes to the park. He likes the park. He brings his computer. Greg works on his computer in the park. He does his homework on the computer. Sometimes he studies for tests. He doesn't like to study at his apartment. Greg's roommate is friendly, but he's too loud. Greg doesn't like loud noises. Greg is very intelligent and gets good grades.

1. He has a full-time job.   ○ True   ○ False
2. He is a student.   ○ True   ○ False
3. He likes loud people.   ○ True   ○ False
4. He goes to the park every day.   ○ True   ○ False
5. He has a computer.   ○ True   ○ False
6. He lives with two roommates.   ○ True   ○ False

B. Answer the questions.

1. Does Greg have blond hair?   _____
2. Does he have a beard?   _____
3. Is he old or young?   _____
4. Is he at a table or near the slide? _____
5. What does he bring to the park?   _____
6. Is he a good student?   _____

Unit 1: Lesson 4 Big Picture Expansion Activity

WORKSHEET #2

Name: _____   Date: _____

Grammar: Simple Present

A. Look at the Big Picture on Student Book pages 8–9. Complete the sentences.

There _____ (are/is) many things to do in Sun County City Park. Some people _____ (play/plays) basketball. Some people _____ (sit/sits) and _____ (talk/talks). Today, two children _____ (are/is) on the slide. Someone _____ (have/has) a camera. One woman _____ (are/is) angry. A man _____ (are/is) tired. Many people _____ (are/is) happy. The park _____ (are/is) a nice place to visit.

B. Look at the Big Picture. Answer the questions.

1. Are there twenty-seven people at the park? _____
2. Does Mei have a toy? _____
3. Is Hector tired? _____
4. Does Tim have a camera? _____
5. Is Rob bored? _____
6. Does Alice have a book? _____
7. Do people play basketball in the park? _____
8. Does Sam have brown hair? _____
9. Does Pat have a mustache? _____
10. Is Adam old? _____

Unit 2: Lesson 3 Big Picture Expansion Activity

WORKSHEET #3

Name: _____   Date: _____

Grammar: *Wh-* Questions

A. Look at the Big Picture on Student Book pages 22–23. Complete the conversations. Answer the questions.

1. A: Where is the information desk?

   B: _____

2. A: How many adults are at the information desk for information?

   B: _____

3. A: Who is buying something at the snack bar?

   B: _____

4. A: What are people buying at the train station?

   B: _____

5. A: Why are people lying down in the waiting area?

   B: _____

B. Look at the Big Picture. Complete the conversations. Write questions.

1. A: (how many) _____?

   B: There are four people in the waiting area.

2. A: (where) _____?

   B: It's between the ticket machine and the ATM.

3. A: (why) _____?

   B: She's standing on the platform because she's waiting for a train.

4. A: (what) _____?

   B: You can buy magazines and newspapers there.

Unit 2: Lesson 4 Big Picture Expansion Activity

WORKSHEET #4

Name: _____   Date: _____

Reading: A Letter Home

A. Look at the Big Picture on Student Book pages 22–23. Read the letter. Someone wrote this letter a few minutes after the action in the Big Picture. Circle the words from the box in the letter.

| benches | suitcase |

Dear Mom and Dad,

   I am writing this letter from the train station. I have a train schedule. I just got it at the information desk. I'm waiting for the 2:30 train to New York. It is 1 o'clock now, so I have an hour and a half to wait. It's cold today. But I'm wearing the pink hat and coat that you gave me, so I'm warm. The train station is nice. There is a snack bar, an information desk, and a newsstand. People buy their tickets at a ticket machine or a ticket office. The waiting area has benches. People can sit or lie down on the benches. I can take my suitcase to baggage check. Then I don't have to carry it with me on the train. I'll write more soon.

Love,

B. Choose the answer. Circle the letter.

1. Who is writing the letter?
   a. a man
   b. a woman

2. Find the person in the picture. What is the person wearing?
   a. boots
   b. a blue shirt

3. Where is the writer standing in the picture?
   a. next to the information desk
   b. at the ATM

4. Where are the benches?
   a. next to the snack bar
   b. in the waiting area

5. How many minutes does this person have to wait for the train?
   a. 60
   b. 90

6. Why do people use the baggage check?
   a. so they don't have to carry their baggage
   b. to buy tickets

Unit 3: Lesson 3 Big Picture Expansion Activity

WORKSHEET #5

Name: _____ Date: _____

Grammar: *Yes/No* Questions + Simple Past

A. Look at the Big Picture on Student Book pages 36–37. Answer the questions.

1. Did a boy bring money to the bank at 2 P.M.? _____
2. Did a woman fill out a deposit slip at 2 P.M.? _____
3. Did three men put something in a safe-deposit box at 2 P.M.? _____
4. Did six people have to stand in line at 2 P.M.? _____
5. Did a girl use the ATM at 2 P.M.? _____
6. Did a woman endorse a check at 2 P.M.? _____

B. Complete the conversations. Write yes/no questions about the Big Picture.

1. A: _____

   B: No, he didn't. Dan deposited coins, not a check.

2. A: _____

   B: No, she didn't. Lea put jewelry in her safe-deposit box, not papers.

3. A: _____

   B: No, he didn't. Al filled out a deposit slip, not a withdrawal slip.

4. A: _____

   B: No, they didn't. The bank tellers didn't stop working until 5.

5. A: _____

   B: Yes, they did. They waited in line for the teller.

Unit 3: Lesson 3 Big Picture Expansion Activity

WORKSHEET #6

Name: _____   Date: _____

Reading: Ali's Day

A. Look at the Big Picture on Student Book pages 36–37. Read the story. Put the events in order. Write the number of each event on the line.

   I am a bank teller at World Savings Bank. Today was a busy day. I went to work at 8:30. First, I counted the cash in my drawer. I have to have different coins and bills so I can give change to the customers. The bank opened at 9. From 9 A.M. until noon I worked at the window for drive-through customers. From 12 to 1 P.M., I had my lunch break. In the afternoon, I worked at the regular teller window. I had lots of customers. A woman needed to open her safe-deposit box. One little boy brought in all the money he had saved. Other customers made deposits and withdrawals. At 5 o'clock the bank closed. I counted the cash again. I left the bank at 5:30.

_____ The bank opened.	_____ I had lunch.	__1__ I went to work.
_____ I worked at the drive-through window.	_____ A woman went to her safe-deposit box.	_____ A boy brought in some cash.
_____ The bank closed.		

B. Answer the questions.

1. What did Ali do at 8:30? _____
2. When did Ali leave the bank? _____
3. What is Ali's job? _____
4. How many hours did Ali work? _____
5. How long did he take for lunch? _____
6. Where did Ali work in the afternoon? _____
7. When did the bank close? _____

Unit 4: Lesson 2 Big Picture Expansion Activity

WORKSHEET #7

Name: _____   Date: _____

Grammar: Future with *be going to*

A. Look at the Big Picture on Student Book pages 50–51. Complete the sentences with *be going to* and a verb from the box.

| change | buy | fall | get | greet | lose | wake |

1. Rich _____ the tire.
2. The salesman _____ the customers at the door.
3. The assistant bookkeeper _____ important papers.
4. The other bookkeeper _____ a promotion.
5. One worker is talking on the phone. He _____ out of his chair.
6. Some customers _____ cars.
7. One worker is sleeping. His boss _____ him up soon.

B. Look at the Big Picture. Complete the sentences to show what the people will do differently tomorrow. Use *be going to*.

1. Today, Jim slept at work. Tomorrow, he<u>'s not going to sleep at work.</u>
2. Today, Ivan didn't come on time. Tomorrow, _____.
3. Today, Arnie wasn't organized. Tomorrow, _____.
4. Today, Susan didn't work very hard. Tomorrow, _____.
5. Today, Mike didn't have a good attitude. Tomorrow, _____.

Unit 4: Lesson 3 Big Picture Expansion Activity

WORKSHEET #8

Name: _____ Date: _____

Reading: Memo on Policies

A. Look at the Big Picture on Student Book pages 50–51. Read the memo and check *True* or *False*. Correct the false statements.

> **Memo**
>
> To: All employees, Allen Motors
>
> From: Donna Tate, manager
>
> Re: Work Policies
>
> The president of Allen Motors, John Allen, is going to visit tomorrow. Please remember the following policies:
>
> 1. **Appearance:** Dress appropriately. You should look professional at all times.
> 2. **Dependability:** Be on time and demonstrate a good attitude.
> 3. **Courtesy:** Remember, customers are very important. Treat them with respect.
> 4. **Diligence:** Remember, hard work sells cars.

	True	False
1. It is okay to wear a T-shirt and jeans in the office.	○	○
2. You should show courtesy to customers.	○	○
3. Being on time is more important than a good attitude.	○	○
4. The president of the United States is going to visit.	○	○
5. Employees should work hard.	○	○
6. The memo is from John Allen.	○	○
7. The memo is about work schedules.	○	○

B. Look at the Big Picture. You are John Allen. Describe these workers to the manager.

1. Ken: _____
2. Tim: _____
3. Laura: _____
4. Mike: _____

Unit 5: Lesson 3 Big Picture Expansion Activity

WORKSHEET #9

Name: _____   Date: _____

Reading: Mall Information

A. Look at the Big Picture on Student Book pages 62–63. Read the ads. Write the name of the store on the line.

Going out of Business!

Everything must go!
Prices drastically reduced.
Most items 75% off.

Great deals on
dresses, shirts, skirts,
and more.

Conveniently located near the Food Court

1. _____

Two Days Only

Buy 2 Get 1 Free
on selected merchandise

coffeemakers, blenders,
toaster ovens, electric can openers

3. _____

Once a year sale

On dishwashers!

All dishwashers half price.

Other appliances marked down.

2. _____

Getting Ready for Spring Sale

Come in now for great prices
on winter shoes.

25–50% off most styles.

4. _____

B. Answer the questions.

1. Which store has a sale on dishwashers?   _____
2. Where can you find half-price shoes?   _____
3. What store sells electric can openers?   _____
4. Which store above is near the Food Court?   _____
5. How long is the sale on kitchen items?   _____

Unit 5: Lesson 4 — Big Picture Expansion Activity

WORKSHEET #10

Name: _____   Date: _____

Grammar: Which one is the cheapest?

A. Look at the Big Picture on Student Book pages 62–63. Choose the correct word. Write the comparative form on the line.

1. May's Department Store is _____ (big/small) than Le Chic Clothing.

2. Le Chic Clothing is _____ (big/small) than May's Department Store.

3. Dishwashers at Sam's are _____ (cheap/expensive) now than they were before.

4. Clothing at May's is probably _____ (cheap/expensive) than clothing at Le Chic today.

5. The items at Kitchen Galore are _____ (useful/pretty) than the items at Gemma's Jewels.

B. Look at the Big Picture. Write the superlative form of words in parentheses to complete the story.

Today I went to the mall. First I went to May's Department Store because it is the _____ (big) store at the mall and has the _____ (good) selection. Then I went to Arches because it has the _____ (cheap) shoes. After Arches, I went to Jingle's Toys. It has the _____ (interesting) toys. I wanted to go to Le Chic because it had the _____ (low) prices on women's clothing, but it was the _____ (busy) store in the mall. It was the _____ (bad) time to go because so many people were there. So I decided to eat lunch. I got something at the bagel place. I think the food there is the _____ (healthy).

Unit 6: Lesson 3 Big Picture Expansion Activity

WORKSHEET #11

Name: _____   Date: _____

Reading: Sam's Family Restaurant

A. Look at the Big Picture on Student Book pages 76–77. Complete the story with information from the picture.

Sam's Family _____ is a fun and friendly place to eat. I went to the restaurant with my daughter and husband. The food was very good. The meatballs are my favorite main dish. The restaurant has great baked desserts, too. Sam's has both tables and _____. You can even sit at the _____ and watch the cook work. Sam's has a lot of hostesses and waiters—there were _____ of them working last night. Susan and _____ served our table. They did a great job, but some of the other waiters had problems. One of them tripped and dropped a _____ right next to our table. Sam's is usually full of people. Only _____ table was empty. I saw _____ other families with children, and one family even brought their dog!

Food ★★★★

Service ★★

★★★★ = excellent, ★★★ = good, ★★ = fair, ★ = poor

B. Answer the questions.

1. What does the writer of the review look like?
   _____

2. Why did the writer rate the service as "fair"?
   _____

3. The writer didn't say anything about how clean the restaurant was. How would you rate Sam's for cleanliness? Why?
   _____
   _____

Unit 6: Lesson 3 Big Picture Expansion Activity

WORKSHEET #12

Name: _____   Date: _____

Grammar: Quantifiers

A. Look at the Big Picture on Student Book pages 76–77. Complete the questions with *How many* or *How much*.

1. _____ bowls are still on Janet's table?
2. _____ water did the baby behind Janet spill?
3. _____ food is Dot carrying on her tray?
4. _____ customers are in the restaurant?
5. _____ waiters are spilling something?
6. _____ soup is there in the picture?
7. _____ water is Leo carrying?
8. _____ people are looking at menus?

B. Answer the questions in complete sentences. Use quantity words before noncount nouns.

1. _____
2. _____
3. _____
4. _____
5. _____
6. _____
7. _____
8. _____

Unit 7: Lesson 4 Big Picture Expansion Activity

WORKSHEET #13

Name: _____   Date: _____

Reading: Sylvia's Story

A. Read Sylvia's story. Check *True* or *False*.

My name is Sylvia. Today my daughter Lisa is getting married. It is a very happy day for my family. I remember my own wedding day. I wore a long white dress. When I married Ron, we had a formal dinner. The guests sat at round tables and waiters served the food. We also had music. One musician played the piano and another played the violin. I danced with my father for the first dance. Later, the musicians played a special song for my husband and me, and we danced too. About 200 guests came to our wedding, and they all brought gifts. Our wedding was at night. Because it was a formal wedding, we did not invite children. We had a beautiful pink and white wedding cake.

1. Sylvia is getting married today.	○ True	○ False
2. Sylvia wore a white dress at her wedding.	○ True	○ False
3. Sylvia has a daughter.	○ True	○ False
4. Sylvia danced with her father at her wedding.	○ True	○ False
5. Sylvia's husband's name is Juan.	○ True	○ False
6. Her daughter's name is Lisa.	○ True	○ False

B. Look at the Big Picture on Student Book pages 90–91. Complete the chart. Write three more things in each column.

At Sylvia's Wedding	At Both Sylvia's and Lisa's Weddings	At Lisa's Wedding
Waiters served the food.	The bride wore a white dress.	The food was on a big table.

Unit 7: Lesson 5 Big Picture Expansion Activity

WORKSHEET #14

Name: _____   Date: _____

Grammar: Word Forms

A. Look at the Big Picture on Student Book pages 90–91. and review the vocabulary. Look at the words below. Complete the sentences using the correct form.

Verbs	Nouns	Adjectives
	custom	customary
	music/musician	musical
photograph	photographer	photographic
employ	employer	
apologize	apology	apologetic
	religion	religious
invite	invitation	
	problem	problematic
respect	respect	respectful

1. We have many wedding _____ (customs/customary).

2. It is _____ (customs/customary) to bring a gift to a wedding.

3. We hired someone to _____ (photograph/photographic) the ceremony.

4. Our _____ (religion/religious) services are very formal.

5. In many cultures, young people show _____ (respect/respectful) to older people.

6. My sister is very _____ (musician/musical). She plays the piano and sings.

7. It was a very large wedding. They _____ (invited/invitation) 300 people.

8. Juan's _____ (employ/employer) came to the wedding.

9. He was very late. He _____ (apologized/apology) many times.

10. It wasn't _____ (problem/problematic). No one even noticed.

Unit 8: Lesson 3 Big Picture Expansion Activity

WORKSHEET #15

Name: _____   Date: _____

Grammar: *Should* and *Shouldn't*

A. Look at the Big Picture on Student Book pages 106–107. Match the problems and solutions. Write the letter on the line.

Problem   **Solution**

1. _____ If you sprain your knee,   a. you should put a bandage on it.
2. _____ If you go to the emergency room,   b. you should get an x-ray.
3. _____ If you cut your hand,   c. you should put an ice pack on it.
4. _____ If you break a leg,   d. you should use crutches.
5. _____ If you can't stand on your own,   e. you should stay calm.

B. Look at the Big Picture. Complete the sentences with *should* or *shouldn't*. Write the name of the correct person on the first line.

1. _____ is holding his stomach. He _____ eat or drink anything.
2. _____ hurt her foot dancing. She _____ walk or stand on it.
3. _____ hurt his knee. He _____ put ice on it.
4. _____ is wearing a sling. He _____ play sports for a while.
5. _____ has a bad cut on her hand. She _____ get stitches.
6. _____ has a sick child. She _____ see a doctor as soon as possible.

C. Write your ideas to complete the sentences. Share your ideas with a partner.

1. When you go to the emergency room, you should _____
   _____.

2. When you go to the emergency room, you shouldn't _____
   _____.

Unit 8: Lesson 4 Big Picture Expansion Activity

WORKSHEET #16

Name: _____   Date: _____

Reading: Doctor's Orders

Read the doctor's suggested treatment for each patient in the Big Picture on Student Book pages 106–107. Write a problem from the box next to each suggested treatment. Then write the patient's name.

> a leg fracture   a wrist sprain   a bad cut   a burn

1.
- Keep the bandage on for three days.
- Keep the area clean and dry.
- If the blisters open, you should use an antibacterial cream to prevent infection.
- Take acetaminophen or aspirin as needed for the pain.

Patient: _____
Problem: _____
_____

2.
- The cast should stay on for six weeks.
- Do not get the cast wet.
- Use the crutches for three days.
- Take acetaminophen for pain as needed.

Patient: _____
Problem: _____
_____

3.
- Wear the bandage for three days.
- Keep the area clean and dry.
- Watch for redness or other signs of infection.
- Have the clinic remove the stitches in one week.

Patient: _____
Problem: _____
_____

4.
- Use the splint and the sling until the next appointment.
- Keep the wrist elevated when possible (on a pillow).
- Take OTC pain relievers as needed for pain.

Patient: _____
Problem: _____
_____

Worksheet #16   239

Unit 9: Lesson 3 Big Picture Expansion Activity

WORKSHEET #17

Name: _____   Date: _____

Grammar: What happened?

A. Look at the Big Picture on Student Book pages 120–121. Complete the sentences with the simple past of a verb from the box. Use each word only once.

| get | put | have | take | fly |
| stand | fight | come | hold | hear |

1. The news reporters _____ to the fire in a helicopter
2. Many people _____ on the fire escapes, waiting for help.
3. The firefighters _____ the fire for many hours.
4. The woman _____ a cloth over her mouth.
5. A firefighter _____ the baby from his mother.
6. A man _____ out his cat for it to be rescued.
7. The firefighters _____ as soon as they _____ about the fire.
8. Everyone _____ out of the building safely.
9. The window _____ a ladder that a man climbed down.

B. Answer the questions. Use the words suggested.

1. What did the doctor do? (drive / ambulance)

    She _____

2. What did the grandmother do? (go down / fire escape)

    She _____

3. What did the reporter do? (tell)

    He _____

4. What did the firefighter see? (see)

    He _____

Unit 9: Lesson 4 Big Picture Expansion Activity

WORKSHEET #18

Name: _____ Date: _____

Reading: How to Escape from a Fire

A. Look at the Big Picture on Student Book pages 120–121. Check *True*, *False*, or *I don't know*.

1. Everyone was able to go down the fire escape.   ○ True ○ False ○ I don't know.
2. No one from the building went to the roof.   ○ True ○ False ○ I don't know.
3. Six people are at the windows.   ○ True ○ False ○ I don't know.
4. Someone called 911.   ○ True ○ False ○ I don't know.
5. A man and his cat are trapped in his apartment.   ○ True ○ False ○ I don't know.
6. Two people are crawling on the ground.   ○ True ○ False ○ I don't know.

B. Look at the Big Picture. Read the information. Answer the questions.

How to Escape from a Fire in Your Apartment Building

- Call 911. Alert everyone in the apartment.
- Unplug and shut off cooking and heating appliances.
- Check the doors before you open them. If the door is hot, find another escape route. If the door is cool, open slowly.
- Shut doors and take your key.
- Use stairways or fire escapes. Do not use the elevators.
- Never go to the roof. You may get trapped there.
- If you can't leave your apartment, use towels and clothes to block the spaces around the door. Go to a window and let someone know you are there.
- If there is a lot of smoke, crawl on the ground where the air is clearer. If your escape is blocked by too much smoke or fire, go back and try to find another way.

---

1. What safety rules do you see followed in the picture?

   _____

2. Do you think everyone is acting in a safe way? Why or why not?

   _____

Unit 10: Lesson 1 Big Picture Expansion Activity

WORKSHEET #19

Name: _____ Date: _____

Grammar: What do we have to do?

A. Look at the Big Picture on Student Book pages 134–135. Complete the sentences. Write *has to/have to*, or *doesn't have to/don't have to*.

1. The welder _____ work 40 hours a week.
2. The machine operator _____ work 40 hours a week.
3. Three people in the waiting room are neatly dressed. One person _____ change his clothes if he wants to get a job.
4. Sam _____ stand up when he is talking to John.
5. In the Career Center, people _____ sit down.
6. Mia _____ stand up to reach the shelf.
7. If you want water in the conference room, you _____ bring your own.
8. If you want to get overtime pay, you _____ work more than 40 hours a week.

B. Look at the Big Picture on Student Book pages 134–135. Complete the advice. Use the ideas below and *have to/don't have to*.

> If you want to get a job through this career center, you _____ dress neatly, but you _____ wear a suit. You _____ come on time. Before the interview, you _____ fill out an application. You can bring a résumé, but you _____ bring photos or evaluations. These aren't necessary. You _____ be a certain age or gender. We employ men and women of all ages. For our machine operator positions, you _____ work from 3 to 7 P.M.

Unit 10: Lesson 4 Big Picture Expansion Activity

WORKSHEET #20

Name: _____ Date: _____

Reading: My New Job

A. Look at the Big Picture on Student Book pages 134–135. Read the story and answer the questions.

Today was my first day at my new job. What a day! I was so excited I went to work an hour early. I am an administrative assistant in a career center. At my old job, I always wore casual clothes. Today I wore casual clothes, too. I wore a pair of brown jeans, sneakers, and a T-shirt. That was a mistake. All the other men were wearing ties. I was embarrassed. But John let me wear one of his shirts and one of his ties. I met many people, but I can't remember all the names. My boss's name is Mia. I spend most of my time in her office. She told me about the procedures that employees need to follow. I think I will like my new job. I hope tomorrow is easier.

1. Look at the picture and find the new employee. What color shirt is he wearing?
   _____

2. What does his boss look like?
   _____

3. What did the new employee do wrong on his first day?
   _____

4. What did he do right?
   _____

5. How did he feel about his first day?
   _____

B. You work in the career center. Look at the Big Picture on Student Book pages 134–135. Answer a job applicant's questions.

1. A: How many hours is full-time?

   You: _____

2. A: Will I get overtime if I work more than that?

   You: _____

3. A: When is the night shift?

   You: _____

TARGET GRAMMAR

Introduction To The Target Grammar Pages

The Second Edition of *All-Star* features all new Target Grammar pages at the end of every student book. The Target Grammar pages offer presentation and practice of three to four grammar points that arise naturally in the content of each unit. This separate grammar section allows teachers the flexibility to tailor the content to their class needs. Teachers may choose to do the target grammar practice immediately after completing the lesson, after completing the entire unit, or not at all. They may also revisit grammar points later in the course if students need review.

The following features make it easy to use the grammar section.

★ The target grammar point is used in a natural context within a lesson.
★ Within a lesson, a target grammar point is identified and a reference to the specific grammar pages in the Target Grammar Pages is provided.
★ The Target Grammar pages are cross-referenced to the pages of the lesson in which the grammar point appears.
★ The Work-Out CD-ROM provides additional practice for the students on each unit's grammar points.

There are four to six pages of grammar practice for each unit, depending on the number of grammar points appearing in the unit. These pages include:

★ Grammar presentation in the form of charts [paradigms] that show the form and function of a structure and provide simple and clear explanation.
★ Grammar practice progressing from more controlled activities to more open-ended and personalized production. More controlled activities include matching, fill-in-the-blank, and multiple choice. The more open-ended activities might require creating sentences, answering questions, or interviewing a partner.
★ Interactive grammar practice in the Work-Out CD-ROM

Suggested Strategies for Teaching Grammar

Chart presentation: You may find that some students need help to understand the information in grammar charts. Have these students point to the target structure as you read the chart examples aloud, or have them repeat the examples after you. If charts have questions and answers, ask questions and call on students to elicit the answers given in the chart. You can also provide part of an example sentence in a chart and elicit the completion.

Practice: Where possible, multiple activities follow the presentation of the grammar point to facilitate practice. Go over the directions and examples eliciting questions. As students work through the items, walk around the room to monitor the activity and provide help as needed. Have students compare answers with one or more classmates before you go over the answers with the class as a whole. This facilitates communication, and allows students to share their expertise.

In addition to the activities that follow the charts in the grammar pages, the lessons of the Student Book provide practice, especially the Big Picture grammar expansions. Each grammar point appears in the content of the Workbook and is practiced through activities. The Work-Out CD-ROM reinforces the grammar points through interactive, engaging, and self-paced activities.

TARGET GRAMMAR

Modeling: The first item in each activity is usually an example that provides students with a model of the structure and the task. For more open-ended, personalized activities, you can provide a model by demonstrating how the task can be completed. For example, if a question asks "What is one goal you have?" you can read the question aloud and then answer it for yourself.

Pair/group work: Many activities are set up in the form of a question and answer. These activities allow students to make the task more communicative by taking turns asking and answering with a partner. Having students check their answers with a partner or in a small group also leads to more interaction and better understanding.

Expansions: The Teacher's Edition provides expansion activities within the unit in the form of Big Picture grammar expansions. There are also Expansion Activities in the grammar section that follows. The expansion activities in the grammar section provide more communicative practice and may be project-based.

Teachable moments: Just as every student has unique needs and experiences, so does each class. Because the grammar section is separate from the units themselves, you can tailor the presentation and practice to meet the needs of your learners. Some classes may need to spend more time on one grammar point, while others may cover it quickly. Most students will benefit from review and recycling. When appropriate and helpful, review a grammar presentation quickly, and then have students practice it in a new context, for example by describing a Big Picture in a later unit.

TARGET GRAMMAR

Unit 1: Lesson 1 Simple Present of *Be*, Statements page 144

Grammar Note:
- Although the simple present with *Be* is not generally considered as difficult as other structures, students may become confused about when to use an article. Point out that in the first chart, the article *a* is used in front of singular nouns.

1. is; 2. isn't; 3. aren't; 4. is; 5. is; 6. are; 7. is; 8. are; 9. is; 10. aren't

Unit 1: Lesson 2 Simple Present of *Have*, Statements page 145

1. has; 2. have; 3. have; 4. has; 5. have; 6. has; 7. have; 8. has

True/False answers will vary.

Answers will vary. Possible answers:
1. I don't have a mustache.
2. I have long hair.
3. My teacher has brown eyes.
4. My teacher has a big smile.
5. All of my classmates have hair.
6. The person next to me has curly hair.

Unit 1: Lesson 3 Simple Present, Questions pages 146–147

1. d/Are; 2. h/is; 3. b/Am; 4. e/Are; 5. f/is; 6. a/Are; 7. c/Is; 8. g/is

1. What is your middle name?
2. Are you bored?
3. Where are your books?

Answers to questions will vary.

Yes/No Questions in Simple Present
Information Questions in Simple Present

1. Ahmed works in a restaurant.
2. Yes, they do.
3. He is a waiter.
4. He goes to work at 4:00 P.M.
5. Yes, he does.

1. Do; 2. do; 3. do; 4. Do; 5. does; 6. Do; 7. Does; 8. Do

Answers to questions will vary.

Unit 1: Lesson 4 Simple Present, Statements

pages 148–149

1. wants; 2. lives; 3. don't/do not go; 4. live; 5. likes; 6. don't/do not have; 7. need

1. He doesn't speak Chinese.
2. They don't like cold weather.
3. I don't need a car.
4. She lives in New York.
5. We don't like swimming.
6. We want ice cream.

TARGET GRAMMAR

1. I don't like ice cream.
2. They don't wear glasses.
3. He doesn't need a high school diploma.
4. Matt and Kelly don't live in Florida.
5. Monica doesn't speak Korean.
6. I don't need a driver's license.
7. We don't like music.
8. Joe doesn't want a motorcycle.
9. Rich doesn't hate flying.
10. I don't need a job.
11. We don't live in Texas.
12. Nicole doesn't speak German.

Answers will vary. Possible answers:

	Me	**My Friend**	**My Friend and I**
1. like	*I like pizza.*	*Julia likes rice.*	*We like ice cream.*
2. like / not	*I don't like hot dogs.*	*Martin likes spaghetti.*	*We like movies.*
3. speak	I speak Japanese.	Mary speaks French.	We speak English.
4. speak / not	I don't speak Arabic.	Mary doesn't speak Turkish.	We don't speak German.
5. need	I need a new car.	June needs money for school.	We need more time.
6. need / not	I don't need homework help.	Sam doesn't need food.	We don't need an apartment.
7. want	I want a piece of cake.	Nathan wants some soup.	We want sandwiches.
8. want/not	I don't want a pencil.	Mark doesn't want a pen.	We don't want paper.
9. live	I live in a dormitory.	Martina lives in an apartment.	We live in Los Angeles.
10. live / not	I don't live in Tokyo.	Kevin doesn't live in Paris.	We don't live in Moscow.

TARGET GRAMMAR

> **EXPANSION ACTIVITY: Your Friend**
> - Write the following questions on the board:
>   - *What is your friend's name?*
>   - *Where is your friend from?*
>   - *Where does your friend live now?*
>   - *What color are your friend's eyes? Hair?*
>   - *Is your friend tall, short, or medium height?*
>   - *Does your friend work or study?*
>   - *What languages does your friend speak?*
>   - *What other information do you want to give about your friend.*
> - Ask for a volunteer to be your partner. Tell the student to think of a close friend. Ask the student each of the questions on the board. Write one or two word answers next to each question. Then tell the class about the volunteer's friend.
> - Put the students in pairs and tell each partner to think of a close friend. Have the partners ask each other all of the questions. They may write one or two word answers.
> - When the pairs have finished, have each student tell the class about his or her partner's friend.

Unit 2: Lesson 1 Present Continuous pages 150–151

> **Grammar Note:**
> - Spelling verbs in the present continuous tense can sometimes be tricky. If the base verb is one syllable and ends in consonant + vowel + consonant, the final consonant must be doubled before adding *–ing*. Common examples include *swim/swimming, hit/hitting, stop/stopping,* and *run/running*. This rule also applies for a word that has more than one syllable, the consonant +vowel + consonant pattern, and stress on the final syllable. A common example is *begin/beginning*.

1. is cashing; 2. aren't eating; 3. isn't working;
4. is walking; 5. isn't watching; is playing
6. 'm not buying/'m mailing; 7. are getting;
8. aren't doing/are socializing; 10. are studying;

Answers will vary. Possible answers:
1. My teacher is standing up.
2. I am thinking.
3. The person next to me is reading.
4. My classmates are working hard.
5. My friend is writing.

1. b/are you going
2. e/When is it closing?
3. d/Who is she visiting?
4. a/What are we buying?
5. c/are they going?

1. What are you eating?
2. Where are you going?
3. What is the cashier doing?
4. What is he doing?
5. What are they buying?
6. What are you doing?
7. Who is she talking to?

Unit 2: Lesson 2 Prepositions of Place and Direction pages 152–153

1. The police station is next to the fire station.
2. The senior center is between the drugstore and the supermarket.
3. The post office is across from the bank.
4. The medical center is across from the drugstore.
5. The fire station is between the police station and the community center.
6. The supermarket is next to the senior center.
7. The library is across from the drugstore.

248 Target Grammar

TARGET GRAMMAR

Answers will vary. Possible answers:
1. The bank is next to the supermarket.
2. The supermarket is across from the bus station.
3. The post office is between the bus station and the drugstore.
4. The fire station is next to the supermarket.
5. The library is across from the drugstore.

1. Tina and Maura are going into the community center.
2. Jeff is running away from a big dog.
3. Barbara is walking out of the post office.
4. The train is going through a tunnel.
5. Joshua and Zoe are walking toward the hotel.

Unit 2: Lesson 3 Wh- Questions Review page 154

1. d; 2. a; 3. g; 4. e; 5. b; 6. c; 7. f

Answers will vary. Possible answers:
1. My birthday is August 23.
2. I study for English class three times a week.
3. I live in New York City.
4. Bon Jovi is my favorite singer.
5. My favorite kind of food is Italian.
6. I usually wake up at 6:30.
7. I'm studying English to get a better job.
8. I shop at Best Buy and Macy's.
9. I usually eat a sandwich for lunch.
10. I use a computer every day.

Unit 2: Lesson 4 Prepositions of Time page 155

1. on Friday; 2. in June; 3. at 3:30 P.M.; 4. from 6:00 P.M. to 8:00 P.M.; 5. in 2003; 6. on December 31; 7. from 7:00 P.M. to 9:30 P.M. 8. at 6:30 P.M.

Answers will vary. Possible answers:
1. at 11:00 P.M.; 2. from 8:00 A.M. to 11:00 A.M.; 3. on Mondays; 4. on November 16; 5. at 1:00 P.M.; 6. in the summer; 7. on June 1; 8. from 11:00 P.M. to 7:00 A.M.

EXPANSION ACTIVITY: What's happening?

- Write the following example sentences on the board:
  - *Some children are playing in the park.*
  - *A man is walking toward the supermarket.*
- Tell the students that they are going to do an exercise in observation. Tell them that they are going to walk around outside the school for ten minutes and look at everything that is happening in the area.
- Tell them that each student will write at least five sentences with the present continuous describing what is happening. Encourage them to include prepositions of place and direction.
- Elicit from students the words that express the present continuous in the sentences you wrote on the board. Underline those words.
- Elicit the prepositions of place and direction in your sentences on the board. Circle them.
- After the students return from outside, give them several minutes to write down their observations.
- Put the students in pairs and tell them to read their sentences to each other.
- When the pairs have finished, have each student read one sentence to the class. Alternatively, you might want each student to write one sentence on the board, underlining the present continuous and circling the prepositions of place and direction.

Target Grammar **249**

TARGET GRAMMAR

Unit 3: Lesson 1 Simple Past, Statements pages 156–157

1

1. cashed; 2. deposited; 3. endorsed; 4. opened; 5. helped; 6. closed; 7. studied; 8. worked

2

1. She didn't open a checking account.
2. They didn't wait in line for 15 minutes.
3. I asked you a question.
4. I didn't endorse my paycheck.
5. We talked to the bank teller.
6. We stopped to use the ATM.

3

1. went; 2. didn't buy; 3. wrote; 4. didn't make; 5. took; 6. ate; 7. paid; 8. didn't spend

True/False answers will vary.

4

wanted; went; put; typed; asked; wanted; typed; came; took; put; asked; wanted; pressed; took; checked; put

5

Answers will vary. Possible answers:
1. I took a walk.
2. I wrote a letter.
3. I paid bills.

Unit 3: Lesson 2 Simple Past *Be*, Statements

page 158

1

1. was; 2. was; 3. were; 4. was; 5. was; 6. was; 7. were; 8. was; 9. was; 10. were; 11. was; 12. wasn't

2

Answers will vary. Possible answers:
1. My mother was tired last night.
2. They were bored yesterday.
3. He was angry at the bank.
4. The streets were crowded this morning.
5. My teacher was busy last week.

Unit 3: Lesson 3 Simple Past, *Yes/No* Questions pages 159–160

1

1. Did you use; 2. Did you spend; 3. Did you make; 4. Did you write; 5. Did you cash; 6. Did you buy; 7. Did you go; 8. Did you pay

2

1. Did John cash a check yesterday?
2. Did they open an account yesterday?
3. Did I buy a car last week?
4. Did we pay our bill?
5. Did Alison use the ATM yesterday?
6. Did Jacob talk to a bank officer?
7. Did you endorse your check?
8. Did they make a withdrawal last week?

3

1. Was Gina sad? Yes, she was.
2. Were the flowers red? No, they weren't.
3. Was he relaxed? Yes, he was.
4. Was Jason thirsty? No, he wasn't.
5. Was it sunny? No, it wasn't.
6. Were they happy? Yes, they were.

Unit 3: Lesson 4 Simple Past, *Wh-* Questions page 161

1

1. e/did/buy; 2. c/did/have; 3. a/was; 4. f/was; 5. b/did/eat; 6. d/were

2

1. Who did you call last week?
2. Where did you live last year?
3. How much did you pay for groceries last month?
4. What did you do on Friday night?

TARGET GRAMMAR

Student answers will vary. Possible answers.
1. I called my mother.
2. I lived in Hawaii.
3. I paid about $800.
4. I went to the movies.

> **EXPANSION ACTIVITY: What did you do last weekend?**
> - Write the following example questions on the board:
>   - *What did you do Friday night?*
>   - *What did you do Saturday morning?*
> - Tell the students that they are going to talk about their weekend. Explain that you want them to give as much detail about what they did as possible.
> - Go over the two sample questions on the board. Elicit from the students other times of the weekend, such as *Saturday afternoon, Saturday night, Sunday morning, Sunday afternoon, and Sunday night.*
> - Ask for a volunteer to model the activity with you. After each *wh-* question, ask a clarifying *yes/no* question in the simple past.
> - Put the students in pairs and tell them to interview each other about their weekends. Each partner has to ask 4 simple past *wh-* questions and 4 simple past *yes/no* questions for clarification.
> - When the pairs have finished, have each student report the most interesting thing that his or her partner did last weekend.

Unit 4: Lesson 1 Want to, Like to, Would Like to

page 162

1. to be; 2. to get; 3. to do; 4. to start; 5. to buy; 6. to graduate; 7. to become; 8. to study

Student answers will vary. Possible answers.
1. I want to graduate from college.
2. I need to buy a car.
3. I like to play sports.
4. I hate to walk.
5. I would like to take a trip.
6. My best friend needs to rent an apartment.
7. My teacher likes to sing.

Unit 4: Lesson 2 Future with *be going to* pages 163–164

1. is going to become; 2. am going to save; 3. are not going to come; 4. are going to get married; 5. is not going to teach; 6. aren't going to graduate; 7. is going to become; 8. are going to learn

Answers will vary. Possible answers:
1. I'm going to go to a party
2. John and Jenny are going to fly to Rome
3. We're going to the beach
4. He is going to have a big test
5. They're going to visit their family in Bolivia

❸

1. Are you going to cook dinner tonight?
2. Are you going to wake up early tomorrow morning?
3. Are you going to study English next year?
4. Are you going to see your family tonight?
5. Are your friends going to come to your house next weekend?
6. Is it going to rain tonight?
7. Are we going to learn something new in this class?

Student answers will vary. Possible answers:
1. No, I'm going to go to a restaurant.
2. Yes, I'm going to get up at 6:00.
3. No, I'm going to study accounting next year.

Target Grammar 251

TARGET GRAMMAR

4. Yes, they're going to come over for dinner.
5. No, they're not. They're going to go to the beach.
6. It is probably going to rain tonight.
7. Yes, we are going to learn a lot of new things.

Unit 4: Lesson 3 Future with *will* page 165

1. won't/promise; 2. won't/promise; 3. 'll/offer; 4. 'll/offer; 5. will/predict; 6. 'll/offer

Answers will vary. Possible answers:
1. Yes, I will.
2. No, they won't.
3. No, he won't.
4. Yes, I will.

Unit 4: Lesson 4 *Because* and *to* for reasons pages 166–167

1. He's taking English classes because he wants to get a promotion.
2. I'm eating lunch early because I didn't eat breakfast.
3. He's going to be late because the roads are snowy.
4. They are studying hard because they want to get good grades.
5. He reads to his children every day because he wants to be a good parent.
6. I'm not going to work today because I'm sick.

Answers will vary. Possible answers:
1. I study English because I want to get a good job.
2. I live in this city because it's beautiful and because I have many friends here.
3. I don't want to live in another country because my family lives here.
4. I'm working because I have a lot of bills to pay.

1. to get; 2. to sign up; 3. to buy; 4. to visit; 5. to save; 6. to learn; 7. to spend

Answers will vary. Possible answers:
1. I take English classes to get a better job.
2. I save money to buy a house someday.
3. I watch TV to relax.
4. I do my homework to learn important things.

> **EXPANSION ACTIVITY: Where are you going to be in the future?**
>
> - Write the following example sentences on the board:
>   - *Where are you going to be in ten years?*
>   - *In ten years, I am going to be working in an office as a manager.*
>   - *What are you going to do to make that happen?*
>   - *To make that happen, I am going to get a business degree.*
> - Go over the four sentences to make sure that the students understand them.
> - Tell the students that they are going to talk about their future. Explain that you want them to talk about their goals for ten years in the future AND what they are going to do to get there.
> - Put the students in pairs and tell them to interview each other about their future plans.
> - When the pairs have finished, have each student report where his or her partner will be in ten years and what he or she is going to do to make that happen.

TARGET GRAMMAR

Unit 5: Lesson 1 *Go + verb + -ing* page 168

1

1. go horseback riding; 2. go skiing; 3. goes running; 4. went sailing; 5. went shopping; 6. going dancing

2

Answers will vary. Possible answers:
1. I like to go hiking.
2. I don't like to go dancing.
3. Last weekend, I went skiing.
4. Last summer, I went camping for three days.
5. Next weekend, I'm going bicycling.

Unit 5: Lesson 2 Comparative Adjectives

pages 169–170

1

1. happier; 2. bigger; 3. better; 4. newer; 5. heavier; 6. worse; 7. angrier; 8. wetter; 9. more beautiful; 10. more modern

2

Answers will vary. Possible answers:
1. more convenient/safer; 2. warmer; 3. more handsome/more intelligent; 4. easier to use

3

1. younger than; 2. more serious than; 3. longer than; 4. shorter than; 5. more beautiful than; 6. happier than

4

1. John is older than Jessica.
2. John is more mature than Jessica.
3. John is more tired than Jessica.
4. Jessica is more relaxed than John.

Unit 5: Lesson 3 *There was* and *There were* page 171

1

1. There weren't; 2. There were; 3. There was; 4. There was; 5. There wasn't; 6. There weren't; 7. There were

2

Answers will vary. Possible answers:
1. There wasn't a pizza shop.
2. There was a bagel shop.
3. There wasn't a salad bar.
4. There were four people sitting at tables.
5. There weren't any stores near the restaurants.

Unit 5: Lesson 4 Superlative Adjectives

pages 172–173

1

1. the prettiest; 2. the newest; 3. the most nervous; 4. the biggest; 5. the most exciting; 6. the tightest; 7. the worst; 8. the sickest; 9. the farthest; 10. the loosest; 11. the heaviest; 12. the curliest; 13. the slimmest; 14. the most intelligent; 15. the best; 16. the angriest

2

1. The oldest; 2. the most famous; 3. the longest; 4. the largest; 5. the fastest; 6. The sunniest; 7. the smallest; 8. the most beautiful; 9. the hottest; 10. The tallest

3

1. the youngest; 2. the tallest; 3. the best; 4. the worst; 5. the most beautiful; 6. the most expensive; 7. the shortest; 8. the happiest; 9. the highest; 10. the best

Answers to the questions will vary.

TARGET GRAMMAR

EXPANSION ACTIVITY: The Best Place in the World for a Vacation

- Write the following questions on the board:
  - *What is the best place in the world for a vacation?*
  - *Paris is the best because it has so many museums.*
  - *Yes, but Rome is more beautiful than Paris.*
  - *I know, but Paris has more interesting food. It's the most interesting food in Europe.*
  - *That's true but…*
- Go over the sentences to make sure that the students understand them.
- Ask for a volunteer to model the activity with you.
- Have each student decide on the best place in the world for a vacation.
- Put the students in pairs and tell them to tell each other their choice for the best vacation spot. Tell them that they must compare the two places that they have chosen. Encourage the students to try to persuade their partner to agree to his or her viewpoint.
- When the pairs have finished, have each student pair report on their two places and whether or not they finally agreed on one place.

Unit 6: Lesson 1 Count and noncount nouns

pages 174–175

Count: banana, book, cellphone, house, pen, ticket, basketball, tree

Noncount: oil, bread, coffee, milk, peace, sugar

1. a; 2. Ø; 3. an; Ø 4. Ø; 5. Ø; 6. a; 7. Ø; 8. an

1. a carton of; 2. four cups of; 3. a can of; 4. a bag of; 5. a bowl of; 6. two bottles of; 7. a bag of

254   Target Grammar

Answers will vary. Possible answers:
1. beans; 2. milk; 3. flour; 4. jar of mayonnaise; 5. orange; 6. ketchup

Unit 6: Lesson 2 *One, each, some, another,* and *the other(s)* page 176

1. some; 2. The others; 3. one; 4. another; 5. each; 6. the other; 7. some; 8. one; 9. one

Unit 6: Lesson 3 Quantifiers page 177

Grammar Note:
- Although in formal English, the word *some* is not used with questions or negatives, in common usage, people do use it in sentences like, *Do you want some milk?*

1. a little; 2. a few; 3. some; 4. any; 5. a little; 6. any; 7. a little; 8. some

1. Last night I had a hamburger and some french fries for dinner.
2. You need a little flour and some eggs to make a cake.
3. I am making some soup, so I need a few potatoes.
4. I had a few cookies this afternoon.

Quantifiers: *many, much, a lot (of),* and *every*

1. much; 2. A little/a lot of; 3. Every/some; 4. many; 5. much

TARGET GRAMMAR

Answers will vary. Possible answers:
1. I eat some cereal. I don't eat any eggs or bacon.
2. I eat a lot of vegetables and grains.
3. I buy a few apples and a lot of spaghetti.
4. I don't get much sleep at night.

Unit 6: Lesson 4 Adjective + Noun page 179

1. I ate some hot soup for dinner last night.
2. There are three red apples in the refrigerator.
3. I ate a delicious dessert after dinner.
4. There is some hot coffee in the kitchen.
5. I bought some expensive cheese at the store.
6. I'd like a hot sandwich please.

Answers to the questions will vary. Possible answers:
1. I eat two scrambled eggs.
2. I have three warm blankets.
3. I'm a tall, middle-aged, man.

> **EXPANSION ACTIVITY: My Shopping List**
> - Write the following conversation on the board:
>   - A: Don't forget to get some beans! B: OK. I'll get a can of beans.
>   - A: And buy a few eggs. B: Is one carton of eggs OK?
>   - A: Yes, but we need a lot of cereal. B: OK. I'll get three boxes of cereal.
>   - A: Do you want any rice? B: No, but I'll get a bag of potatoes.
> - Choose two students to read the conversation to the class or ask for a volunteer to model it with you.
> - Tell each student to make a shopping list with four items on it. Tell them that the items must have quantifiers, like *some* and *any*, and quantity phrases, like *a box of* and *a jar of*.
> - Put the students in pairs and have them tell each other what to buy at the store.
> - Ask for volunteers to do their conversations in front of the class.

Unit 7: Lesson 1 *It's, its* and *'s* page 180

My name's Robert and I think my family's great. My mother(s) name is Maria and my father(s) name is Peter. I have one sister. Her name's Sonia. She's married and has two children. Her husband(s) name is Tom. Their son(s) name is Bobby. He's my nephew. Their daughter(s) name is Tina. She's my niece. They live in an apartment. It's new but its living room is very small. I live at my parent(s') house. It's big, so we have room for my sister(s) family to stay with us when they visit. It's great when they do!

1. (It's) my birthday.
2. (It's) a beautiful day.
3. N/A
4. I hate my computer! (It's) not working.
5. N/A
6. N/A

Answers will vary. Possible answers:
1. My mother's name's Elizabeth. My father's name's Gerald.
2. It's sunny and warm.
3. It's blue and there's a picture of a mountain on its cover.

Target Grammar   255

TARGET GRAMMAR

Unit 7: Lesson 2 Possessive Pronouns and Object Pronouns pages 181–182

1. your, his, his; his, our, his; his
2. your; Its; mine, theirs
3. your, its; mine; my

2

1. That's not hers. It's mine.
2. That's not ours. It's theirs.
3. That's not yours. It's mine.
4. That's not yours. It's his.
5. That's not mine. It's hers.
6. That's not mine. It's theirs.
7. He's not ours. He's hers.
8. That's not mine. It's his.

3

1. them; 2. him; 3. it/us; 4. them/you; 5. it/them; 6. it/her

4

1. I gave her the present.
2. Bob showed me the picture.
3. She told them the secret.
4. We gave it to you yesterday.

Unit 7: Lesson 3 Indefinite Pronouns page 183

someone (or somebody)/anyone (or anybody)/something/Everything/anything/no one (or nobody)/Everyone (or everybody)/nothing

Answers will vary. Possible answers:
1. My mother is someone (or somebody) I ask for advice.
2. No, there's nothing I'd like to do.
3. No, I didn't apologize to anyone today.
4. Everyone (or everybody) should visit a foreign country.
5. Yes, I do take care of someone (or somebody). My son lives with me.

Unit 7: Lesson 4 Can, Could, Would and May for requests and offers

pages 184–185

1. Can; 2. Would you; 3. Could you; 4. Can you; 5. May I; 6. Could I

Answers to the questions will vary.
1. Excuse me, could I have a menu, please? Yes, you could.
2. Excuse me, would you take a picture of us? Yes, I would.
3. Can I please borrow your bike? No, you can't.
4. Could you help me please? Yes, I could.
5. Could I bring you anything else? No, you couldn't.
6. Will you please close the window? Yes, I will.
7. May I ask you a few questions? Yes, you may.

3

1. Can I bring you the check?
2. May I use your laptop, please?
3. I would like a bowl of soup, please.
4. Will you call me later?
5. Could I see your driver's license, please?
6. Could/May I take your picture, Mr. President?

EXPANSION ACTIVITY: Making Requests
- Write the following phrases on the board:
  - Would you…
  - Could you…
  - Can you…
  - May I…
  - Will you…

TARGET GRAMMAR

- Tell the students that they must each write four requests that are questions. They must use three of the phrases that you wrote on the board.
- Put the students in pairs. Have them read their requests to their partners. Have their partners respond to the requests positively or negatively.
- Have each student read one request to the class and have his or her partner answer.
- Have each student tell the class in what kind of setting the request might be used.

Unit 8: Lesson 1 *Can* and *Could* for Ability pages 186–187

Grammar Note:
- The difference in pronunciation between *can* and *can't* is often very difficult for learners. Make sure that the students understand that the word *can* generally does not receive stress. The "a" in can is pronounced as a schwa /ə/. To help the students hear these two words, write the following two sentences on the left and right of the board: *I can swim.* and *I can't swim.* Have the students stand up in front of the board while you move to the middle of the room. Say one of the sentences and have the students move to the right or left, according to what they heard. Continue until the students have no problem distinguishing between the two words.

1. can go; 2. can't see; 3. can't run; 4. can move; 5. can hear; 6. can do; 7. can't fix; 8. can help

1. Can you swim
2. Can you speak
3. Can you touch
4. Can you drive
5. Can you read
6. Can you run

Answers to questions will vary.

1. could stay; 2. couldn't go; 3. couldn't read/can; 4. could dance/can't; 5. Could you do/could; 6. Can they see/can't

4

1. When I was young, I couldn't drive.
2. Yesterday, I couldn't remember his name, but now I can.
3. William was sick yesterday, so he couldn't go to work.
4. A: Can Joshua speak Chinese? B: No, he can't.
5. A: Could they fix your car? B: Yes, they could.

Unit 8: Lesson 2 *Should* and *Shouldn't* for Advice page 188

1. shouldn't go; 2. should wear; 3. should sit; 4. should drink; 5. Should he play/shouldn't; 6. Should she see/shouldn't

Answers will vary. Possible answers:
1. lie down.
2. see a doctor?
3. take some medicine.
4. drink ginger ale.

Unit 8: Lesson 3 Adverbs of Degree page 189

1

1. a little; 2. really long; 3. old enough; 4. really; 5. very bad; 6. hot enough

2

1. I have a really high fever right now.
2. My muscles are very strong.

Target Grammar 257

TARGET GRAMMAR

3. I have really good eyes.
4. I can't run very well. My knees aren't strong enough.
5. I can't order from the children's menu. I am too old.

True/False answers will vary.

Unit 8: Lesson 4 Adverbs of Frequency pages 190–191

Answers will vary.

1. always eat; 2. always or usually; sometimes; 3. sometimes or usually uses; 4. never eats; 5. rarely see

Questions with Adverbs of Frequency

1. How often do you get a cold?
2. When do you usually get sick?
3. How often do you take medicine?
4. How often do you miss school?
5. When do you usually use an ice pack?

Answers to the questions will vary.

Answers to the questions will vary. Possible answers:
1. I usually go to the doctor twice a year.
2. I sometimes take aspirins.
3. My doctor never gives me a prescription.
4. A baby often gets a fever.
5. I rarely wear a bandage.

EXPANSION ACTIVITY: When I Was a Child
- Write the following questions and answers on the board:
  - A: *What could you do when you were a child?*
    B: *When I was a child, I could play the piano.*
  - A: *What couldn't you do when you were a child?*
    B: *I couldn't speak English.*
- Ask for two student volunteers to read the mini-dialogue.
- Put the students in pairs. Have them ask their partners the questions on the board.
- Have students report to the class on what their partners said they *could* and *couldn't* do.

Unit 9: Lesson 1 Simple Past Review pages 192–193

Grammar Note:
- Negative forms of past tense verbs can be a serious problem for students because the past is reflected in the auxiliary verb *did* rather than the base form verb, e.g., *did not go*. Be sure to point out these grammar features to the students and check that they understand them.

1. drink/drank; 2. shuts/didn't shut; 3. sleeps/slept; 4. shut/shut; 5. meets/met; 6. sees/didn't see

1. went; 2. left; 3. was; 4. didn't do; 5. put; 6. didn't put; 7. ate; 8. didn't do; 9. turned; 10. shut

TARGET GRAMMAR

Answers will vary. Possible answers:
1. I washed the dishes.
2. I ate cereal with fruit and milk.
3. I left at 7:00.
4. I took the bus to work.
5. I saw my friend Bob.

Unit 9: Lesson 3 Series of Commands page 194

Answers will vary. Possible answers.
1. Call 911, leave the building, and go outside with your class.
2. Get the plunger, take it to the bathroom, and unclog the toilet.
3. Leave the house as quickly as possible, go to a neighbor's house, and call 911.
4. Stay calm, press the emergency button, and wait patiently for help to arrive.
5. Stay calm, exit the car on the side away from the road, and call 911.
6. Walk to shelter and stay inside the shelter until the storm ends. Don't go outside.

Answers will vary. Possible answers:
1. Let's close the windows.
2. Let's call a plumber.
3. Let's open the door and windows.
4. Let's take her to a doctor.
5. Let's leave the house and call 911.

Unit 9: Lesson 4 Adverbs of Point in Time pages 195–196

1. last week; 2. last week; 3. last Saturday; 4. last Monday or four days ago; 5. Wednesday or two days ago; 6. last Sunday/last Thursday

Answers will vary.

1. next Saturday/in eight days; 2. in a week/next Friday; 3. next Wednesday; 4. next Monday; 5. next Sunday/in two days/the day after tomorrow

Answers will vary.

Answers will vary. Possible answers.
1. I'm going to eat in three hours.
2. I'm going to go on vacation next year.
3. I'm going to see them in three weeks.

> **EXPANSION ACTIVITY: Last Weekend and Next Weekend**
>
> - Write the following phrases on the board:
> - *What did you do last…?*
> - *What are you going to do next…?*
> - *Friday night, Saturday morning, Saturday afternoon, Saturday night, Sunday morning, Sunday afternoon, Sunday night*
> - Ask a couple of students sample questions, e.g. *What did you do last Saturday night?* and *What are you going to do next Sunday morning?*
> - Tell the students that they are going to walk around and ask other students about their last weekend and their next weekend.
> - Tell the students to stand up and mingle. Have them ask other students about their weekends. Emphasize that they should give as many details as possible and talk about specific times in the weekends, e.g., *last Sunday morning and next Saturday night*.
> - Have each student tell the class about one interesting activity or event that they learned about.

TARGET GRAMMAR

Unit 10: Lesson 1 Have to, Don't Have to, and Must pages 197–198

> **Grammar Note:**
> • Corpus studies of actual language use have shown that native speakers use *have to* to express necessity far more frequently than they use *must*.

1. must/have to; 2. don't have to; 3. must not;
4. must not; 5. must/has to; 6. must not;
7. has to/must; 8. don't have to

1. must/has to; 2. have to/must/don't have to; 3. must/have to/don't have to; 4. have to/must/don't have to; 5. must/have to; 6. don't have to; 7. don't have to; 8. must/have to; 9. don't have to; 10. must/has to; 11. must/has to; 12. doesn't have to; 13. must/has to

Answers will vary. Possible answers:
1. I have to study.
2. You must not talk when the teacher is explaining something.
3. I have to cook dinner.

Unit 10: Lesson 2 Adverbs of Manner pages 199–200

1. appropriately; 2. carefully; 3. early; 4. efficiently;
5. fast; 6. well; 7. hard; 8. independently;
9. intelligently; 10. loudly; 11. neatly; 12. politely;
13. slowly; 14. thoroughly

1. slowly; 2. politely; 3. independently; 4. fast;
5. hard; 6. carefully; 7. appropriately; 8. well

Name	Positive evaluations	Negative evaluations
Jim	He answers customers' questions politely. He can work independently.	He works very slowly. He drives too fast.
Nancy	She works hard. She writes carefully.	She doesn't dress appropriately. She doesn't communicate well with her supervisor.

Answers will vary. Possible answers:
1. I prefer to work with a group of people.
2. I think that it's more important to work thoroughly in order to avoid mistakes.
3. Communicating well means that other people understand your ideas.
4. Dressing appropriately communicates to your colleagues that you take your job seriously.
5. The biggest problem with working fast is that you make a lot of mistakes.

TARGET GRAMMAR

Unit 10: Lesson 3
Compound Sentences with *and, but,* and *or* page 201

1

1. Michael is an accountant, and I am too.
2. Do you want to work the day shift, or would you prefer the evening shift?
3. I was a chef in my last job, and you were too.
4. Tania likes to work, but Luis doesn't.
5. Henry traveled a lot as a salesperson, and Martha did too.
6. Did he quit, or was he fired?
7. Will you start next week, or do you have to wait for paperwork?
8. I worked very hard, but I didn't get a promotion.

Unit 10: Lesson 4
Negative Compound Sentences page 202

1

1. An accountant doesn't have to be strong, and a teacher doesn't either.
2. I can't drive a forklift or use a computer.
3. Marcia didn't get to work on time or dress appropriately.
4. Linda's supervisor didn't welcome her on the first day, and her co-workers didn't either.
5. Karl doesn't work full-time and Greg doesn't either.
6. The company doesn't give us computers or telephones.
7. My co-workers don't work quickly, and I don't either.

2

Answers will vary. Possible answers.
1. I don't answer phones or talk to customers.
2. At work, I don't watch TV, and I don't listen to the radio either.
3. I don't use a copier or a fax machine at home.
4. I don't leave my door or windows unlocked at home.

EXPANSION ACTIVITY: Next Week

- Write the following phrases on the board:
  - *Next week, I have to…*
  - *Next week, I must…*
  - *I don't have to…*
  - *I must not…*
- Tell the students that they are going to talk about the coming week. They will have to write eight sentences about their activities next week, two sentences with each of the phrases on the board.
- Start the activity by telling the students eight things about your next week. Have the students combine each pair of your sentences with the same phrases into one sentence. For example:
  - You: *Next week, I have to go shopping. Next week, I have to pay my rent.*
  - Student: *Next week, our teacher has to go shopping and pay her rent.*
- Give the students ten minutes to write eight things about their next week.
- Put the students in pairs. Have them read their eight sentences to each other.
- Tell their partners to combine the eight sentences into four sentences.
- Have each student say one of their combined sentences about their partner to the class.

Workbook Answer Key

Pre-Unit

A.
CPU, Keyboard, Printer, Cable, Mouse, Monitor

B.
Student Name: Paul Ming
Date of birth: 10/14/76

C.
4 – Click on "Submit."
5 – Create a password.
2 – Click on "Create Account."
3 – Type in your name and date of birth.
1 – Go to the school website.

Unit 1

Lesson 1

A.
1. birth certificate
2. driver's license
3. diploma
4. building pass

B.
1. b   5. c
2. f   6. h
3. e   7. d
4. g   8. a

C.
1. is   5. isn't
2. are   6. is
3. aren't, are   7. isn't
4. is

D.
Answers may vary.

E.
Birth Certificate: birthplace, date of birth, mother's name, father's name
Driver's License: address, date of birth, height, weight, photo

Lesson 2

A.
1. Cristina   4. Berta
2. Adam   5. Dan
3. Eli

B.
Possible answers :
Dan only : He has long hair. He has blue eyes.
Cristina only : She has short hair. She has brown eyes.
Dan and Cristina : They don't have curly hair. They don't have mustaches.

C.
1. doesn't have   5. doesn't have
2. has   6. have
3. have   7. don't have
4. has

D.
1. are   4. has
2. is   5. have
3. is

E.
Answers may vary.

F.
Answers may vary.

Lesson 3

A.

```
c e l l p h o n e m a x z e
b a s k e t b a l l f g d n
o l a s t o a n p g r a y b
r f d e j y l g c n a r s w
e   t i r e d d r a d i o u k
d i p h a p p y m a d u t o
r e l a x e d n e r v o u s
l   l a p t o p e r s w i n g
p l a s l i d e a i r e d x
```

B.
1. nervous
2. basketball
3. camera
4. cell phone
5. tired
6. sad
7. laptop
8. bored

C.
1. a   4. a
2. b   5. b
3. a   6. b

D.
Answers may vary.

262 Workbook Answer Key

Workbook Answer Key

Lesson 4

A.
1. housework
2. pet
3. music
4. swimming
5. baseball
6. motorcycle

B.
1. c
2. a
3. f
4. b
5. d
6. e

C.
1. no
2. no
3. yes
4. yes
5. yes
6. no

D.
Answers may vary.

Alternate Application: Family: Understanding School Forms and Personnel

A.
1. A principal
2. A nurse
3. A librarian
4. A lab assistant
5. An art teacher
6. A tutor
7. A counselor
8. A secretary

B.
1. b
2. a
3. b
4. a

C.
1. Sayed Nasser
2. Mr. Todd
3. 4th
4. 203
5. (614) 555-8115

D.
Answers may vary.

Alternate Application: Community: Understanding Forms and Documents

A.
1. Eric Amine Houngbo
2. 1532 S. Beacon St.
3. brown
4. 5'10"
5. ehounbay@kpcc.edu
6. H-99304

B.
Answers may vary.

C.
Answers may vary.

Practice Test

1. c
2. c
3. c
4. a
5. c
6. a
7. c
8. c
9. b
10. b

Unit 2

Lesson 1

A.
1. mail packages
2. check out books
3. get a prescription
4. buy groceries
5. get cash
6. get something to eat

B.
Answers may vary.

C.
Answers may vary.

D.
1. are
2. are
3. is
4. are
5. am

E.
Answers may vary. Possible answers:
1. He is mailing letters.
2. They're reading a book.

Workbook Answer Key 263

Workbook Answer Key

3. They are eating.
4. They're buying groceries.

Lesson 2
A.
1. False
2. False
3. True
4. True
5. False
6. True
7. False

B.
1. e
2. a
3. b
4. c
5. d
6. f

C.
1. next to
2. across from
3. across from
4. between

D.
Answers may vary.

E.
Answers may vary.

Lesson 3
A.
1. snack bar
2. waiting area
3. newsstand
4. baggage check
5. pay phone
6. information desk

B.
1. a
2. a
3. b
4. b
5. a
6. a
7. b

C.
2—At the baggage check.
5—Thank you.
1—Excuse me. Where can I check my luggage?
6—You're welcome.
3—Where's the baggage check?
4—It's next to the newsstand.

D.
1. c
2. e
3. a
4. d
5. b
6. f

E.
Answers may vary.

Lesson 4
A.
1. no
2. no
3. yes
4. no
5. yes
6. no

B.
1. c
2. b
3. a

C.
Only trains 1 and 2 stop there: Waldo, Ocala, Wildwood, Dade City, Tampa, Lakeland

All trains stop there: Savannah, Jacksonville, Winter Haven, West Palm Beach, Delray Beach, Fort Lauderdale, Hollywood, Miami

Only trains 3 and 4 stop there: Palatka, Deland, Sanford, Winter Park, Orlando, Kissimmee

D.
1. 16 minutes
2. 23 minutes
3. Train #3
4. 3 hours 10 minutes
5. 32 minutes

Alternate Application:
Work: Understanding Driving Safety
A.
1. False
2. True
3. False
4. True
5. False
6. True

B.
Things Helen does right: always has her registration and insurance card in the car, always has her driver's license with her, always wears her seatbelt, doesn't drink alcohol

Things Helen does wrong: drives while tired, often talks on the cell phone while driving

C.
1. d
2. a
3. b
4. c

Workbook Answer Key

Alternate Application:
Family: Understanding Telephone Services

A.
Circle: Galveston, Texas, Mexico, Houston, San Antonio, Waco, Dallas

B.
1. Dallas
2. parents
3. San Antonio
4. Frank

C.
Check: long distance, call waiting, prepaid telephone cards, caller ID, three-way calling

D.
1. f
2. d
3. b
4. a
5. c
6. e

E.
1. 512
2. 214, 972, 469
3. 915
4. 254
5. 713, 281, 832
6. 817, 682

F.
Answers may vary.

Practice Test
1. b
2. d
3. a
4. a
5. c
6. c
7. d
8. c
9. c
10. b

Spotlight: Writing

A.
left side : greeting

right side from top to bottom : heading, body, closing, signature

B.
left side : return address

right side from top to bottom : stamp, address

C.
Answers may vary.

D.
Answer's may vary.

Unit 3

Lesson 1

A.

Across
1. groceries
3. bus fare
4. toiletries
6. car
7. utilities
8. cash
9. rent

Down
1. gas
2. electricity
5. recreation

B.

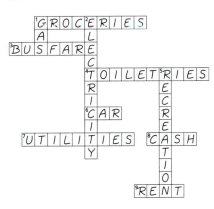

C.
Answers may vary.

D.
1. f
2. d
3. g
4. h
5. a
6. b
7. j
8. e
9. i
10. c

E.
1. a
2. a
3. a
4. b

Lesson 2

A.
Toothbrush; razor and shaving cream

Workbook Answer Key

B.
1. $15.00
2. $3.50
3. $2.25
4. $3.89
5. $4.29
6. $28.93
7. $50.00
8. $21.07

C.
1. bought
2. didn't buy
3. spent
4. filled
5. left

D.
3 – No, it wasn't.
1 – I bought the toiletries you wanted at the drugstore.
4 – That's strange. Were the razors on sale?
6 – Good, razors can be expensive.
2 – Was the shampoo on sale?
5 – Yes, they were.

E.
Answers may vary.

F.
1. $3.89
2. Parker Drugs
3. 7:43 P.M.
4. razor
5. tax
6. cash
7. $6.68

Lesson 3

A.
1. c
2. d
3. b
4. a

B.
1. ATM
2. withdrawal slip
3. savings account
4. paycheck
5. bank teller
6. checkbook
7. safe-deposit box

C.
1. c
2. b
3. d
4. e
5. a

D.
Answers may vary, but will use *Yes, I do, No, I don't, Yes, I did,* or *No, I didn't.*

E.
Answers may vary.

Lesson 4

A.
1. no
2. yes
3. yes
4. yes
5. no

B.
Answers may vary.
1. I know what fees the bank charges.
2. I check my bank statement monthly.
3. I write my ATM withdrawals in my check register.
4. For small items like candy.
5. In my neighborhood bank.

C.
1. a
2. b
3. a
4. b
5. b

D.
Answers may vary.

Alternate Application: Family: Understanding Credit History and Budgets

B.
1. house
2. down payment
3. borrow
4. credit card
5. credit history
6. have too much debt / owe too much money

C.

EXPENSE	JANUARY
rent	$850
food	$400
train pass	$90
gas	$25
day care	$300
utilities	$80
savings	$500
monthly total	$2,245

Workbook Answer Key

Take It Outside, page 43
Answers may vary.

Alternate Application: Community: Understanding bills

A.
Check: internet, voice mail, cable television, phone

B.
1. Hugo Martinez
2. 12/29/11
3. 165.36
4. 188200100-33782X
5. 12/16 – 1/15
6. $10.76
7. cable television
8. $0.00

C.
Answers may vary.

D.
Answers may vary.

Practice Test
1. c
2. d
3. b
4. d
5. c
6. b
7. b
8. c
9. d
10. d

Unit 4

Lesson 1

A.
1. get a job
2. get a raise
3. buy a house
4. become a U.S. citizen
5. be a good parent

B.
1. a
2. a
3. b
4. b
5. a
6. a

C.
Answers may vary.

D.
1. b
2. d
3. a

Lesson 2

A.
1. b
2. f
3. a
4. e
5. d
6. c

B.
1. Yes
2. Yes
3. No
4. I don't know.
5. No

C.
1. Education, language and literacy
2. Volunteer opportunities
3. Housing
4. Libraries
5. Employment
6. Starting a business
7. Education, language, and literacy

D.
1. am going to move
2. is going to go
3. are going to start
4. are going to learn
5. is going to get

E.
Answers may vary.

Lesson 3

A.
1. opposite
2. same
3. opposite
4. opposite
5. same
6. opposite
7. same
8. opposite
9. opposite
10. same

B.
Answers may vary.

Workbook Answer Key   **267**

Workbook Answer Key

C.
Answers may vary.

D.
Answers may vary.

Lesson 4

A.
1. writer
2. Port-au-Prince, Haiti
3. New York
4. Creole, French
5. her aunt
6. to live with her parents
7. 1995

B.
1. her father moved to New York
2. she wrote her first story
3. she moved to New York
4. she lived with her aunt
5. she published her first book of stories

C.
Answers may vary.

D.
Answers may vary.

E.
1. 1981
2. 26
3. 3 years

Alternate Application:
Work: Promotions and Evaluations

A.
Answers may vary.

B.
ways to get a promotion; how to make plans; the qualities you need for a better job; what to wear to an interview; the importance of skills and achievements

C.
1. Follow the seven steps from the article.
2. Get extra training or education.
3. Be positive, responsible, and hard working.
4. Make a plan.
5. Dress professionally.

D.
Answers may vary.

Alternate Application:
Community: Understanding a School Calendar

A.
5 – Semester ends
3 – Academic classes begin
1 – New student registration
6 – Graduation
4 – Final exam period
2 – GED and Adult ESL classes begin

B.
on January 8 – GED and ESL classes begin
on January 17 – Martin Luther King, Jr. Holiday
from March 5 to March 11 – Spring Break
on May 11 – Graduation
from May 4 to May 10 – Final Exam Period
new student registration: December 6 to January 7
Spring Holiday: March 25
graduation: May 11

C.
Answers may vary.

Practice Test

1. d
2. b
3. a
4. d
5. a
6. b
7. d
8. d
9. b
10. d

Spotlight: Writing

A.
from left to right : 6, 2, 3, 1, 5, 4
timeline :

1. Jame's wife started labor.
2. He drove her to the hospital.
3. He put on a hospital gown.
4. They took them into the delivery room.
5. He cut the umbilical cord.
6. James held his baby for the first time.

B.
Underline : on March 12, December 2001, several days, three months, finally

C.
Answers may vary.

Workbook Answer Key

Unit 5

Lesson 1

A.
1. bucket, mop
2. coat
3. boots
4. vacuum cleaner
5. blender

B.
Answers may vary.

C.
1. b
2. e
3. a
4. c
5. f
6. d

D.
1. a
2. b
3. a
4. b
5. a

E.
Answers may vary.

Lesson 2

A.

```
w  a  p  p  l  i  a  n  c  e
p  n  e  u  o  b  r  e  a  k
u  s  j  e  w  e  l  r  y  n  t
s  i  l  t  e  c  h  o  o  w
h  r  e  v  u  e  m  o  p  e
   c  a  r  r  y  s  a  l  e  r
o  d  z  e  q  c  l  a  n  p
a  v  s  t  r  o  l  l  e  r
t  f  u  r  n  i  t  u  r  e
u  n  b  u  s  i  n  e  s  s
```

B.
1. d
2. f
3. b
4. c
5. e
6. a

C.
Answers may vary.

D.
1. no
2. yes
3. yes
4. yes
5. yes
6. no

Lesson 3

A.
4—I think so. I saved twelve dollars.
2—Yes. There was one at Barb's.
5—That's a good deal.
3—Really? Did you get a good deal?
1—Did you get a new blender?

B.
1. a
2. b
3. a
4. b
5. a

C.
1. $50.00
2. $250.00
3. $50.00
4. $40.00
5. $3.50
6. $256.00

D.
1. $12.80
2. $15.00
3. $26.10
4. $15.00

E.
1. There was
2. There weren't
3. There were
4. There were
5. There were
6. There were
7. There weren't

F.
Answers may vary.

Lesson 4

A.
Answers may vary.

B.
1. no
2. yes
3. yes
4. no
5. yes

C.
1. a
2. b
3. a
4. b
5. b

Workbook Answer Key 269

Workbook Answer Key

D.
1. Toastee
2. My Toast
3. My Toast
4. Answers will vary.
5. Lap-2
6. EZ Comp
7. Answers will vary.

**Alternate Application:
Work: Buying Uniforms**

A.
Nurse's cap, Police officer's shirt, Painter's overalls, Waiter's jacket, Flight attendant's jacket

B.
1. $17.00   4. $20.00
2. $39.00   5. $32.00
3. $27.00

C.
Answers may vary
1. dress/cap/pants/shirt/white shoes
2. waiters/flight attendants/doctor/hotel workers/bus drivers
3. nurses/doctors/nursing assistants/dental assistants/painters/waiters

Take It Outside, page 73
Answers will vary.

**Alternate Application:
Family: Understanding Warning Labels**

A.

Cleaning Supplies	Laundry Supplies	Small Appliances
bleach	bleach	hairdryer
vacuum cleaner	iron	toilet brush
oven cleaner		microwave oven
toilet brush		iron

B.
1. a cleaning supply and a laundry supply
2. small appliance
3. A toilet brush
4. small appliances

C.
1. hairdryer
2. bleach
3. vacuum cleaner
4. microwave oven

D.
1. bleach
2. vacuum cleaner
3. microwave oven and/or iron
4. hairdryer

E.
1. D; 2. B; 3. A; 4. C

Practice Test
1. c   6. b
2. a   7. c
3. b   8. c
4. c   9. d
5. d   10. a

Unit 6

Lesson 1

A.
1. red meat
2. fruit
3. turkey
4. vegetables
5. ice cream
6. fish

B.
Answers may vary.

C.
1. b   4. c
2. a   5. f
3. d   6. e
Some answers may vary.

D.
Answers may vary.

E.
Answers may vary.

Lesson 2

A.
A waiter, customers, a table, a plate, a napkin, serving, smiling

Workbook Answer Key

B.
Answers may vary.

C.
1. d
2. a
3. f
4. b
5. c
6. e

D.
1. waiter
2. bowl
3. spill
4. menu
5. napkin

E.
Answers may vary.

Lesson 3

A.
Across
1. beverages
4. ice cream
5. tray
6. dessert
8. main dish

Down
2. vegetables
3. appetizer
7. salad

B.

```
¹B E ²V E R ³A G E S
    E       P
    G       P
⁴I C E C R  E A M
    T       T
⁵T R A Y    I
    B       Z
    L    ⁶D E S ⁷S E R T
    E       R   A
    S           L
                A
           ⁸M A I N D I S H
```

C.
2—Yes. I'd like a small garden salad and a hamburger.
5—Large or small?
3—Do you want something to drink with your hamburger?
1—Are you ready to order?
4—Yes, I'd like some milk please.
6—Large, please.

D.
1. any
2. some
3. any
4. a little
5. some; some
6. some
7. some
8. any

E.
1. $1.50
2. $6.40
3. $0.75
4. $0.56

Lesson 4

A.
Answers may vary. Examples include the following:
1. The cook is measuring the ingredients.
2. The cook is mixing the ingredients.
3. The cook is cutting up vegetables.
4. The cook is frying up some chicken.
5. The cook is baking a desert.

B.
1 cup of butter; ½ cup of sugar, 2 tsp. of water, 2 tsp. of vanilla, 2 cups of flour, ½ cup of nuts

C.
Left column: Adjective
Right column: Noun
Possible answers:
1. delicious meal
2. easy recipe
3. cold water
4. warm water
5. soft butter
6. sweet desserts

**Alternate Application:
Work: Food Containers and Measurements**

A.
a bottle of: olive oil, water, orange soda
a jar of: peanut butter, pickles
a carton of: milk, orange juice
2 cups of: water, flour
a dozen: eggs
2 pounds of: potatoes, tomatoes

Workbook Answer Key

B.
1. two pounds of
2. a dozen
3. cartons
4. bottle
5. jar

C.
1. 32
2. 32
3. 8
4. 128
5. 20

D.
1. 30
2. 50
3. 15
4. 640
5. 15
6. 20

The total dollar amount is: $48.97

**Alternate Application:
Family: The FDA and Food Labels**

A.
1. False – The FDA is a government agency.
2. True
3. False – The FDA is responsible for labels on food.
4. False – An ingredient list appears on any food with two or more ingredients.
5. False – Tomato Puree is the main ingredient in Mark's Pizza Sauce. Wheat flour is the main ingredient for the crust.
6. False – Tomato Puree is made with water and tomato paste.

B.
top row: 2, 1
bottom row: 4, 5

C.
1. tomato sauce and diced tomatoes
2. dry roasted peanuts and trail mix
3. salt
4. oatmeal cookies
5. three out of the four

Practice Test
1. c
2. a
3. c
4. c
5. d
6. a
7. b
8. c
9. b
10. b

Spotlight: Writing

A.
Answers will vary.

B.
1. No
2. meatloaf, green beans, and mashed potatoes
3. It's unhealthy.

C & D.
Answers may vary.

Unit 7

Lesson 1

A.
Across
1. brother-in-law
3. niece
6. fiancée
7. uncle
9. friend
10. boss
11. grandparents

Down
2. landlord
3. nephew
4. coworker
5. parents
8. neighbor

B.

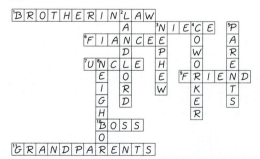

Note: 2 Down could also be LANDLADY.

C.
1. Isha
2. Ivan
3. Richard
4. Anita
5. Isha
6. Jerome

Workbook Answer Key

D.
Answers may vary.

Lesson 2

A.
1. have dinner
2. dance
3. shake hands
4. cut cake

B.
Answers may vary.

C.
1. a
2. b
3. a
4. b
5. b

D.
1. That's the mother of the groom.
2. Who's your father dancing with?
3. In this picture I am hugging my wife's mother or I am hugging my wife's mother in this picture.
4. My brother's fiancée is from China.
5. Lalo made a toast at my wedding.

Lesson 3

A.
1. ask for advice
2. apologize
3. compliment
4. criticize
5. disagree
6. talk back

B.
1. should
2. shouldn't
3. shouldn't
4. shouldn't
5. shouldn't
6. should
7. should

C.
You have a meeting with your boss. → She criticizes your work. → You apologize. → You ask for advice on how to do a better job. → You leave the meeting with a good attitude. You have a meeting with your boss. → She compliments your work. → You thank your boss. → You leave the meeting with a good attitude.

D.
1. someone, anything, someone
2. something, something, someone, everyone

Lesson 4

A.
1. five
2. birthday
3. the child's
4. family (parents and grandparents)
5. opening presents/celebrating a birthday

B.
Answers may vary.

C.
1. first month
2. red eggs
3. envelopes
4. ancestors
5. red
6. hair

D.
Answers may vary.

Alternate Application: Family: Parental Responsibilities

A.
Problems (Mad Mom's): son hits sister, daughter doesn't listen to mother, mom gets angry

Solutions (Dr. Dina's Ideas): use simple rules, help children use words, ignore small problems, use time outs, reward good behavior

B.
1. 2
2. 6, 4
3. The son hits his sister.
4. The daughter doesn't listen to her mother.
5. to ask for advice
6. to keep children safe and help them learn

C.
Answers may vary.

D.
Answers may vary.

Take It Outside, page 103
Answers may vary.

Workbook Answer Key

Alternate Application: Community: Postal Services

A.
1. postcard
2. letter
3. large envelope
4. package

B.
1. True
2. False
3. True
4. False
5. False
6. False
7. False

C.
Situation #1: Express Mail
Situation #2: First-Class Mail
Situation #3: Parcel Post

D.
Answers may vary.

Practice Test

1. a
2. c
3. c
4. b
5. a
6. b
7. b
8. c
9. d
10. d

Unit 8

Lesson 1

A.

[word search puzzle]

B.
1. joints
2. legs
3. skin
4. teeth
5. brain
6. heart
7. bones
8. ears
9. waist
10. back

C.
1. f
2. g
3. a
4. d
5. c
6. b
7. e

D.
Answers may vary.

Lesson 2

A.
1. d
2. c
3. e
4. a
5. b

B.
1. a
2. b
3. b
4. b
5. a

C.
Answers may vary.

D.
1. shouldn't
2. should
3. should
4. should
5. shouldn't
6. should

E.

I Should	I Shouldn't
Exercise often	Eat fatty food
Get 8 hours of sleep	Work too many hours
Eat nutritious food	Smoke cigarettes
See a doctor regularly	
Brush my teeth every day	

Workbook Answer Key

Lesson 3

A.
1. a
2. c
3. f
4. b
5. e
6. d

B.
1. bandage
2. x-ray
3. crutch
4. wheelchair
5. examining room

C.
3—Did you have to go to the emergency room?
4—Yes, a friend took me.
1—What happened to your elbow?
5—Did they put ice on it?
2—I sprained it.
6—Yes, and they gave me this sling.

D.
Answers may vary.

E.
I sprained my ankle in 2010. I was running down a hill very fast when I slipped. I went to the emergency room. The doctors were very nice. They took x-rays, but they said I didn't have a fracture. The doctor put a bandage on my ankle and gave me some crutches.

F.
Answers may vary.

Lesson 4

A.
1. cream
2. capsule
3. tablet
4. teaspoon

B.
1. 3
2. 4
3. 2
4. 12
5. 1.5

C.
1. 3
2. ½
3. 8

D.
1. yes
2. no
3. no
4. yes
5. no

E.
Answers may vary.

**Alternate Application:
Work: Accident Reports**

A.
1. Daniel Young
2. He slipped on the wet floor.
3. 6/15
4. back
5. bruise

B.
Address: 1521 Market Street
D.O.B: 03/02/75
Workplace: San Francisco General Hospital
Position: Nursing Assistant
Date of accident: today
Time of accident: 9:30
Primary Insurance: GoodHealth Insurance
Group Number: 83351
Policy Number: P3397X
Policy Holder: Robert Garza

**Alternate Application:
Family: Medical History**

A.
1. Grace Park
2. heart disease
3. no
4. Elizabeth Park, Grace's sister
5. earaches

B.
Answers may vary.

Take It Outside, page 119
Answers may vary.

Practice Test
1. a
2. c
3. c
4. b
5. c
6. c
7. a
8. c
9. a
10. c

Workbook Answer Key

Spotlight : Writing

A:
Cause: rain, Effect: car hit tree
Cause: cut on face from crash, Effect: stitches
Cause: broken bone in hand, Effect: pin placed in hand

B & C:
Answers may vary.

Unit 9

Lesson 1

A.
1. pan, pot, juice cup
2. heat, stove
3. refrigerator
4. door
5. stove
6. pan, eggs, pot, juice cup

B.
Answers may vary.

C.
Answers may vary.

D.
1. had
2. took out
3. cooked
4. put
5. played
6. came
7. shut off
8. went
9. locked
10. forgot
11. got

E.
1. False – Waifa had friends over last night.
2. True
3. False – The neighbors came over to ask them to turn the music down.
4. True
5. False – Waifa left the cake in the oven, and it got burned.
6. False – Waifa locked the door.

Lesson 2

A.
Answers may vary.

B.
Answers may vary.

C.
3—Could you please take a look at my shower again?
5—No. This time it's clogged up.
1—Hello. This is Mike Burnett in apartment 2H.
4—Is it leaking again?
6—Okay. I'll be over as soon as I can.
2—Hi. What can I do for you?

D.
Date: 3-12-12
Time: 10:00 A.M.
Name: Carrie Wesley
Address: 201 Appleton Lane, Apartment 10J
Problem: Toilet is leaking.

E.
1. sent
2. got
3. Did, look
4. read
5. did, see
6. noticed
7. Did, put

Lesson 3

A.
firefighter, fire truck, hose, ladder, smoke

B.
Across
1. ambulance
3. truck
6. ladder
7. hose
8. spray

Down
1. attach
2. crawl
4. cover
5. hydrant
8. smoke

C.

Workbook Answer Key

D.
1. b
2. a
3. a
4. a

Lesson 4

A.
earthquake

B.
1. Don't stand
2. Go
3. Don't use
4. Don't go
5. Don't turn

C.
1. b
2. a
3. c

D.
1. b
2. b
3. a
4. a
5. a

E.
1. 212
2. 32
3. 15
4. 25

F.
1. b
2. a
3. a
4. b
5. a
6. a
7. a

**Alternate Application:
Work: Emergencies at Work**

A.
1. fire alarm
2. smoke detector
3. fire extinguisher

B.
1. b
2. c
3. a

C.
1. False
2. True
3. True
4. False
5. False

D.
Answers may vary.

Take It Outside, page 133
Answers may vary.

**Alternate Application:
Community: Weather Emergencies**

A.
1. Answers may vary. Possible answers.
Spring: rain, lightening, thunderstorm
Summer: hurricane, tornado, thunderstorm
Fall: wind, fog, rain
Winter: hail, snow, sleet

B.

EMERGENCY	THINGS YOU SHOULD DO	THINGS YOU SHOULDN'T DO
A tornado	Go to basement or small room Protect neck and head	Be near windows Drive near a tornado
A hurricane	Stay calm Stay indoors & away from windows Listen to radio Save water	Stay by windows Leave large objects outside Be near dangling power lines Panic
A thunderstorm	Get indoors Secure windows and outdoor objects Avoid electricity	Be in a body of water Use electrical equipment Be outside

Practice Test
1. c
2. d
3. d
4. b
5. c
6. b
7. a
8. c
9. c
10. a

Workbook Answer Key

Unit 10

Lesson 1

A.
1. hospitality
2. building and construction
3. manufacturing
4. health care

B.
Answers may vary.

C.
1. a
2. c
3. d
4. b
5. f
6. e

D.
1. has to
2. have to
3. don't have to
4. doesn't have to
5. have to
6. have to
7. don't have to
8. has to
9. doesn't have to
10. don't have to

E.
Answers may vary.

Lesson 2

A.
Answers may vary.

B.
1. a
2. b
3. b
4. a
5. a

C.
Answers may vary.

D.
Answers may vary.

E.
1. diligently
2. quickly
3. politely
4. appropriately
5. well

F.
Answers may vary.

Lesson 3

A.

a	c	o	m	p	u	t	e	r	i	z	e	k
p	u	n	c	t	u	a	l	e	n	d	s	c
a	b	s	g	c	a	r	e	g	i	v	e	r
s	i	u	o	f	f	i	c	e	x	i	t	e
s	c	p	p	s	h	i	f	t	u	p	o	t	a
e	l	p	i	o	c	p	r	o	b	l	e	m
m	e	l	n	e	p	a	i	n	t	e	r	s
b	a	y	g	y	z	i	c	v	u	t	h	e
l	r	n	m	a	c	h	i	n	e	s	v	t
e	w	e	l	d	e	r	a	b	l	e	n	d
r	u	l	i	k	e	a	n	i	g	h	t	x

B.
1. b
2. c
3. a
4. e
5. d

C.
Answers may vary.

D.
1. False
2. True
3. False
4. True
5. True

Lesson 4

A.
Answers may vary.

B.
What to Wear: Go to a thrift store for better prices. Look in the telephone book for uniforms.

Childcare: Talk to other parents. Fill out medical forms.

Transportation: Call if you are going to be late. Have a backup plan. Plan for extra time.

C.
You don't have much money for clothes: Go to a thrift store for better prices.

Your car won't start the first day: Have a back-up plan.

Your child has an emergency at childcare and you aren't available: Have emergency contact information available.

Workbook Answer Key

You need a uniform: Look in the telephone book for uniforms.

You're not sure how long it takes to get to your new job: Do a practice trip so you know how long it will take.

D.
Answers may vary.

**Alternate Application:
Work: Understanding Time Cards**

A.
Monday: 8 hours
Tuesday: 8 hours
Wednesday: 8.5 hours
Thursday: 7.5 hours
Friday: 8 hours
Saturday: 4 hours
Weekly Regular: 40 hours
Overtime: 4

B.
1. Hong
2. Southside Distributors
3. Maintenance
4. 44
5. 4
6. 6
7. 1 hour

C.
Tuesday: 8:00 A.M. to noon
Wednesday: 1 P.M. to 6 P.M.
Thursday & Friday: 8 A.M. to 1 P.M.

Take It Outside, page 147
Answers may vary.

**Alternate Application:
Community: Official Holidays**

A.
Answers may vary.

B.
1. Labor Day
2. New Year's Day
3. Veteran's Day
4. Independence Day
5. Columbus Day
6. Memorial Day
7. Martin Luther King, Jr. Day
8. Washington's Birthday
9. Election Day

C.
Answers may vary.

Practice Test

1. d
2. b
3. c
4. b
5. c
6. d
7. a
8. b
9. b
10. c

Spotlight: Writing

A.
1. administrative assistant
2. administrative assistant to firm partner
3. math teacher

B.
4, 1, 3, 2

C.
Answers may vary.

Unit 1 Test

Name: _____ Date: _____ Score: _____

LISTENING: Listen to the conversations. Then choose the correct answer for each question.

Conversation 1 153

1. What is the man's name in this conversation?
   A. Robert
   B. Martin
   C. Mr. Carter

2. What is he doing?
   A. greeting a friend
   B. introducing himself
   C. introducing a friend

3. Where are they?
   A. At school.
   B. At work.
   C. At home.

Conversation 2

4. Who should get the book?
   A. Mark
   B. Rick
   C. Sam

5. What does he look like?
   A. He has short hair.
   B. He has blond hair.
   C. He has long hair.

6. Do Mark and Sam know each other?
   A. yes
   B. no
   C. I don't know

GRAMMAR: Choose the word or words that correctly complete each sentence.

7. Adam _____ bald.
   A. is
   B. has
   C. doesn't have

8. He _____ a beard.
   A. is
   B. has
   C. doesn't have

9. Yuko _____ swimming.
   A. liking
   B. likes
   C. like

ADAM   YUKO

280 Unit 1 Test

Unit 1 Test

10. Yuko _____ dark hair.
   A. has
   B. have
   C. don't have

11. Adam _____ pets.
   A. doesn't like
   B. don't like
   C. doesn't likes

12. _____ you _____ Yuko and Adam?
   A. Does ... know
   B. Does ... knows
   C. Do ... know

READING/VOCABULARY: Read the driver's license application. Then choose the correct answer for each question below.

13. What is her last name?
   A. Ann
   B. Sophie
   C. Patel

14. What is her address?
   A. 105 Fairview Road
   B. 1035 Fairway Road
   C. 1035 Fairview Road

15. What is her date of birth?
   A. 03/12/87
   B. 5'4"
   C. 08601

16. What is her weight?
   A. 120 lbs.
   B. 54 lbs.
   C. Heavy

17. What color are her eyes?
   A. brown
   B. blue
   C. green

18. What is the application for?
   A. birth certificate
   B. driver's license
   C. diploma

DRIVER'S LICENSE APPLICATION

LICENSE NEEDED
- OPERATOR
- CHAFFEUR
- MOPED

1. (none) — Present Driver License No.
2. Full name: Ann (First) Sophie (Middle) Patel (Last)
3. 1035 Fairview Rd. Apt. 6G (Residence Address, Apt. or Lot Number) Mercer (County)
4. Trenton (Town or City) 08601 (Zip Code)
5. Brown (Eye Color) 5'4 (Height) 120 lbs (Weight) F (Sex) 03/12/87 (Birth Date)
6. 8/15/12 (Date) Ann Patel (Signature of Applicant)

19–20. WRITING: Write two sentences that describe what you look like.

_____

_____

Unit 2 Test

Name: _____   Date: _____   Score: _____

LISTENING: Listen to the conversations. Then choose the correct answer for each question.

Conversation 1 154

1. Where does the woman want to go?
   A. Cedar
   B. the library
   C. the hospital

2. Where is she going to start?
   A. at the library
   B. on Central Boulevard
   C. at the hospital

3. What street is the hospital on?
   A. Central Boulevard
   B. Cedar Street
   C. Elm Street

Conversation 2

4. Who is speaking?
   A. two friends
   B. a student and teacher
   C. a customer and ticket agent

5. Where does the man want to go?
   A. Trenton
   B. Roundtrip
   C. Miami

6. When is the train coming?
   A. 9:30
   B. 9:15
   C. 9:50

GRAMMAR: Choose the word or phrase that correctly completes each sentence.

7. I _____ a ticket now.
   A. is buying
   B. are buying
   C. am buying

8. We _____ English at school.
   A. am studying
   B. are studying
   C. is studying

9. Tina and Donna _____ in Texas.
   A. am living
   B. is living
   C. are living

10. _____ is the supermarket?
    A. Where
    B. Who
    C. When

11. _____ is the bus leaving?
    A. Who
    B. When
    C. What

12. Why _____ to the medical center?
    A. are you going
    B. you are going
    C. you go

282   Unit 2 Test

Unit 2 Test

READING/VOCABULARY: Read the following train schedule. Then choose the correct answer for each question below.

13. What time is the train scheduled to leave Cleburne?
    A. 4:00
    B. 4:42
    C. 5:50

14. How many hours is it usually from Fort Worth to Austin?
    A. almost 8
    B. 2.5
    C. between 4 and 5

15. What is the name of the train?
    A. San Antonio Eagle
    B. Texas Eagle
    C. Destination

The Texas Eagle Train Schedule

- On-line Tickets
- Route Map
- General Information
- Links
- Contact Us

THE TEXAS EAGLE TRAIN

Time	Destination
4:00	Fort Worth
4:42	Cleburne
5:50	McGregor
6:30	Temple
7:26	Taylor
8:20	Austin
9:02	San Marcos
11:45	San Antonio

16. The train is 40 minutes late today. When will it be in Austin?
    A. 8:20
    B. 8:40
    C. 9:00

17. You arrive at the train station in Temple at 6:45. Are you there in time for the train?
    A. Yes. I'm right on time
    B. No. I'm 15 minutes late.
    C. Yes. I'm 15 minutes early.

18. It's now 7:30. Miguel is on the Texas Eagle train. The train is on time. Where is Miguel?
    A. between Temple and Taylor
    B. between Taylor and Austin
    C. between Austin and San Marcos

19–20. WRITING: Write two sentences about what people are doing in your class right now.

_____

_____

Unit 3 Test

Name: _____   Date: _____   Score: _____

LISTENING: Listen to the conversations. Then choose the correct answer for each question.

Conversation 1 🎧 155

1. How much is the purchase?
   - A. $20.00
   - B. $5.25
   - C. $15.75

2. Does the clerk give the correct change at first?
   - A. Yes.
   - B. No. He gives more than he should.
   - C. No. He gives less money than he should.

3. How much is the correct change?
   - A. $15.75
   - B. $4.25
   - C. $5.25

Conversation 2

4. What does the woman want to do?
   - A. cash a check
   - B. open an account
   - C. get change

5. What kind of photo ID does she have?
   - A. a building pass
   - B. a driver's license
   - C. a passport

6. How many bills does she get?
   - A. 20
   - B. 100
   - C. 5

GRAMMAR: Choose the word or phrase that correctly completes each sentence.

7. Susan _____ to the store yesterday.
   - A. went
   - B. ate
   - C. did

8. She _____ some toothpaste and a razor for $4.30.
   - A. buy
   - B. bought
   - C. does buy

9. She _____ with a check. She paid with a twenty.
   - A. didn't pay
   - B. doesn't pay
   - C. don't pay

10. The cashier _____ her $5.30 in change.
    - A. don't give
    - B. give
    - C. gave

11. _____ you a twenty? I think I should get $15.30." Susan asked.
    - A. Don't I give
    - B. Did I give
    - C. I did give

12. "Yes, you _____. I'm sorry. Here's another $10," said the cashier.
    - A. are
    - B. do
    - C. did

Unit 3 Test

READING/VOCABULARY: Read John's check register. Then choose the correct answer for each question below.

13. How much does John pay for rent?
    A. $800.00
    B. $758.99
    C. $1577.50

14. Are utilities included in the rent?
    A. yes
    B. no
    C. I don't know

Check Register

CHECK NO. or ATM	DATE	DESCRIPTION	TRANSACTION AMOUNT	DEPOSIT AMOUNT	BALANCE
411	6/27	Harper Electric Power Co.	$80.39		$1632.70
412	6/28	Harper gas	$42.60		$1591.10
413	6/29	Southern telephone	$32.11		$1558.99
414	6/30	Downtown Rental company (rent)	$800.00		$758.99
ATM	7/2	cash withdrawal	$100.00		$658.99
	7/3	deposit		$1577.50	$2236.49
415	7/4	AJ's Supermart (groceries)	$76.40		$2160.09

15. What is John's balance at the end of June 30?
    A. $1558.99
    B. $758.99
    C. $658.99

16. How much did John withdraw in cash between 6/27 and 7/4?
    A. $100.00
    B. $1632.70
    C. $800.00

17. How much did John deposit the same week?
    A. $100.00
    B. $1577.50
    C. $2160.09

18. How much was the check for groceries?
    A. $80.39
    B. $42.60
    C. $76.40

19–20. WRITING: Write two sentences about what you did yesterday.

_____

_____

Unit 4 Test

Name: _____ Date: _____ Score: _____

LISTENING: Listen to the conversations. Then choose the correct answer for each question.

Conversation 1 🎧 156

1. What job are they talking about?
   A. tailor
   B. supervisor
   C. cook

2. How do the speakers feel about Ben Taylor?
   A. They like him.
   B. They don't like him.
   C. I don't know.

3. Which of the following is not one of Ben's qualities?
   A. bad attitude
   B. hardworking
   C. good with people

Conversation 2

4. What are the speakers talking about?
   A. courses at school
   B. ways to use the computer
   C. how Rita got a promotion

5. How does Rita feel?
   A. sad
   B. disorganized
   C. happy

6. What do you think Carl is going to do?
   A. go back to school
   B. give advice
   C. buy a computer

GRAMMAR: Choose the word or phrase that correctly completes each sentence.

7. A: What is your goal?
   B: I _____ a good parent.
   A. would like be
   B. would like to be
   C. like to be

8. Don't worry! I _____ late for class!
   A. willn't be
   B. will be not
   C. won't be

9. Why did she go home?
   A. Because she was sick.
   B. She went home to be sick.
   C. She would like to be sick.

10. She's taking classes _____ a better job.
    A. to get
    B. because she gets
    C. because she likes

11. You _____ more time with your children.
    A. are going spend
    B. go to spending
    C. are going to spend

12. Mike and I _____ a house.
    A. are going to buy
    B. is going to buy
    C. am going to buy

286   Unit 4 Test

Unit 4 Test

READING/VOCABULARY: Read the story. Then choose the correct answer to complete the sentences below.

Madeleine Albright—A Successful Immigrant

Madeleine Albright moved to the United States as a young girl and became very successful in the U.S. government. She was born in Czechoslovakia in 1937 and came to the United States in 1948. Her father was a diplomat. Albright graduated from Wellesley College in 1959 and later got her master's degree and doctorate in law and government. She married and had twin daughters. She taught at Georgetown University. Albright was appointed ambassador to the United Nations in 1993. President Clinton asked Albright to be secretary of state in 1996. She was the first woman to have that job. In 2001, she started the Albright Group, an international consulting firm.

13. Madeleine Albright moved to the United States in _____.
    A. 1937
    B. 1948
    C. 1959

14. She graduated from _____.
    A. Wellesley College
    B. Georgetown University
    C. doctorate

15. Albright was very successful in _____.
    A. law
    B. government
    C. the presidency

16. When Clinton was president, Albright was _____.
    A. a teacher
    B. in college
    C. secretary of state

17. Albright is probably _____.
    A. hardworking
    B. disorganized
    C. lazy

18. Albright is well known because she was _____.
    A. a good mother
    B. the best teacher
    C. the first female secretary of state in the U.S.

19–20. WRITING: Write two sentences about what you are going to do tomorrow.

_____

_____

Unit 5 Test

Name: _____   Date: _____   Score: _____

LISTENING: Listen to the conversations. Then choose the correct answer for each question.

Conversation 1 157

1. What did he buy?
    A. a coffeemaker
    B. a broom
    C. a vacuum cleaner

2. How much was it marked down?
    A. 20%
    B. 45%
    C. 50%

3. What was the price before it was marked down?
    A. $45
    B. $50
    C. $90

Conversation 2

4. What are they talking about?
    A. a coat
    B. boots
    C. the weather

5. What does the customer want to do?
    A. get a refund
    B. make an exchange
    C. buy a new jacket

6. Why is the second coat better?
    A. It's smaller and warmer.
    B. It's bigger and nicer.
    C. It's warmer and bigger.

GRAMMAR: Choose the word or phrase that correctly completes each sentence.

7. My brother is _____ my sister.
    A. the oldest
    B. oldest
    C. older than

8. I went _____ in the mountains last week.
    A. to hiking
    B. hiked
    C. hiking

9. I didn't buy anything because _____ any stores open.
    A. there weren't
    B. there wasn't
    C. there were

10. I would like _____ next weekend.
    A. go to skiing
    B. to go skiing
    C. go skiing

11. Maria is _____ her family
    A. smaller than
    B. the smallest in
    C. the smallest

12. Jack is _____ man I know.
    A. more interesting
    B. the most interesting
    C. interesting than

Unit 5 Test

READING/VOCABULARY: Read the story. Then choose the correct answer to complete each sentence.

13. This information is mostly about _____.
    A. grocery shopping
    B. shopping for school
    C. making good decisions

> **Save on Back-to-School Shopping**
> www.saveonline4school.com
>
> A few simple ideas can help you save money on back to school clothing and supplies:
>
> - If the school sends home a list, look at it carefully. If you have more than one child, maybe they can reuse items. Make a list of what you have and what you need to buy.
>
> - Comparison shop. Go to several stores to find the best price.
>
> - Figure how much you can afford. Don't spend more than that amount. Tell your children how much they can spend on certain items, and help them make smart choices.
>
> - Don't go shopping when you're tired. You need to be able to make good decisions and avoid buying things without thinking.

14. You can save money on back-to-school shopping if you _____.
    A. buy everything on the school's list
    B. go shopping when you're tired
    C. figure out how much money you can spend and only spend that amount

15. You may spend too much money if you _____.
    A. buy without thinking about it first
    B. make good decisions
    C. make a list of what you need

16. Your children can help you save money if they _____.
    A. use items more than once
    B. buy what they want
    C. ask for lots of things

17. You can find this information _____.
    A. on the Internet
    B. on a coupon
    C. in an ad

18. _____ should do the back-to-school shopping.
    A. Mothers
    B. Children
    C. Parents and children

19–20. WRITING: Write two sentences and compare the place you live now to a place you lived before.

_____

_____

Unit 6 Test

Name: _____   Date: _____   Score: _____

LISTENING: Listen to the conversations. Then choose the correct answer for each question.

Conversation 1 158

1. Where are they?
   A. at home
   B. at a train station
   C. at a restaurant

2. What does the customer want?
   A. a menu
   B. to order
   C. a cup of coffee

3. What is the waiter doing?
   A. writing down the order
   B. taking someone else's order to another table
   C. getting a cup of coffee

Conversation 2

4. Who is speaking?
   A. a customer and a waitress
   B. a student and a teacher
   C. a customer and a salesclerk

5. What does he want to eat?
   A. chicken salad sandwich
   B. chicken sandwich and soup
   C. a salad and a chicken sandwich

6. What size drink does he want?
   A. root beer
   B. large
   C. small

GRAMMAR: Choose the word or phrase that correctly completes each sentence.

7. I'd like _____ of coffee.
   A. a piece
   B. a cup
   C. a slice

8. He ate three _____.
   A. rices
   B. pieces of bread
   C. porks

9. We need _____.
   A. flour
   B. apple
   C. pound of meat

10. A: Would you like a piece of cake?
    B: Yes, I'd love _____.
    A. each
    B. one
    C. the other

11. _____ poultry do Americans eat?
    A. How much
    B. How many

12. She made _____ last night.
    A. some delicious soup
    B. delicious some soup
    C. some soup delicious

Unit 6 Test

READING/VOCABULARY: Read the menu. Then choose the correct answer to complete each sentence below.

13. Which of the following is a type of salad?
    - A. vegetable
    - B. steak
    - C. tuna

14. How much is a large coffee?
    - A. $.75
    - B. $1.00
    - C. $1.50

15. What is the cheapest dessert?
    - A. ice cream
    - B. pie
    - C. cake

16. Which sandwich is $6.95?
    - A. chicken
    - B. tuna
    - C. steak

McCarthy's Family Restaurant

Soups
- Onion $2.50
- Chicken noodle $3.00
- Vegetable $2.50

Salads
- Garden $3.00
- Fruit $3.50
- Tuna $4.50

Sandwiches
- Chicken $5.95
- Tuna $5.25
- Steak $6.95

Desserts
- Ice cream $1.50
- Pie $2.00
- Cake $2.25

Beverages
- Coffee $.75/1.00
- Tea $.75/1.00
- Milk $1.00/1.50

Thank you! Come again!

17. Which item costs $3.00?
    - A. a salad
    - B. a dessert
    - C. a sandwich

18. How much is a large tea and a chicken sandwich?
    - A. $6.95
    - B. $6.70
    - C. $5.95

19–20. WRITING: Write two sentences about what you ate yesterday. Use quantity words with noncount nouns.

_____

_____

Unit 7 Test

Name: _____ Date: _____ Score: _____

LISTENING: Listen to the conversations. Then choose the correct answer for each question.

Conversation 1 159

1. Who is talking?
   A. two friends
   B. a boss and a worker
   C. a father and son

2. How was Bob's day?
   A. good
   B. bad
   C. great

3. What did his boss do?
   A. He apologized
   B. He complimented Bob.
   C. He criticized Bob.

Conversation 2

4. When do you think this conversation takes place?
   A. before dinner
   B. during breakfast
   C. after a meal

5. What is the woman going to do?
   A. wash the dishes
   B. clear the table
   C. set the table

6. What does "I'm all set" mean?
   A. I don't need help.
   B. I would like some help.
   C. I am ready to help.

GRAMMAR: Choose the word or phrase that correctly completes each sentence.

7. A: Is this your coat?
   B: No, _____ his.
   A. it's
   B. its
   C. it

8. A: Your car is beautiful!
   B: Actually, it's not _____. It's my son's car.
   A. my
   B. mine
   C. me

9. I gave _____ some water.
   A. he
   B. his
   C. him

10. That's _____ car.
    A. mine
    B. my
    C. me

11. Because I was in a hurry, I didn't eat _____ for breakfast.
    A. something
    B. nothing
    C. anything

12. _____ you help me clean the kitchen?
    A. Could
    B. May
    C. When

Unit 7 Test

READING/VOCABULARY: Read the information about family traditions. Then choose the correct answer to complete each sentence below.

In our family, we have many traditions. When one of us four kids has a birthday, we wake up early and give presents. Later, our aunts and uncles and cousins come over. My mother makes a big cake and puts candles on it. Then we sing Happy Birthday. On your birthday, you can choose what to have for your birthday dinner. I always pick cheeseburgers and hash browns. At night we have fireworks. Birthdays are a lot of fun.

13. This story is about _____.
   A. fireworks
   B. birthday traditions
   C. favorite meals

14. The writer _____ birthdays.
   A. likes
   B. dislikes
   C. is bored by

15. The family gives presents _____.
   A. in the morning
   B. after dinner
   C. at lunch

16. The mother always makes _____ for birthdays.
   A. a birthday dinner
   B. cheeseburgers
   C. a cake

17. Hash browns are _____.
   A. something to eat
   B. a kind of firework
   C. a birthday song

18. How many brothers and sisters does the writer have?
   A. 2
   B. 3
   C. 4

19–20. WRITING: Write two sentences about your family traditions.

_____

_____

Unit 8 Test

Name: _____ Date: _____ Score: _____

LISTENING: Listen to the conversations. Then choose the correct answer for each question.

Conversation 1 🎧 160

1. What are the speakers talking about?
   A. a cold
   B. an infection
   C. a sprain

2. What do you think their relationship is?
   A. two friends
   B. patient and receptionist
   C. doctor and nurse

3. What happened?
   A. She hurt her ankle in a basketball game.
   B. She hurt her ankle playing soccer.
   C. She hurt her ankle opening the door.

Conversation 2

4. Where are the speakers?
   A. the emergency room
   B. at home
   C. at school

5. What does the patient need to use until the next appointment?
   A. an ice pack
   B. crutches
   C. cold medication

6. How many tablets can he take?
   A. four in one day
   B. one a day for four days
   C. four tablets twice a day

GRAMMAR: Choose the word that correctly completes each sentence.

7. John has a sprain. He _____ play basketball.
   A. can
   B. can't
   C. should

8. I have a bad fever. I _____ see a doctor.
   A. should
   B. shouldn't
   C. can't

9. He _____ run five miles last year, but now he can.
   A. can
   B. can't
   C. couldn't

10. Mario arrived at 11:05 for his 11:00 appointment. He was _____ late.
    A. too
    B. very
    C. a little

11. I sprained my ankle and can't walk. My ankle isn't strong _____.
    A. enough
    B. pretty
    C. very

12. How _____ do you have to take your medicine?
    A. usually
    B. often
    C. sometimes

294   Unit 8 Test

Unit 8 Test

READING/VOCABULARY: Read the medicine label. Then choose the correct answer for each question below.

13. Which sentence is true?
    A. This is an OTC medicine.
    B. This is a prescription medicine.
    C. This medicine is in tablet form.

14. Who can take this medicine?
    A. adults
    B. children
    C. people with heart disease

15. Which problem is this medicine for?
    A. flu
    B. infection
    C. breathing problems

16. How many capsules can you take in one day?
    A. 1
    B. 2
    C. 12

17. Is this medicine good for dizziness?
    A. No
    B. Yes

18. What should you do after seven days?
    A. buy another package of Cold Away
    B. stop using the medicine
    C. take two capsules

COLD AWAY
For Cold and Flu Symptoms

For headache, body aches, fever, runny nose, sneezing, coughing and sore throat associated with cold or flu.

12 capsules   Take 1 capsule every 12 hours.

Warnings:
Ask a doctor before use if you have breathing problems, lung disease or heart disease.
Do not use for more than 7 days.
Do not give to children under 12 years of age.

19-20. WRITING: Look at the picture. Write two sentences about the woman's injury and what happened at the emergency room.

_____
_____
_____

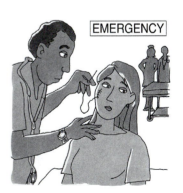

Unit 9 Test

Name: _____ Date: _____ Score: _____

LISTENING: Listen to the conversations. Then choose the correct answer for each question.

Conversation 1 161

1. Who is calling?
   A. a neighbor
   B. a tenant
   C. an apartment manager

2. Why is she calling?
   A. The kitchen sink is plugged up.
   B. The sink is leaking
   C. The sink will run over soon.

3. What has happened before?
   A. Margo has fixed the sink.
   B. The sink got plugged up.
   C. The sink leaked.

Conversation 2

4. What is the problem?
   A. There's a fire.
   B. There's a car accident.
   C. Someone is hurt.

5. Where is the fire?
   A. On 15th Street.
   B. On 42nd Street.
   C. On 5th Street.

6. What is the other problem that the woman talks about?
   A. Some people are injured.
   B. There are some people in the building.
   C. Some electrical wires fell on a car.

GRAMMAR: Choose the correct answer for each question.

7. Yesterday, I _____ a fire.
   A. saw
   B. see
   C. seen

8. There's a fire. _____ 911!
   A. Calls
   B. Let's
   C. Call

9. That pot is very hot. _____ it up!
   A. Pick
   B. Don't pick
   C. Don't picks

10. There's a leak in the faucet. _____ call the landlord.
    A. Let's
    B. Should
    C. Must

11. I had a problem with my refrigerator _____.
    A. in a week
    B. next week
    C. last week

12. I'm going to meet the landlord _____.
    A. tomorrow
    B. yesterday
    C. two days ago

296   Unit 9 Test

Unit 9 Test

READING/VOCABULARY: Read the information. Then choose the correct answer for each question below.

> Dear Mom and Dad,
>
> I am writing to tell you that I am OK. I know that you were worried when I told you about the fire. This is what happened. My smoke alarm woke me up around 3:00 A.M. and I ran down the fire escape with my neighbors. I breathed in some smoke and the fire burned my left elbow a little bit. I had a bad cough for a few days. My neighbor called 911 very quickly. The fire department came in about 15 minutes, but the building is gone. I lost all of my things. An ambulance got me to the emergency room around 4:00. The doctors treated my burns. I was there about six hours. I'm staying with my friend Martina now. I can't email because the fire destroyed my computer. I am already back at my job, so I can buy new clothes and other things. My arm is feeling fine.
>
> Please call me at Martina's apartment. The phone number is 555-6789.
>
> Love,
>
> Mary

13. Why is Mary writing her parents?
    A. To tell them about Martina
    B. To tell them she is safe
    C. To ask for help

14. How did Mary get out of the apartment?
    A. She used the stairs to escape.
    B. She went down the elevator.
    C. She went down the fire escape.

15. What injuries did Mary have?
    A. A minor burn and smoke in her lungs
    B. Serious burns on her left arm
    C. A bad cough and a broken arm

16. What woke Mary up?
    A. Her neighbors
    B. Her smoke alarm
    C. Her parents

17. About what time did Mary get out of the emergency room?
    A. 10:00 A.M.
    B. 11:00 A.M.
    C. noon

18. Where is Mary staying now?
    A. She's still in the hospital.
    B. She's staying with a friend.
    C. She's back in her apartment.

19–20. WRITING: Write two sentences about an emergency you have had at home.

_____

_____

Unit 10 Test

Name: _____ Date: _____ Score: _____

LISTENING: Listen to the conversations. Then choose the correct answer for each question.

Conversation 1 162

1. Who is speaking?
   A. two friends
   B. a supervisor and an employee
   C. an interviewer and a job applicant

2. What job are they talking about?
   A. accountant
   B. businessman
   C. administrative assistant

3. How many years of experience does he have in that type of job?
   A. a long time
   B. a year
   C. three years

Conversation 2

4. Who is talking?
   A. two friends
   B. a supervisor and an employee
   C. a husband and wife

5. Why is she calling?
   A. to apologize
   B. to explain why she won't be at work
   C. to make an appointment

6. What is the problem?
   A. She'll feel better soon.
   B. She had an accident.
   C. She's sick.

GRAMMAR: Choose the word or phrase that correctly completes each sentence.

7. Mechanics _____ be able to fix things.
   A. has to
   B. doesn't have to
   C. have to

8. A welder _____ be good with numbers.
   A. has to
   B. doesn't have to
   C. have to

9. Jim works very _____.
   A. hard
   B. hardly
   C. harder

10. She is walking _____.
    A. slow
    B. slowly
    C. slowed

11. June is willing to work long hours, _____ I'm not.
    A. or
    B. and
    C. but

12. Do you have a job, _____ are you unemployed?
    A. or
    B. and
    C. but

Unit 10 Test

READING/VOCABULARY: Read the résumé about Adam Barker's job experience. Then choose the correct answer to each question below.

13. What street does Adam live on?
    - A. Southville
    - B. Barker
    - C. Pleasant

14. What job does Adam Barker want?
    - A. construction worker
    - B. administrative assistant
    - C. office manager

15. How many years experience does he have in office work?
    - A. Six and a half
    - B. Five and a half
    - C. One

16. Can Adam use a computer?
    - A. yes
    - B. no
    - C. I don't know.

17. Which would Adam probably rather do?
    - A. work inside
    - B. work outside
    - C. I don't know.

18. Which of these skills are on the résumé above?
    - A. ability to solve problems, work independently, and be punctual
    - B. computer skills, ability to solve problems, good people skills
    - C. ability to follow directions, work well with others, computer skills

---

Adam Barker
1305 Pleasant St.
Southville, ND

Position Desired: Office manager in construction company

SKILLS
- Excellent computer skills
- Great communication skills, both oral and written
- Good with customers, coworkers, and supervisors
- Organizational and problem-solving ability

WORK EXPERIENCE
Office Manager, R&K Building Co. 1/2000–7/2005
   Managed the office, supervised administrative assistant, wrote letters to customers, maintained computer information system.
Administrative Assistant, R&K Building Co. 1/1999–1/2000
   Took telephone messages, helped office manager, order supplies

---

19–20. WRITING: Write two sentences about what would you like to do in a job?

_____

_____

Unit Test Audio Scripts

Unit 1

Conversation 1

Male:	Hi. My name is Robert. I'm in Ms. Martin's class.
Female:	Hi. Nice to meet you. I'm Linda. I'm in Mr. Carter's class.
Male:	Nice to meet you, Linda. How's your class?
Female:	Good. I like it.

Conversation 2

Female:	Mark, would you give this book to Sam?
Male:	I'm sorry. I don't know Sam.
Female:	He works in the cafeteria and has long straight hair.
Male:	Long straight hair?
Female:	Right.

Unit 2

Conversation 1

Female:	Excuse me. Where's the hospital?
Male:	It's on Central Boulevard, between Cedar and Elm.
Female:	How do I get there from the library?
Male:	Go north on Cedar and take a left on Central.

Conversation 2

Male 1:	I'd like a round-trip ticket to Miami.
Male 2:	Did you say round-trip?
Male 1:	Yes. What's the next train?
Male 2:	The 9:30 train.
Male 1:	Is it on time?
Male 2:	No, it's about 20 minutes late today.

Unit 3

Conversation 1

Male:	That'll be $15.75.
Female:	I have a twenty.
Male:	Great. Your change is $5.25.
Female:	Shouldn't that be $4.25?
Male:	You're right. Thanks.

Conversation 2

Female:	I'd like to cash this check for $100.
Male:	Do you have an account here and a photo ID?
Female:	Yes, I do. Here's my driver's license.
Male:	How do you want it?
Female:	Can I have twenties please?
Male:	Sure. Here you are—twenty, forty, sixty, eighty, one hundred.
Female:	Thanks.

Unit 4

Conversation 1

Male:	Who is going to get the job as the new supervisor?
Female:	I think Ben Taylor will. He is hardworking and good with people.
Male:	Yes, and he has a great attitude.
Female:	That's true.

Conversation 2

Male:	Hi, Rita. You look happy. What's up?
Female:	Hey, Carl. I am happy—I just got a promotion.
Male:	That's great! I want to get a promotion too. How did you do it?
Female:	I went back to school last year and learned to use a computer.
Male:	That sounds like a good idea.

Unit Test Audio Scripts

Unit 5

Conversation 1

Female: Did you get a new vacuum?
Male: Yes. I got one that was half-price at Al's Superstore.
Female: That's sounds like a good deal. How much was it?
Male: $45.
Female: That's great.

Conversation 2

Male 1: Can I help you?
Male 2: Yes. I want to return this coat. It's too small.
Male 1: Do you want to exchange it or do you want a refund?
Male 2: I think I want to exchange it for this one.
Male 1: Yes, that one is bigger, and a little warmer too.
Male 2: Okay. I'll exchange it.

Unit 6

Conversation 1

Male 1: Excuse me.
Male 2: Yes. Can I help you?
Male 1: Yes, please. Can you bring me a cup of coffee?
Male 2: Sure. I'll get some right away, as soon as I take this order to that table.
Male 1: Thanks.

Conversation 2

Female: Are you ready to order?
Male: Yes, I'd like a chicken sandwich and a small salad.
Female: What would you like to drink?
Male: I'd like a root beer.
Female: Large or small?
Male: Large, please.

Unit 7

Conversation 1

Male 1: Hey, Bob. How was your day?
Male 2: Terrible.
Male 1: What happened?
Male 2: My boss yelled at me.
Male 1: Really? What did he say?
Male 2: He said I wasn't being safe.

Conversation 2

Female: Can I help you with the dishes?
Male: Thanks for offering but I'm all set.
Female: Can I clear the table?
Male: Thank you. That would be a big help.

Unit 8

Conversation 1

Female: I'd like to make an appointment as soon as I can.
Male: What's the problem?
Female: I hurt my ankle in a soccer game. I think I have a sprain.
Male: Can you walk?
Female: No.
Male: I have an opening this morning at eleven.
Female: I'll take it.

Conversation 2

Female: You need to use crutches until the next appointment. And here's a prescription for some pain medication.
Male: How often do I take it?
Female: Take one tablet four times a day. Don't take more than that.
Male: Can I drive my car?
Female: No. Not until I see you again.

Unit Test Audio Scripts

Unit 9

Conversation 1

Female: Hi. This is Margo Ruiz in Apartment 296.
Male: Hi. What can I do for you?
Female: Could you please take a look at my kitchen sink?
Male: What's wrong with it? Is it plugged up again?
Female: No. This time it's leaking.
Male: Okay. I'll be over soon.

Conversation 2

Female: Is this 911?
Male: Yes, how can I help you?
Female: I'm calling to report a fire at 1542 5th Street. It's an office building.
Male: OK. That's 1542 5th Street. We'll send some fire trucks over.
Female: There's one more thing.
Male: Yes?
Female: There are still people inside the building.
Male: OK. I'll tell the fire department. Thanks!

Unit 10

Conversation 1

Female: Why are you applying for the accountant's position?
Male: I like working with numbers.
Female: Are you willing to work long hours?
Male: Yes, I am. In my last job I had to work long hours a lot.
Female: Tell me about your accounting experience.
Male: Well, I was an accountant for three years before I went back to college to study business.

Conversation 2

Female: Hello, is this Mr. Atkins?
Male: Yes, it is.
Female: This is Lupe Reyes. I'm sorry but I can't work tonight. I feel terrible. I think I have the flu.
Male: I hope you feel better soon.
Female: Thank you.

Unit Test Answer Key

Unit 1

1. a; 2. b; 3. a; 4. c; 5. c; 6. b; 7. a; 8. b; 9. b; 10. a; 11. a; 12. c; 13. c; 14. c; 15. a; 16. a; 17. a 18. b;

19 and 20. Answers will vary. Possible answers may include similar sentences:

> I am tall. I have long brown hair.
>
> I am short and heavy. I have curly black hair.

Unit 2

1. c; 2. a; 3. a; 4. c; 5. c; 6. c; 7. c; 8. b; 9. c; 10. a; 11. b; 12. a; 13. b; 14. c; 15. b; 16. c; 17. b; 18. b;

19 and 20. Answers will vary. Possible answers may include similar sentences:

> Kumiko is asking the teacher a question. Jorge is writing on his test.
>
> The students are taking the test. The teacher is watching them.

Unit 3

1. c; 2. b; 3. b; 4. a; 5. b; 6. c; 7. a; 8. b; 9. a; 10. c; 11. b; 12. c; 13. a; 14. b; 15. b; 16. a; 17. b; 18. c;

19 and 20. Answers will vary. Possible answers may include similar sentences:

> I did my homework. I watched TV.
>
> I picked up my children after school. I took them home and made dinner.

Unit 4

1. b; 2. a; 3. a; 4. c; 5. c; 6. a; 7. b; 8. c; 9. a; 10. a; 11. c; 12. a; 13. b; 14. a; 15. b; 16. c; 17. a; 18. c;

19 and 20. Answers will vary. Possible answers may include similar sentences:

> I am going to go to the supermarket. I am going to do laundry.
>
> I'm going to come to class. After class I am going to go to the cafeteria with Ron.

Unit 5

1. c; 2. c; 3. c; 4. a; 5. b; 6. c; 7. c; 8. c; 9. a; 10. b; 11. b; 12. b; 13. b; 14. c; 15. a; 16. a; 17. a; 18. c;

19 and 20. Answers will vary. Possible answers may include similar sentences:

> The house I live in now is smaller than my old house. It is newer than my old house.
>
> My new apartment is more expensive than my old apartment. But it is closer to my job.

Unit 6

1. c; 2. c; 3. b; 4. a; 5. c; 6. b; 7. b; 8. b; 9. a; 10. b; 11. a; 12. a; 13. c; 14. b; 15. a; 16. c; 17. a; 18. a;

19 and 20. Answers will vary. Possible answers may include similar sentences:

> Yesterday for breakfast I had some cereal and some juice. For lunch, I had a sandwich, a salad, and some French fries.
>
> For dinner I had two pieces of chicken and some beans. For dessert I had some cake and ice cream.

Unit 7

1. a; 2. b; 3. c; 4. c; 5. b; 6. a; 7. a; 8. b; 9. c; 10. b; 11. c; 12. a; 13. b; 14. a; 15. a; 16. c; 17. a; 18. b;

19 and 20. Answers will vary. Possible answers may include similar sentences:

> At New Year's, everyone in my family goes to my grandmother's house. My grandmother cooks delicious food and we play games and sing songs.
>
> On Christmas Eve my whole family goes to church together. Then we come home and have a big meal and give each other presents.

Unit Test Answer Key

Unit 8

1. c; 2. b; 3. b; 4. a; 5. b; 6. a; 7. b; 8. a; 9. c; 10. c; 11. a; 12. b; 13. a; 14. a; 15. a; 16. b; 17. a; 18. b;

19 and 20. Answers will vary. Possible answers may include similar sentences:

> The woman cut her face. She came to the emergency room and a nurse gave her stitches.

> The woman fell into a window and cut her face. She came to the hospital, and a nurse put stitches in her cheek.

Unit 9

1. b; 2. b; 3. b; 4. a; 5. c; 6. b; 7. a; 8. c; 9. b; 10. a; 11. c; 12. a; 13. b; 14. c; 15. a; 16. b; 17. a; 18. b;

19 and 20. Answers will vary. Possible answers may include similar sentences:

> One day I tried to cook something with oil but it caught fire and started to burn. I had to use a fire extinguisher to put out the fire.

> My daughter slipped in the bathtub and hit her head. We had to take her to the hospital to get stitches.

Unit 10

1. c; 2. a; 3. c; 4. b; 5. b; 6. c; 7. c; 8. b; 9. a; 10. b; 11. c; 12. a; 13. c; 14. c; 15. a; 16. a; 17. a; 18. b;

19 and 20. Answers will vary. Possible answers may include similar sentences:

> I would like to work with many different people in my job. I would like to speak English and my native language.

> I would like to work outside in my job. I would like to build things and work with my hands.